THE BATTLE OF TRAFALGAR

Admiral Lord Horatio Nelson. History's greatest sea warrior was determined to annihilate the French and Spanish fleets at Trafalgar as the surest way of protecting the freedom and liberties of Britain. (CPL)

THE BATTLE OF TRAFALGAR

MARTIN ROBSON

CONWAY MARITIME PRESS

Copyright © Conway Maritime Press, 2005

First published in 2005 by Conway Maritime Press

An imprint of **Chrysalis** Books Group plc
The Chrysalis Building, Bramley Road,
London W10 6SP

Distributed in North America by:
Casemate Publishers, 2114 Darby Road, Havertown,
PA 19083, USA

Martin Robson has asserted his moral right
to be identified as the author of this work.

British Library Cataloguing in Publication Data
A catalogue record for this book is available
from the British Library

Library of Congress Cataloging in Publication Data available

ISBN 0 85177 979 4

Printed in China

CONTENTS

THE BATTLE OF TRAFALGAR

ACKNOWLEDGMENTS

Many people have provided direct or indirect assistance in production of this book. On a professional note I must thank Professor Andrew Lambert of the Laughton Naval History Unit, King's College London, for opening my eyes to the importance of naval and maritime history. His guidance and assistance proved invaluable during my undergraduate and postgraduate years. Colin White kindly brought my attention to his discovery of 'Nelson's Battle Plan' during my time as Editor of the *Age of Sail* annual. My co-editor of that publication, Nicholas Tracy, provided many useful ideas and explanations regarding fleet tactics. Peter Goodwin, Keeper and Curator of HMS *Victory*, has, in the course of numerous professional (and some social) conversations, provided me with a wealth of information relating to ship construction and seamanship. My former colleagues at Conway Maritime Press, Stuart Robertson and John Lee, have proved to be a valuable and understanding team. John Lee in particular deserves much credit for bringing to fruition the Conway Compass Series. Of course any errors that are contained in the text are entirely my own.

On a more personal level I must express my extreme gratitude to my parents, who have proved to be immensely understanding and generous supporters of my chosen career. Without their help I would not be in the position to write this book. Last, and certainly not least, I offer Charlotte my heartfelt thanks and apologies. The former for her constant support and encouragement; the latter for tolerating my all-consuming interest in Nelson, Trafalgar and things naval and maritime. It is to her that this book is dedicated.

Martin Robson, Gosforth, December 2004

INTRODUCTION

On 21 October 1805 the combined fleets of France and Spain were dealt a crushing blow by the Royal Navy under the command of Admiral Lord Horatio Nelson. The battle itself was fought within the wider war between France, in 1805 led by the powerful figure of the Emperor Napoleon Bonaparte, and her various continental allies, and the island nation of Great Britain. The wars lasted from 1793 until Napoleon's final defeat in 1815, and Trafalgar may seem a small event when compared to the epic struggles and battles fought on land. Moreover, there is already a vast literature on the battle and Lord Nelson. More books are being published now and throughout 2005. This begs the question, one that all historians working in this field must ask of themselves, is there room for another book?

There clearly is, for a number of reasons. Many of the existing studies are out of date; since their publication new material has come to the fore, allowing us to approach the battle from a more complete viewpoint. Biographies of Nelson, appearing with increasing regularity over the past few years, concentrate on his role in the battle without examining the wider experience of the French, Spanish and British crews who fought and died that day. Of course one cannot examine Trafalgar without the shadow of Nelson looming over the subject. Nearly 200 years after his death he remains one of the greatest Britons, an iconic, larger than life character, whose story still has many things to say to the twenty-first century. Yet, as this book will prove, there is much more to Trafalgar than the story of Nelson. Recent studies that attempt to examine the battle as a whole do just that, without any reference to the wider strategic context of the campaign. The events that led to Trafalgar began several years before, and the effects of the battle have echoed down through almost 200 years of naval history.

Throughout this book one thing will become clear, that the subject under consideration is not purely one of naval history. The aim is to examine the battle of Trafalgar within a wider context: an analysis of how it fits into the global struggle fought between Great Britain and France and her allies during the late eighteenth and early nineteenth centuries. In doing so it attempts to provide the reader with sound understanding of how and why the battle was fought, the tactics employed, what the short and long term effects were, the background information on the important individuals concerned and technical details of the ships involved. The key to this is the presentation of important French, Spanish and British documentary evidence in the form of eye-witness accounts, private writings and official orders.

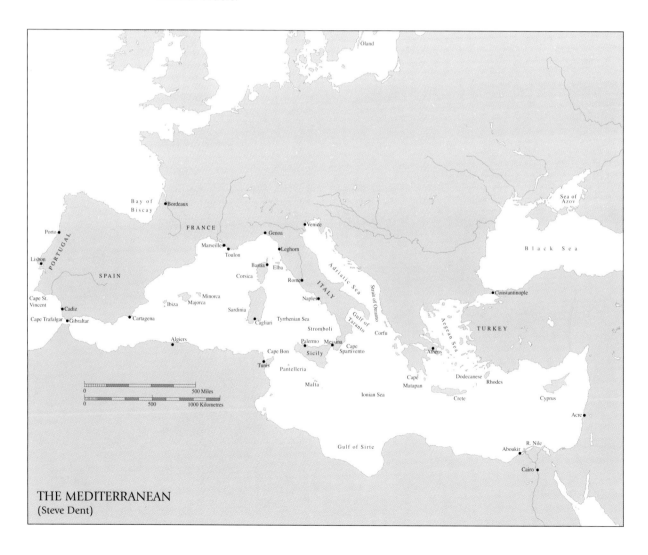

THE MEDITERRANEAN
(Steve Dent)

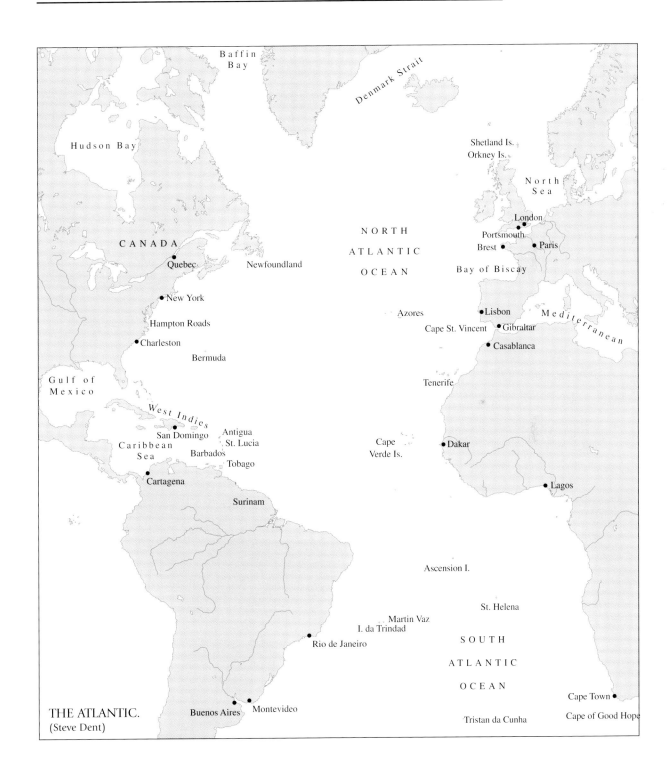

Baffin Bay

Denmark Strait

Hudson Bay

Shetland Is.
Orkney Is.

North Sea

CANADA

London
Portsmouth
Brest ● ● Paris

NORTH

ATLANTIC

OCEAN

Bay of Biscay

Quebec

Newfoundland

New York

Lisbon

Mediterranean

Hampton Roads

Azores

Cape St. Vincent ● Gibraltar

Charleston

Casablanca

Bermuda

Gulf of
Mexico

Tenerife

West Indies

San Domingo
Caribbean
Sea

Antigua
St. Lucia
Barbados
Tobago

Cape
Verde Is.

Dakar

Cartagena

Surinam

Lagos

Ascension I.

St. Helena

Martin Vaz
I. da Trindad

SOUTH

ATLANTIC

OCEAN

Rio de Janeiro

Cape Town ●

THE ATLANTIC.
(Steve Dent)

Buenos Aires   Montevideo

Tristan da Cunha

Cape of Good Hope

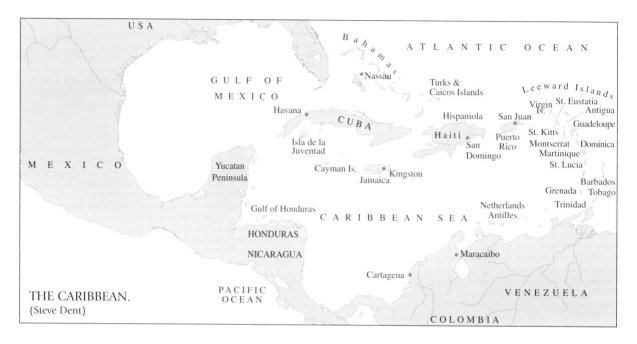

THE CARIBBEAN.
(Steve Dent)

EUROPE.
(Steve Dent)

THE FRENCH INVASION THREAT

The battle of Trafalgar had its root cause in the French threat to invade England that reached a crisis point in the summer of 1805. For more than two years the forces of, to paraphrase A. T. Mahan, the whale and the elephant faced each other across a narrow stretch of water. Ever since the forces of Revolutionary France had taken up arms in 1793, England had remained a stout opponent of France, providing European nations with money to fight the revolution and assisting where possible with her land and naval forces. All attempts to force the British government to accept a powerful France on the European mainland had been rebuffed by London. Even a short-lived peace negotiated at Amiens in 1802 had only been a breathing space, allowing France and England to regroup their forces. By the spring of 1805 the continental situation was certainly favourable for Napoleon to concentrate on England: the threat of war with Austria had declined during the winter months; Napoleon had crushed the Royalist plots of early 1804 which threatened his dictatorship and had crowned himself Emperor of France at a coronation ceremony on 2 December, thereby stabilising post-revolutionary France.

With no clouds on the horizon, Napoleon could concentrate all efforts on finally solving the problem of Britain. He gathered a huge French army around the port of Boulogne, ready at a moment's notice to strike a deadly blow to the country and people that continued to defy French arms. On the clear fine days, as Napoleon's invasion force practised their manoeuvres, visible in the distance were the white cliffs and beyond them the rolling countryside of their ultimate prize. Many of those stationed in the military camps around Boulogne must have believed that they would shortly be landing on the shores of their old and hated enemy, 'Perfidious

Napoleon Bonaparte, Emperor of the French. By the summer of 1805 it seemed as if Napoleon's lengthy preparations for the invasion of England might bear fruit; only the Royal Navy stood as a check to his ambitions. (CPL)

NAPOLEON BONAPARTE, EMPEROR OF THE FRENCH (1769–1821)

In the year 1805 Napoleon was at the height of his formidable powers. A successful general in the armies of Revolutionary France, by 1800 he was virtual dictator of France, a situation confirmed by his coronation as Emperor Napoleon I in December 1804.

Born on 15 August 1769 in Corsica to poor aristocracy, his drive and ambition propelled him to a military career in mainland France. When the Revolution came in 1789 Napoleon, serving in the artillery, seized his opportunity. At Toulon in 1793 he gained the attention of his superiors, leading to his employment in Paris during 1795 to suppress a conservative uprising with a 'whiff of grapeshot'. His campaigns in Northern Italy during 1796–7 brought him to national attention and lead to his commanding an expedition to Egypt in 1798, partly to keep him away from home politics. During the voyage to Egypt another facet of Napoleon's career was evident: he was extremely lucky. The overcrowded French fleet narrowly missed the British fleet under Nelson. Returning to France after Nelson had destroyed the French fleet at Aboukir Bay, in a *coup d'état* of 9–10 November 1799 Napoleon became First Consul and, effectively, dictator of France. His second Italian campaign resulted in his famous victory at Marengo, the events of which were massaged by his effective publicity machine. By 1802 the continent was at his mercy and England agreed to peace.

With war renewed in 1803 Napoleon had the opportunity to solve the problem of England once and for all by direct invasion. His plans were foiled by Villeneuve's inability to push past Admiral Robert Calder into the English Channel on 22 July 1805. Napoleon had already made the decision to head east and fight Austria before news of Trafalgar reached him. His victories over the Austrians and Russians at Ulm and then at Austerlitz in 1805, followed by the crushing of Prussia in 1806, had significantly greater effects on the continent than Nelson's great victory at Trafalgar. Unable to invade England, Napoleon turned to economic warfare by implementing a Europe-wide blockade of British goods. By invading Portugal in 1807 to enforce the blockade, and desiring to reform his ally Spain, Napoleon was himself to blame for the Spanish uprising and Peninsular War which would contribute a great deal to his eventual downfall. Despite another victory over Austria in 1809, Napoleon's powers were on the wane. The disastrous invasion of Russia in 1812 proved that he could be beaten, though it took until 1814 for a Coalition of all the major European powers to force his abdication. The 'Hundred Days' of 1815 saw his escape from exile and his final defeat at the hands of an Anglo–Prussian force at Waterloo on 18 June 1815. Exiled to St. Helena under the guard of British forces, he remained a threat to European peace until his death in 1821.

Albion'. On 6 July 1805 many must also have looked west, out to sea, awaiting the appearance of a mighty fleet that would escort them across the Channel, for on that date the invasion flotilla was ready to sail.

'The Plum Pudding in Danger'. Gillray's cartoon depicts Napoleon helping himself to continental Europe, while William Pitt carves off Britain and the West Indies. (CPL)

It had taken Napoleon more than two years of work to reach a position where the flotilla could strike. Once war had broken out after the failure of the Peace of Amiens in 1803, Napoleon looked to direct invasion as a way to solve the problem of England's continued defiance of his ideas for a French-controlled Europe. Aware that the traditional British strategy of coalition-building would lead to continental threats to France, Napoleon needed to complete the subjugation of England before British diplomacy and money could divert the resources necessary for the invasion to other theatres. In its simplest form the plan was for French armies to be transported across the Channel, land in southern England, crush any opposition and march on London to overthrow the government and King George III. We should not let the fact that the planned invasion never took place cloud the issue, for Napoleon took it seriously and undertook extensive and expensive preparations.[1]

In September 1803 Napoleon had initially expected the invasion army to consist of 114,000 men and 7,000 horses with accompanying artillery. By the August of 1805 the required invasion force had been increased to a total of 167,000 men. Such large numbers would require a massive effort to construct the necessary vessels to ferry them across the Channel. Ships-of-the-line and frigates were not suitable for this task, being unable to work close inshore. Instead, what were needed were shallow-draught, flat-bottomed vessels, fitted with both sail and oars, capable of landing troops on a beach in some semblance of order. They also had to be sturdy enough to survive the Channel crossing intact.

As Minister of the Navy and Colonies, Rear Admiral Denis Decrès was the man charged by Napoleon to organise and implement the plan to invade England. (Warwick Leadlay Gallery)

REAR ADMIRAL DENIS DECRÈS (1761–1820)

Eight years older than Napoleon, Decrès served as Minister of the Navy and Colonies and was responsible for the administration of the French Navy. Born into an aristocratic family from Champagne, he went to sea aged seventeen and gained a reputation as a tough fighter during several engagements in the West Indies. Decisive of mind, he was nevertheless a willing subordinate and a practical seaman. Returning from the Indian Ocean in 1794, upon his arrival back in Revolutionary France he was arrested and held in Paris for a few months until intervention from senior naval figures saw him released. His internment did his career no lasting damage and he was promoted to Rear Admiral in 1797. The following year, commanding a squadron under Admiral Brueys, he participated in the successful attack on Malta and landed troops on the island. He sprang to national fame when during the British siege to retake Malta he broke through the British blockade in the 74-gun *Guillaume Tell*, engaged a superior force and surrendered only after his ship

was completely dismasted and had lost half her crew. Typically Decrès was in the thick of the fighting and received several wounds. Exchanged, he was decorated by Napoleon in April 1801 but was unable to serve again at sea because of his injuries. Genuinely respected by Napoleon, who perhaps noted that his rise through the ranks by ability and hard work mirrored his own, Decrès was now appointed to a desk job as Maritime Prefect of Lorient, the very port where he had been arrested in 1794! As successful in an administrative role as he had been at sea, Decrès became Naval Minister in October 1801 and played a key role in organising the naval forces for the invasion of England, though expressing grave doubts as to the practicality of the plans and denouncing Pierre-Alexandre Farfait's contribution. Not especially liked, but certainly feared by his own subordinates, whom he expected to work as hard as he did, he tried his utmost to implement Napoleon's often-impossible demands. Decrès' arrogance towards his employees, professional and personal, may have led to his murder in 1820 by an explosive charge planted under his bed, possibly by his valet.

In fact even before the Peace of Amiens officially broke down, Napoleon had already turned to the naval aspect of the invasion plans. Perhaps to add leverage to the increasingly strained talks taking place between Paris and London, in March 1803 Napoleon ordered the construction of several types of invasion craft. On the same day that war was declared by Britain, 18 May, he confirmed orders for the building of the first 57 vessels. On 24 May he appointed the former Pierre-Alexandre Farfait, to the position of Inspector-General of the National Flotilla. Farfait had held the post of Minister of Marine before Rear Admiral Denis Decrès succeeded him in 1801. Other notable appointments followed: Vice Admiral Bruix was put in overall command of the Flotilla on 7 September 1803, with Rear Admirals Magon and Emeriau as his subordinates.

Upon the outbreak of war, efforts were made to collect a force of shallow-draught vessels from the existing ships stationed in the French Atlantic ports, all of which were to be converted to landing-craft. More than 1,000 vessels of various types, many of them fishing vessels, were assembled and provided enough tonnage to ferry nearly 13,000 men and more than 5,000 horses across the Channel.[2] Although in the end these proved to be the most reliable vessels designated for the invasion force, it was obvious that alone their numbers were nowhere near enough for the scale of operations intended by Napoleon.

This heavily stylised image portrays the Boulogne Flotilla at sea. In reality the invasion craft suffered numerous difficulties even in the most advantageous weather conditions. (CPL)

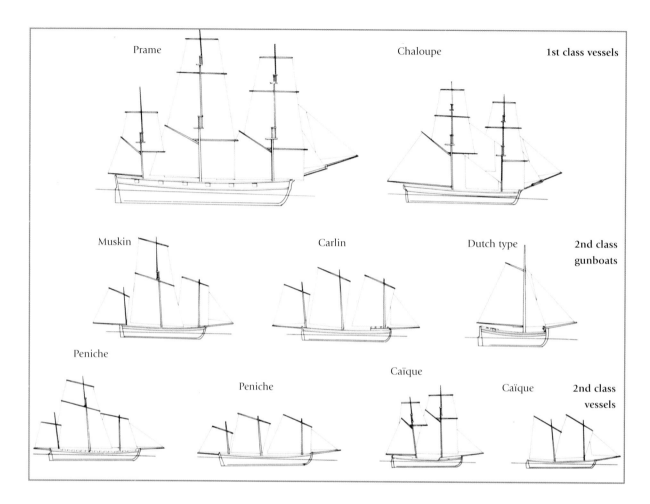

Types of vessels of
the French invasion
flotilla.
(CPL)

Throughout the remainder of 1803 and the early months of 1804 the dockyards, private shipyards and rivers of western coastal France were a hive of activity. In June 1803, 700 vessels were laid down in the Channel ports and rivers. In early July construction orders for a total of 2,410 vessels were dispatched. As the building project intensified the costs spiralled beyond all initial calculations, 29,917,500 francs for the hulls and rigging alone.[3]

Construction on such a massive scale required an immense administrative and industrial effort, and vessels were also built in Toulouse, Grenoble, Rouen, on the Rhine, in Liège, Ghent, Bruges, Namur in the Low Countries, and as far inland as Paris and Versailles.[4] Moreover, the newly acquired Dutch territories, now renamed the Batavian Republic, were available to assist the construction effort. On 25 June instructions were sent for the construction of 100 *chaloupes canonnières*, 250 *bateaux canonniers* and a further 100 transports. Delivery of these vessels was severely delayed because of the limited *matériel* available to the Batavian authorities.

NAPOLEON'S INVASION FLOTILLA

50 *prames* (shallow draught corvette), 117ft x 26½ft x 8½ft, crew 38, armament 12 x 24pdr, lift 120 men, false keels indicate that they were to beach with the first wave; cost per vessel – 70,000 francs

300 *chaloupes canonnières* (gun brig), 80ft x 20ft x 6ft, crew 22, armament 1 x 18pdr aft, 2 x 18 or 24pdr forward on sliding mounts, lift 130 men plus 1 x 6 or 8in howitzer; cost per vessel – 32–42,000 francs

300 *bateaux canonniers* (lug rigged), 64ft x 14½ft x 5ft, crew 6, armament none?, lift 106 men, 2 horses, 1 x 24pdr, 1 howitzer, 1 field gun; cost per vessel – 18–23,000 francs

700 *péniches* (lug rigged), 64ft x 11ft x 4ft, crew 5, armament none, lift 66 men plus 2 small howitzers or 8in mortar; cost per vessel – 8–9,000 francs

1,000 *chasses-marées* (coasting lugger)

50 *caïques* (warship longboat) armed with 1 x 24pdr

10 *bombardes* (bomb vessel)

As well as the regular invasion craft, a number of wild and wholly impracticable schemes were put forward to facilitate the invasion. One envisaged 3,000 men floating over the Channel in a huge balloon filled with hot air. A tunnel to be dug under the Channel to allow the safe passage of troops was another popular but unpractical idea. Robert Fulton, the American inventor, proposed a submersible vessel and in April 1800 tested his self-funded *Nautilus* in the River Seine. The following year at Le Havre *Nautilus* successfully placed explosives and then detonated explosive devices against ships in the harbour. But despite the apparent success, Napoleon eventually decided against Fulton's plans so the enterprising American offered his inventions to the British government!

By May 1804 there were 1,273 vessels ready to ferry French troops, horses, artillery and the necessary equipment across the Channel for a landing in England. Napoleon was a frequent visitor, inspecting the technical preparations and inspiring the men. On 20 July he was ready to attempt an embarkation and ordered the flotilla to sea, but with the weather deteriorating rapidly Admiral Bruix refused and was dismissed from his post. The exercises went ahead and were a shambles, 20 vessels were wrecked and between 200 and 400 men were killed. Even worse was the fact that such disastrous exercises could be seen from the opposite shore.

A major cause of the loss of life was the poor qualities of the vessels themselves. Many were built of unseasoned timber, which quickly degenerated and required extensive repair and rebuilding. Moreover, all had less than desirable sea-keeping qualities because of their shallow draughts, low freeboard and in particular the absence of proper keels. The *prames* were, according to one French officer, 'disastrous'; they could not keep the wind and were difficult to steer; in the end few were used and orders for this vessel were cut back. The *bateaux* were extremely prone to being swamped even while moored. The *chaloupes* also suffered from bad sea-keeping due to the lack of a keel and were not sturdy enough to carry their designated loads.

> ### Gale Hits Invasion Force
> ### Deal, *July 24 [1804]*
>
> *Yesterday evening the weather being clear, and the sun shining upon the French coast, we had a very good view of the enemy, and have clearly ascertained that their loss in the gale of Friday and Saturday last has been very considerable. We distinctly counted nine wrecks on the rocks between Portel and Boulogne; and from the boldness of the coast and the tremendous sea, when they came ashore, it is scarcely possible that any of the people on board, 500 in number at least, could have been saved; the entire coast between Boulogne and Portel was covered with wagons and soldiers, clearing away wrecks, and an immensity of small boats were engaged in searching the bottom for different articles. In the space of fifty yards,*
>
> *close under Portel, there are a Gun-brig and four Luggers dashed to pieces. The few Brigs that succeeded in getting into Boulogne seem to be much damaged in their masts and rigging; indeed from the amazing surf, when getting in, it is impossible that it could be otherwise. Altogether, the loss of the enemy, on Saturday morning, has been the most severe they have met with since the commencement of the war; and it is highly probable that the soldiers will not be so sanguine for the expedition, after having had such convincing proofs of the danger attending it, and having seen our ships ride out gales of wind in perfect safety, when they have invariably suffered, both in Men and Vessels.*
>
> Source: *Naval Chronicle, III, pp. 51–2.*

More than anything else, this waste of life at Napoleon's hands should have highlighted the fact that, in the absence of a large escort force and without any interference from the Royal Navy, to have any chance of success the attempt would still need the very best of weather conditions. Naval opinion inside France was pessimistic as to whether the invasion craft were suitable for the choppy seas of the Channel; Admirals Laurent Truguet and Ganteaume, and even Decrès, had all doubted the feasibility of the invasion.[5]

Besides the weather the French invasion plans suffered from the impossibility of getting all the vessels to sea in one tide. At least two tides, a period of twenty-four hours, would be the bare minimum and would leave at least half the flotilla outside the harbours and therefore vulnerable to attack by the Royal Navy. This partly explains why Boulogne was chosen as the main port for the embarkation. The *Bassure de Basse*, a large sandbank situated about a mile offshore of the harbour, provided an anchorage where the flotilla could be concentrated yet remain partly protected from attack. Measures were undertaken to increase the first wave capability: at Boulogne the narrow and relatively shallow channel leading from the River Liane out to sea was dredged, an artificial basin was excavated and the quayside extended by a kilometre to increase the number troops that could be embarked. At the same time the defences of the invasion ports were strengthened to prevent any British attack from damaging the vessels or facilities. These measures had some success: at Boulogne for instance, 180 artillery pieces were installed within the space of three kilometres while mobile Horse-Artillery columns were deployed as a rapid reaction force to any British attack.[6]

During 1804 Napoleon decided on the distribution of the invasion forces. The right-hand invasion thrust would come from 30,000 men setting out from Ostend and Nieuport in 300 vessels. The left wing was to be the most substantial, comprising 100,000 men and 3,000 horses to be embarked in 2,380 vessels and was centred on Boulogne, Ambleteuse and Étaples. The centre of the invasion flotilla would consist of 300 of the largest vessels held in Dunkirk, Gravelines and Calais. In addition to the above, 100 *chaloupes canonnières* and 200 *bateaux canonniers* were to be held back at Flushing to form a second wave.

Napoleon had refined the plans so that by July 1805 the first wave of the invasion force had been organised as follows. Based twelve miles south of Boulogne at Étaples to convey Marshal Ney's 23,000 men, the 402 landing-craft of the left wing were under the command of Rear Admiral Courand. In the centre, Marshal Soult commanded two army corps comprising 40,000 men to be transported by the 1,000 vessels at Boulogne under the command of Admiral Savary and Captain Leray. The right wing would embark from Wimereux, 276 vessels containing 15,000 men under Marshal Lannes. In the second wave of the invasion another force based a few miles north of Boulogne at Ambleteuse consisted of the 175 ships provided by the Dutch which would take Marshal Davout's 20,000 men across the Channel. Finally, the reserve based at Calais, Dunkirk and Ostend would only sail once a beachhead had been established. It could carry 33,000 men and nearly 3,000 horses.[7]

French Naval Strategy
During 1804 Napoleon began to finalise the strategy that would climax off Cape Trafalgar in late 1805. It was clear that in order to invade the British Isles the Royal Navy had to be drawn away or driven out of home waters, thereby allowing the French invasion flotilla to cross the Channel intact. This necessitated a large concentration of French naval forces in the Channel. However, the main problem for French naval strategists had always been the need to maintain a strong naval presence in both the Atlantic and Mediterranean theatres, thereby splitting available forces in two. The main French fleet bases at Brest and Toulon were separated by hundreds of miles of sea. What Napoleon had to achieve was a concentration of the Brest and Toulon fleets in the Channel to counter the Royal Navy. In order to do this he came up with a typical Napoleonic plan – a high-risk gamble to achieve a decisive victory.

On 25 May 1804 Napoleon wrote to Admiral Latouche Tréville in Toulon asking if he would be ready to sail in July. In June 1804 he appointed Admiral Ganteaume to command the squadron in Brest. On 2 July he began to implement his strategy, informing Latouche Tréville that he was to sail from Toulon to Rochefort and Cherbourg, if necessary attacking Royal Navy squadrons on the way. Once in the Channel the Brest fleet would sally out of port and join with Latouche Tréville, giving the French command of the sea and allowing the invasion flotilla to emerge. Once July came Napoleon wrote again, expressing the hope that the Toulon fleet could sail the following month. On 2 August he

VICE ADMIRAL PIERRE CHARLES JEAN-BAPTISTE SILVESTRE VILLENEUVE (1763–1806)

Villeneuve will forever be remembered as the man who lost to Nelson at Trafalgar. Described by one eye-witness as 'a tallish thin man, a very tranquil, placid, English-looking Frenchman',[8] Villeneuve came from aristocratic stock. He joined the French Navy in 1778 during a period of French naval aggrandisement and success during the American Revolution. Despite his background he had a sympathetic view of the turbulent events following the French Revolution of 1789 and avoided the fate of a large number of his brother officers, many of whom were removed from the navy or emigrated abroad. With a marked lack of experienced officers remaining in the post-revolution navy, Villeneuve benefited from rapid promotion to Captain in 1793 and then Rear Admiral in 1795. At the Nile in 1798 his flagship, the *Guillaume Tell*, was stationed towards the rear of the French battle line. Villeneuve, together with another ship-of-the-line and two frigates, managed to escape the destruction of the French Mediterranean Fleet. Despite criticism of his actions at the Nile, promotion to Vice Admiral followed in May 1804 and the command of the French fleet based at Toulon.

Villeneuve's fleet was to play an integral part in Napoleon's plan to invade the British Isles by escaping from the confines of the Mediterranean, joining with the Spanish fleet at Cadiz and then drawing Nelson's fleet away from European waters by making a dash to the strategically important West Indies. Villeneuve was not convinced that Napoleon's plan would work, but he successfully induced Nelson to pursue him across the Atlantic. Returning to European waters, he was prevented from entering the Channel by Sir Robert Calder and, in direct contradiction of Napoleon's orders to head for Brest, sailed for Cadiz. When news that he was about to be replaced reached him at that

ordered a temporary postponement of the invasion for a few weeks and on 20 August the death of Latouche Tréville dealt the project a major blow. In his stead Napoleon appointed Admiral Pierre Villeneuve, a brave officer and a skilful seaman, but also a man who had grave doubts about the project. Aware of Villeneuve's personal views on the invasion plan, Napoleon relegated the Toulon fleet to creating a diversion to allow the Brest fleet to now take the key role of covering the invasion flotilla.

By the end of September 1804 Napoleon's plans had been expanded into a complicated and ambitious global strategy to include overseas colonial targets to draw British naval forces away from the Channel. On 29 September he instructed Villeneuve to leave Toulon with at least ten battleships. Avoiding any engagement with Nelson, he was to make for Cadiz, pick up the French ships in port there and then head for Surinam in South America. After landing 5,600 troops there, he would be joined by six more battleships under Admiral Missessy, who would have escaped from Rochefort by evading the British blockade, sailed for the West Indies, reinforced the French garrison at Martinique and retaken St. Lucia and Santo Domingo, all before sailing to join Villeneuve. Furthermore, a raiding force would have been sent from Toulon to seize St. Helena, land soldiers in Senegal, recapture Gorée and attack the British settlements along the African coast.

port, Villeneuve took the fateful decision to put to sea on 19 October 1805.

Meeting him after the battle of Trafalgar, Admiral Cuthbert Collingwood remarked: 'Admiral Villeneuve is a well-bred man, and, I believe, a very good officer; he has nothing in his manners of the offensive vapouring and boasting which we, perhaps too often, attribute to Frenchmen.'[9] Villeneuve was held prisoner in England and even attended Nelson's funeral. Paroled in the spring of 1806, on 22 April, only a few days after his arrival back in France, he was found stabbed through the heart in a hotel room in Rennes. According to official French reports Villeneuve took his own life, but there remains the possibility that he was killed by Napoleon's agents.

The much-maligned Vice Admiral Pierre Villeneuve has the dubious record of having been on the receiving end of a Nelson victory twice: at Aboukir Bay in 1798 and Trafalgar in 1805. (CPL)

Napoleon hoped that his complicated and elaborate manoeuvres would panic London into dispatching warships from home waters to counter threats to Britain's widespread overseas interests, leaving the British Isles exposed to the invasion flotilla. Villeneuve and Missessy would then be able to return to European waters, picking up five French battleships from the Spanish port of Ferrol and the remainder of the ships in Rochefort, and sail to Boulogne, there to protect the invasion fleet. Ganteaume would provide the final piece of the jigsaw with the Brest squadron, which would strike out into the Atlantic, then turn towards Ireland where 18,000 troops would be landed, thereby drawing away any remaining Royal Naval squadrons and distracting the British government's attention away from the invasion flotilla. Ganteaume would then return to help cover the invasion either by way of the Channel or by sailing round the north coast of Scotland and down the east coast of England.[10]

This was strategic planning on a fantastic scale, encompassing global fleet movements over thousands of miles of ocean. It was also completely impracticable. A key tenet that Napoleon could never grasp was that, while his high-risk strategies had brought tremendous success on land, matters at sea were immensely more complicated. On land inclement weather might delay the advance of an army, at sea it could completely wreck a fleet. His failure to understand sea warfare doomed all his plans from the outset. While appearing radical and visionary, his plans took no

---

Napoleon to Ganteaume Aix-la-Chapelle,

6 September 1804

Vice-Admiral Ganteaume, Commander-in-Chief of the Brest fleet, I have received your letter of August 27th. I have given orders for the 1,273 men wanting to make up the complement of your squadron to be placed at your disposal, viz.: 200 men of the Marine Artillery, 600 dockyard conscripts, and 500 men from infantry of the line. So the Patriote is in the roadstead at last! With 21 ships, I hope that you will be in a position to do something.

Your sortie has struck the English with great terror. They know well that, having all the seas to defend, a squadron escaping from Brest could do them incalculable harm; and, if you could carry in Brumaire 16,000 men and 500 horses to Ireland, the result would be fatal to our enemies. Tell me if you think you can be ready, and what are the possibilities of success…. [Napoleon continued urging Ganteaume to undertake naval exercises in the roadstead at Brest – 'I have caused these manoeuvres to be carried out by the Boulogne flotilla, with excellent results, and it is still doing them; it is an object of encouragement and of instruction the advantage of which no one can deny.']

Source: Hodges and Hughes, pp. 206–7.

---

account of the influence that time, distance, weather, communications, accidents, disease, and so on, had on naval planning. In order to succeed, all his plans had to run without mishap over huge distances and within the same time-scale so as to achieve a concentration of force against an experienced foe operating on interior lines of communication.[11]

Perhaps Napoleon's plans for the invasion of England were clouded by the apparent success of his 1798 amphibious operation. Taking place in the relatively calm and predictable waters of the Mediterranean, that expedition had been an initial success, as the French evaded Nelson and landed an army in Egypt. What the French Emperor forgot was that the naval escort was destroyed by Nelson once the army had been put ashore and eventually he had to flee back to France with a small group of friends leaving the rest of the army behind.

Spain Joins with France

In late 1804 Napoleon's plans were given a massive boost by the entry of Spain into the war against Britain. Upon the outbreak of war in 1793, Spain had fought against Revolutionary France. In 1796, by the Treaty of San Ildefonso, Spain had changed sides and agreed to supply France with fifteen sail-of-the-line. When the Peace of Amiens broke down, Spain hoped to remain out of the war but was committed to providing naval assistance to France or to pay an indemnity. Napoleon, short of cash, asked for a substantial sum of money. When the Spaniards protested at the size of the payment, Napoleon offered three choices: pay what he asked, declare war on Britain, or have war declared on them by France. Not surprisingly the Spaniards chose the first option, paying the indemnity on 19 October 1803 to preserve nominal neutrality.

When it was rumoured that a further payment would be made to France in late 1804, the British government decided to act. Having already warned Madrid that the original payment was viewed as a *casus belli*, London was concerned over Spanish naval preparations and viewed with suspicion a Spanish squadron of four frigates returning from South America, laden with specie, possibly to pay off the French. The British plan was to present an overwhelming force and peacefully seize the vessels. However, when the Spaniards were intercepted on 5 October 1804, the Royal Navy could only muster four frigates for the attack. The Spanish commander naturally resisted, but after a short engagement one of his frigates, the 34-gun *Mercedes*, exploded sending men, women, children and a large amount of cash to the bottom. The three remaining vessels were seized and valued at £1,000,000.

The Spanish government was outraged at the attack and on 12 December declared war on Britain. This now gave Napoleon access to the Spanish navy, with six battleships at Cartagena, nine at Ferrol and sixteen in the main Spanish fleet base at Cadiz. Spain's entry into the war swung the naval situation back towards France. The key question for the British government was how to counter Napoleon's plans

At the beginning of March 1805, which is when the Trafalgar campaign can be considered to have commenced, the combatants' naval forces were distributed as follows:

French and Spanish – 78 battleships

Texel – nine French battleships, 80 transports, 25,000 men

Boulogne – invasion flotilla, 130,000 men

Brest – 21 French battleships

Rochefort – two French battleships

Lorient – one French battleship

Ferrol – five French battleships, ten Spanish battleships

Cadiz – one French battleship, six Spanish battleships ready to sail

Cartagena – six Spanish French battleships

Toulon – eleven French battleships

At sea in the West Indies – six French battleships under Missiessy

British – 65–69 battleships

The Downs, Lord Keith, watching the Texel and Straits of Dover – eleven small battleships

Channel fleet, Cornwallis, watching Brest – 20–24 battleships (the actual number on station at any one time varied depending on revictualling, watering and repairing)

Blockading Rochefort – no ships, the naval force having been sent after Missiessy

Blockading Ferrol – eight battleships

Blockading Cadiz – Orde, six battleships

Mediterranean Fleet – Nelson, twelve battleships

West Indies – four battleships, plus Cochrane's squadron to arrive with six more.

THE BRITISH DEFENCE AGAINST INVASION

Britain did not await her fate with resignation. In a prime example of how sea power can influence the course of war, the Royal Navy stood as an immovable bulwark against the ambitions of Napoleon. The Royal Navy was central to British maritime security and economic expansion during this period. The British battle fleet was designed for aggressive, offensive strategy and tactics, to destroy the enemy in battle or negate it by blockade. Battle was preferable to destroy the threat, but it was actually quite rare. There were only six major fleet battles during the wars, the Glorious First of June (1794), St. Vincent (14 February 1797), Camperdown (11 October 1797), Nile (1 August 1798) Copenhagen (2 April 1801) and Trafalgar (21 October 1805), with perhaps another half-dozen squadron-size fleet actions.

Unsurprisingly, the enemy's fleets did not always seek to engage the Royal Navy and generally tried to avoided battles and the associated loss of ships and highly skilled sailors. For a large part of the time they remained in harbour, safe from the activities of the British fleets, but by remaining 'in being' they posed a constant threat. Stationed off the main French ports of Brest, Toulon, Rochefort and the Spanish port of Ferrol, stood a mighty 'Wooden Wall', as Royal Navy squadrons blockaded these ports. 'They were dull, weary, uneventful months,' wrote Mahan, 'those months of watching and waiting of the big ships before the French arsenals. Purposeless they surely seemed to many, but they saved England…Those far distant, storm-beaten ships, upon which the Grand Army never looked, stood between it and the domination of the world.'[12]

Although the blockading of Europe's coasts could inflict wear and tear on the Royal Navy, the Admiralty had largely managed to compensate for this. Ships

ADMIRAL SIR WILLIAM CORNWALLIS (1744–1819)

Sir William Cornwallis was the man who commanded the Channel Fleet during the Trafalgar campaign. This command was the cornerstone of Admiralty policy, forming the major pool of ships available for many duties while the fleet's main deployment area was off Ushant, to blockade the French naval base of Brest.

Born in February 1744 to a distinguished and well-connected family, Cornwallis entered the Royal Navy in 1755. A combination of outstanding ability and, of course, the necessary patronage of senior officers, ensured that his early career was meteoric. He saw action during the Seven Years' War, was present at the 1759 victory at Quiberon Bay and was promoted to Post Captain in 1765 at the age of 21. He next entered Parliament and served as an MP until 1807. At Jamaica in 1779, during the War of American Independence, he came into contact with Nelson, and they became firm friends. A great deal of Cornwallis' active service was in the West Indies; in the 74-gun *Canada* he was present at Admiral Sir George Rodney's victory at the Battle of the Saintes (12 April 1782). Stationed in the East Indies when war with revolutionary France broke out, on his return to England Cornwallis was promoted to Rear Admiral in 1793 and Vice Admiral the following year.

Now serving with the Channel Fleet, in 1795 Cornwallis was in command of a detached squadron when he was pursued by a superior French force. Two of his squadron's ships were in trouble and he turned to assist them. The French, thinking British reinforcements were at hand, backed off. Refusing a command in the West Indies in 1798 because of illness, he was court-martialled and censured. Although he spent the next few years ashore, he was promoted to Admiral in 1799 and was back at sea in 1801 as Commander-in-Chief of the Channel Fleet, a post he held until 1806.

A quiet and retiring, plump red-faced bachelor, he once joked that rather than enjoying the delights of London high-society he preferred the seclusion of his country estate and the society of his cabbages! Regarded with affection by his crews, who, among other nicknames, referred to him as 'Billy go tight' because of his paunch, and 'Blue Billy' (the blue pennant, informing his captains that they were to be ready to weigh anchor at any moment, was nearly always flying from his flagship in the Channel). Often overlooked, Cornwallis' contribution to the outcome of the naval war cannot be overstated. It was his fleet that prevented Ganteaume ever getting out of Brest, and acting on Barham's orders, it was his placing of Sir Robert Calder off Cape Finisterre that prevented Villeneuve entering the Channel, thereby ending Napoleon's invasion plan.

As commander of the Channel Fleet, Admiral William Cornwallis played a pivotal role during the months leading up to Trafalgar. His fleet, usually stationed off Ushant, formed the linchpin of British maritime strategy. (CPL)

were supplied on blockading station by a regular system,[13] and by rotating ships between blockade duties and time in port, wear and tear could be repaired. But the need to send ships off station for repairs or to obtain supplies could mean that as many as 50 per cent of the blockading vessels might in fact be engaged elsewhere.

SAILING WARSHIPS

During the age of sail fleets were divided into several ship types. This reflected the various duties that a specific ship was expected to perform. In the Royal Navy the system was known as 'rating' and used the number of guns carried by a ship to provide classification. The system was not rigid, and some vessels were re-rated during their careers, but in general the following holds true:

First Rate – ships of 120, 110, 104 or 100 guns
Second Rate – ships of 98 or 90 guns
Third Rate – ships of 80, 74, 70 or 64 guns
Fourth Rate – ships of 60 or 50 guns
Fifth Rate – ships of 44, 40, 38, 36 or 32 guns
Sixth Rate – ships of 28, 24 or 20 guns
Unrated – ships of fewer than 20 guns, such as sloops, brigs and cutters

Ships of the line

The main line of battle was composed of the heavy First to Third Rate ships. Their role was to engage the enemy's ships with heavy gunfire. These ships formed the majority of both fleets at Trafalgar. First Rates, such as HMS *Victory* and *Royal Sovereign*, and Second Rates, such as *Téméraire*, had three gun decks and hence were known as three-deckers. The one exception at Trafalgar was the Spanish *Santíssima Trinidad*, which carried four gun decks. They were expensive, impressive and prestigious symbols of state power, and hence were popular as Admiral's flagships. Three-deckers had the heaviest guns and were designed for close-quarter work, smashing enemy ships with their broadsides of 32pdrs on the lower, 24pdrs on the middle and 12pdrs on the upper gun decks. At Trafalgar Nelson used his three-deckers to lead his attacks; with their heavy firepower and strong build they packed a powerful punch. Because of the large number of heavy guns and their stout construction it was considered naval opinion that in combat one three-decker was the equivalent of two smaller ships. The most numerous class of ship-of-the-line was the Third Rate, and in particular the two-decked 74-gun ship. Originally conceived by the French, it was a design classic, matching fire power, the ability to carry a full battery of 32pdrs, and speed, making it one of the most useful ship types. They could stand in the line of battle, and their fine lines ensured good seaworthiness. They were also cheaper to build and maintain and required fewer crew than the larger ships. The 64-gun ships carried a lighter battery on their two gun decks than the 74s. Cheaper and quicker to build than larger ships, they were the product of the War of American Independence; none was built after the 1780s. By 1800 they were considered too small for the main fleet, yet two 64-gun ships were in Nelson's fleet at Trafalgar.

The major British naval force was the Channel Fleet, averaging about 33 ships-of-the-line and ten frigates. It was under the command of Admiral Sir William Cornwallis. Usually located off Ushant, blockading the French fleet base at Brest, it covered the possibility of the French Fleet making a thrust at Ireland, or it could follow an enemy up the Channel. But blockade was not infallible. There was a possibility that the Royal Navy might be blown off station and French or Spanish fleets might escape and play havoc with British colonial possessions and commerce.

Fourth Rates were a dying breed; with the advent of three-deckers they were no longer big enough to take their place in the line-of-battle, but they could prove useful, serving as flagships for smaller detached squadrons. During the Trafalgar campaign the Royal Navy's Fourth Rates were concentrated in the North Sea Fleet, where, despite their size, they could have wrought havoc on the French invasion flotilla.

Frigates

The Fifth and Sixth Rates were far too weak to stand in the line of battle. With their main battery carried on a single gun deck, frigates were built for speed and mobility. Their main roles were reconnaissance, commerce protection and raiding, carrying communications and attacking enemy privateers. Using their mobility they could tackle isolated ships-of-the-line, as long as they avoided the devastating broadsides. In battle their role was to pass signals throughout the fleet and provide assistance to their larger sisters. As a consequence of their adventurous and dashing role, Frigate captains came to great prominence. Frigates saw a great deal more action than the ships-of-the-line and crews had a greater chance of claiming prize money for capturing enemy ships, so service in frigates was more popular than the tedious routine of blockade experienced by the larger ships.

Unrated ships

The unrated vessels were usually highly specialised ships carrying fewer than 20 guns. Sloops were the largest warships to be commanded by an officer below the rank of captain and were mainly used to protect commercial ships while raiding those of the enemy. Cheap and quick to build, they were ideal for watching over the French invasion ports. Fireships were designed to crash into enemy ships, setting them alight. They were often small warships or merchant vessels converted for the task. Their material effects were quite small, but they could create panic and fear among an enemy fleet. Bomb vessels were even more specialised, usually carrying two mortars which sent explosive shells on a high trajectory against targets on land.

All of the following smaller vessels could be commanded by a lieutenant. Schooners, named after their sailing rig, were an American design and few served in the Royal Navy, the famous exception being the *Pickle*, which carried news of Trafalgar to England. Cutters had a deep draught for their size and were not suitable for inshore work, but their speed and mobility made them essential for carrying communications and patrol work. Gunboats varied in size from those carrying one single heavy gun which could be traversed, to those carrying a broadside as well. Particularly useful in amphibious landings because of their shallow draught and capability to provide fire support, gunboats would have been important in frustrating any attempt by the French to land in England.

William James noted that even while in port the French and allied fleets would 'occupy the attention of an equal number of British ships' while any French squadron that escaped blockade would be pursued by at least 'two squadrons of equal force'.[14] In this case the Channel Fleet also acted as a strategic naval reserve, for if enemy ships managed to escape, a not uncommon occurrence, they were aggressively hunted down by Royal Naval squadrons detached from the fleet. If these encountered a superior enemy force they could fall back on Cornwallis, concentrating enough naval power in the decisive theatre to prevent any French naval incursion into the Straits of Dover.[15]

This had been the policy of the Seven Years' War, leading to ultimate victory over France in North America. But during the War of American Independence, control of home waters had been lost and the French had made a decisive contribution to the war in the rebellious colonies. This was a reminder that British home and colonial defence was best assured by keeping enemy fleets bottled up in port:

...the blockade of Brest consequently came to complement the great expeditions to the West Indies that characterised the Revolutionary War. After 1795 the principle of maintaining the blockade was consistently applied. Even though the resources that could be devoted to it were at times limited by deployments to other stations, there was full recognition that the blockade was indispensable to the maintenance of the British war effort in other theatres.[16]

The prickly Lord Keith was furious that Nelson was given command of the Mediterranean Fleet in 1803. As commander of the North Sea Fleet during 1805, it was Keith's responsibility to keep watch over the French invasion harbours. (CPL)

GEORGE ELPHINSTONE, ADMIRAL LORD KEITH (1745–1823)

Born to Scottish aristocracy, he was the son of Charles, 10th Lord Elphinstone, and first went to sea in 1761 at the relatively mature age of 16. Promoted to Lieutenant in 1770, he made post captain in 1775 and saw active service during the War of American Independence. After this he entered the world of politics but was back at sea in 1793. Serving with Lord Hood's Mediterranean Fleet in HMS *Robust*, he was actively involved in the occupation of the French naval base of Toulon and was one of the last to leave the city when it was recaptured by French Revolutionaries. Created a Knight of the Bath and promoted to flag rank as Rear Admiral in 1794, in 1795 he commanded a successful operation to seize the Dutch Cape of Good Hope. In 1797 he assisted in subduing the naval mutinies. Ennobled as Baron Keith, he served as second in command of St. Vincent's Mediterranean Fleet in 1798, but the latter's ill health led to his recall in 1799 leaving Keith in command. Here he came into contact with Nelson. Nelson had grown accustomed to having an independent role under St. Vincent, but now his physical and mental health was in turmoil. Keith attempted to use kid gloves in his official dealings with Nelson, but in private was concerned over his subordinate's behaviour in Naples. When Nelson was ordered home Keith continued to command the Mediterranean Fleet until the peace of 1802. With the war renewed in 1803, Keith was furious when Nelson was given the Mediterranean Fleet while he was appointed to the North Sea Fleet. It therefore fell to Keith to command and organise the anti-invasion flotilla in the Channel during the dangerous years of 1803-5, though he held the command until 1807. Suffering from arthritis and gout, Keith spent five years ashore until he was ordered to hoist his flag as commander of the Channel Fleet in 1812. During the next few years Keith's ships provided much needed support to the war being fought by the Duke of Wellington in the Iberian Peninsula. At the end of the wars in 1815, Keith retired. He died in his native Scotland in 1823.

Stationed in the Downs, a secure anchorage between the Kent coast and the Goodwin Sands, the North Sea Fleet was under the command of Admiral Lord Keith. Covering the coast of the Low Countries and Northern France, his command was responsible for watching the main French invasion ports, in particular Boulogne. Keith's fleet numbered 176 vessels in total, including 21 ships-of-the-line and 29 frigates. Some of the battleships were old 50-gun vessels, too small to take part in a full-scale naval battle but would be more than capable of tackling the invasion flotilla. It was Keith's smaller vessels that operated off the enemy coasts, gathering intelligence and harrying the invasion preparations.

The Mediterranean Fleet was under the command of Vice Admiral Lord Horatio Nelson and numbered thirteen ships-of-the-line and twelve frigates. Although behind the Channel and North Sea Fleets in order of importance, it was a key command because, while the North Sea and Channel Fleets were both essentially defensive deployments, the Mediterranean Fleet was the main offensive weapon of the Royal Navy. Due to the distance from the Admiralty the commander was also granted a degree of independence. Promoting British interests along the entire length of the Mediterranean demanded an expertise beyond purely naval considerations. Diplomacy and tact were needed to deal with the many countries and governments upon which British sea power in the region depended. The tasks of the Mediterranean Fleet were: preventing Malta and Sicily (both important for naval supplies and repairs) from falling into French hands; supporting the operations of British land forces or, in support of Prime Minister William Pitt's attempts to build an anti-French coalition, Britain's allies; protecting British trading interests; blockading the French Toulon squadron. The numerous assignments were a constant drain on naval resources, but if the enemy fleets in the region could be destroyed, it would ease the burden of blockading every hostile naval base containing ships. After the Spaniards entered the war Nelson's fleet was divided, and Sir John Orde was stationed off Cadiz to watch over that port. In addition to the fleets in European waters, smaller British squadrons were positioned across the globe to protect British trade and naval bases. These were mainly concentrated in the areas of greatest importance, the West and East Indies.

Defence Against Invasion
The direct response to the French invasion threat during 1803–1805 was a triple layer of naval defence. Earl St. Vincent, the First Lord of the Admiralty until 1804, and his successor Henry Dundas, 1st Viscount Melville, outlined the measures that it was hoped would prevent the French ever setting foot ashore in Britain. On 6 June 1804 Melville declared to Keith: 'I always go on the principle that as we ought to have a threefold naval protection, it is highly essential that we should have as many vessels armed as possible.' The triple layered defence entailed 'that the enemy should be met first at the mouth of their own harbours and on their own coasts; secondly they should be annoyed every inch of their passage in crossing the sea, and lastly that they should be again met by every resistance that can be opposed to them on our own coast when they approach it'.[17]

Vice Admiral Lord Horatio Nelson (1758–1805)

The greatest exponent of naval warfare in British history was born on 29 September 1758 in the small Norfolk village of Burnham Thorpe, the son of the Reverend Edmund and Catherine (née Suckling) Nelson. The young Horatio entered the Royal Navy as a midshipman in *Raisonnable* in 1770, helped by the patronage of his uncle, Captain Maurice Suckling. He served in the West Indies before embarking on an Arctic expedition in a converted bomb vessel, HMS *Carcass*, in 1772. In 1777 he made Lieutenant and was appointed to HMS *Lowestoffe*. The following year Sir Peter Parker promoted him to the rank of commander, the sloop HMS *Badger* being his first independent command, before achieving the post rank of captain and moving into HMS *Hinchinbroke*. He gained valuable experience assisting operations ashore during an expedition to Nicaragua, but fell gravely ill and returned home.

During the years 1784–7 he was back in the West Indies. His controversial anti-contraband measures caused friction with his commander, Admiral Sir Richard Hughes, and many of the rich merchants in the islands. His gauche handling of a dispute between Prince William Henry, son of King George III, and a Lieutenant William Schomberg led to Nelson being unemployed on half-pay. While in the West Indies in March 1787 Nelson had married a wealthy widow, Frances Nisbet, and they now moved to Burnham Thorpe. It was a strained marriage. Frances, or Fanny as she was often referred to, found life hard in cold, rural Norfolk while Nelson was increasingly fractious at his unemployment. Moreover, although Fanny had a son by her first marriage, Josiah Nisbet, it became very obvious that the marriage would produce no children of Nelson's own. Like many Royal Naval officers, the outbreak of war with Revolutionary France provided Nelson with the opportunity for employment, in his case to the 64-gun *Agamemnon*. Stationed in the Mediterranean, he first met Sir William and Lady Emma Hamilton while on a diplomatic mission to Naples. The following year Nelson was wounded at the siege of Calvi, in Corsica. A French cannon-ball struck the ground in front of him, sending gravel flying into his face, which caused the permanent damage to the sight in his right eye.

In 1795 the recovered Nelson, still in *Agamemnon*, operated with the main Mediterranean Fleet under Admiral William Hotham, tasting fleet action at the battle of Genoa in March and showing his aggressive spirit by attacking the larger French ship *Ça Ira*, damaging her so much that she was seized next day. Promoted to Commodore in 1796, Nelson came to national attention in 1797 at the battle of Cape St. Vincent. Commanding HMS *Captain*, he wore out of the loose line of battle formed by Admiral Sir John Jervis, possibly in accordance with Jervis' instructions to assist the British van in its fight with the Spanish rear. In close combat he personally led the boarding-parties which captured two Spanish battleships. Nelson made sure his role in the battle was brought to the fore by writing a letter to his former captain, William Locker, that was specifically designed for newspaper publication. The result was that he was created a Knight of the Bath and promoted to Rear Admiral. Success was followed by failure; he lost his right arm during a headstrong amphibious assault on Santa Cruz in Tenerife which was repelled with heavy losses.

Convalescing ashore, Nelson was deeply depressed but soon overcame his disability with good humour, referring to the stump as his 'fin'. Remaining in London, rather than being with the fleet, Nelson could meet the great and the good, cementing his popular image in the general public's mind, and his professional skill and opinions with the Admiralty. They responded by appointing him to the Mediterranean Fleet under Jervis, now ennobled as Earl St. Vincent. Catching the French fleet at anchor in Aboukir Bay, off the Nile delta, he again displayed aggressive and decisive tactics. Placing great emphasis on the individual judgement of his captains, the British fleet enveloped the head of the French fleet, destroying the enemy in a ferocious engagement. Of the thirteen French battleships, only two escaped capture or destruction. In one evening the balance of power in the Mediterranean had shifted away from France and towards Britain. Having collected another wound, this time to the forehead, Nelson's image was transformed from naval hero to national hero. The man who had thwarted Napoleon Bonaparte's ambitions in the east became the first true 'celebrity'.

After the battle he returned to Naples to convalesce with the Hamiltons, and began his affair with Lady Emma. He became involved in the bloody Neapolitan civil war and was implicated in the decision to execute several revolutionaries, which caused some controversy at home and lead to his recall in 1800. With the Hamiltons Nelson took the long way home, touring European cities, revelling in his popularity as the man who had bloodied the nose of Napoleon. On arrival in England he bought a house in Merton, on the London to Portsmouth road, separated from Fanny and took up residence with the Hamiltons. Emma was now pregnant with Nelson's child and he was concerned for their health until February 1802 when she gave birth to a daughter, Horatia.

In 1801 Nelson had been posted back to sea with the Channel Fleet and led an expedition to Copenhagen to browbeat the pro-French Russians and the Baltic States into re-opening the area to British trade. An attempt to negotiate with the Danes broke down, leading to an attack on their fleet at anchor, a very close-fought battle, during which Nelson famously ignored his superior officer's signal, and brought to a timely conclusion by a brilliant piece of Nelsonic diplomacy. Sensing that things were not going according to plan because of the tenacious fighting of the Danes, he wrote to the Crown Prince of Denmark just as fire from the Danish fleet was slackening. The Prince agreed to a truce which ended the bloody fight. Returning to home waters, the national hero joined the fleet that was thwarting Napoleon's projected invasion until the Peace of Amiens.

When war broke out again in 1803, Nelson was appointed to the Mediterranean Fleet which was blockading Toulon. In April 1804 he moved up in naval seniority to Vice Admiral of the White.

By 1805 Lord Nelson was already the greatest sea warrior of the age of sail and the first true celebrity. His vision and leadership would prove key in any engagement with the enemy. (CPL)

The first line of defence was the deployment along the French and Dutch coastlines of a flotilla consisting of 170 vessels, mainly composed of frigates and gunboats, but including 21 ships-of-the-line. Their key role was to watch the invasion ports and gather intelligence regarding enemy fleet movements while preventing any of the smaller enemy ships getting out of their own harbours. Numerous small-scale skirmishes occurred along the enemy coast, and French ships were driven back into port causing confusion among the invasion forces. The second defensive tier was the squadron of ships-of-the-line and frigates under the direct command of Keith. Their job was to attack the invasion flotilla while it was still at sea, so a large part of the squadron was often stationed off Boulogne. The Sea Fencibles, a naval volunteer service that was to provide 25,000 men and 800 gunboats to protect the various possible landing sites along the south coast from Swansea in the west to Great Yarmouth on the east coast, provided the third and final layer of naval defence.[18]

If the French succeeded in forcing their way through these purely naval measures, they would find that the British government had also been busy preparing defences ashore. Volunteers had flooded recruiting stations in 1803 to assist in Home Defence; a sort of Georgian 'Dad's Army'. The number of Volunteers had swollen to unwieldy heights in late 1804 when they mustered 300,000 in England with a further 70,000 in Ireland. Of extremely dubious military capacity, there is no doubt that Napoleon's veterans would have made short work of them. Their main use was in relieving more regular formations of sentry and transport duties while keeping up morale among the populace. Of more military value were the results of the Militia Act of 1802 which prescribed the recruiting of 51,500 men, with another 25,000 added to this in 1803. Men were tempted into the Militia by a bounty of £7.12s.6d, in return for a period of five years' service within the British Isles. Many who came forward were unfit or, once enrolled, deserted. With many officers having served in the Regular Army, the Militia proved a fertile ground for recruiting for the Regular Army, which in 1803 numbered 132,000 men. Only 81,000 of these were available for Home Defence, as colonial commitments, especially in the Caribbean, absorbed 50,000 men. By the offer of a large bounty, as much as £60 in some instances, the Regular Army had been increased by another 35,000 men by 1805.

Not surprisingly the Militia and the Regular Army were concentrated in the south-east. Military encampments were located at Bexhill, Beachy Head, Rye, Winchelsea, Brighton and Southbourne. In July 1805 the military forces were re-organised to provide, in modern terms, a 'rapid response force' of 10,000 men capable of being deployed in one strategic lift to wherever the French might land.

For many the renewal of war provided an opportunity to return to a military career, such as John Henry Slessor (1777–1850) who kept a diary of his career throughout the Napoleonic Wars:

> All is bustle. The French Ambassador has received his passports and embarked for Calais. Our Navy and Army are immediately to be augmented; the Militia called out, new loans, fresh taxes, etc. The Admiralty and Horse Guards are crowded with applications for employment…

I now got appointed to a company in a Reserve Battn. This was supposed to be an effective way of recruiting the regiments of the line; rather a compulsory act in the first instance, whereby each county was obliged to furnish a quota of men for home service, who after a while, were permitted, with the temptation of an additional bounty, to volunteer into Regular Regiments. The consequence was that all our best men left us'[19]

Alongside the increase in manpower, the government instituted an extensive programme of fortification building. Perhaps the most spectacular was the Royal Military Canal, begun in 1803 behind Romney Marsh (which it was hoped could be flooded). Similarly the building of 74 Martello Towers along the south coast between Eastbourne and Folkestone was designed to hold up an enemy landing for as long as possible. These towers, 30 feet high with walls of between six and nine feet thick, topped off with a bomb-proof roof, were copied from a Corsican design that had successfully resisted attack by the Royal Navy in 1794. They were armed with one or two heavy guns on the roof, giving them a wide field of fire. However, none of these engineering projects were completed until after the battle of Trafalgar and their defensive properties may have been overstated.

In any military operation, speed of communication and intelligence are key elements. News that the invasion attempt was underway would invariably come from the Royal Navy. The British government had already addressed this need with the construction of a series of shutter telegraph stations, linking the Admiralty with the

---

T. Birch, Lieut. Col. A.Q.M., Gen. Eastern District, to the Reverend H. Bate Dudley, Inspector, &c. &c., Colchester, July 3 1804

Sir – I have the honour to inform you, by the direction of Lieutenant-General Sir James Craig, that the Primary Signal Stations are now established, throughout the County of Essex at the following places:

Colchester	*Mum's Hedge*	*Brightlingsea*
White Notley	*Earls Colne*	*Ongar Park*
Gosfield	*Meffing*	*Sewer's End*
Rettenden	*Littlebury*	*Danbury*
Thaxted	*Langdon Hill*	*Hatfield Broad Oak*
Come Green		

A white Flag is constantly flying at the stations merely to point it out more clearly to the sentinels on guard at the communicating stations. The hoisting of the Red Flag is in future to be considered the signal for general alarm, and will be a sufficient authority for lighting any beacons already established, and hoisting the Red Flags that may have been provided at the different towns and villages for the same purpose.
Source: Naval Chronicle, III, p. 48.

key naval bases of Portsmouth, Plymouth, Sheerness and Chatham (this latter line actually finished at Keith's headquarters). As had occurred in 1588, when England was threatened by the Spanish Armada, beacons were built throughout the countryside, which could be lit to signal the dreaded news that the French were coming. Posters were printed entitled 'In case of actual invasion', which detailed the measures the public were to implement including the evacuation of women and children from coastal areas and the removal of carts, horses, foodstuffs, in fact anything that would benefit the invader.

While there had been several unconventional plans to cross the Channel put forward in France, in Britain the combination of the ever-present threat of invasion, industrial progress, the violent bloodletting of the French Revolution and the deliberate spreading of misinformation from the French government, had provided fertile ground for producers of popular prints. Imagination ran riot during the 1790s and 1800s as a whole host of fiendishly cunning, yet entirely impracticable ideas were credited to the French. These included an enormous 600-foot long raft capable of carrying 15,000 men, powered by windmills and containing a powerful castle-like construction fortified with 500 artillery pieces! Another was 'The Dread of Albion', a huge turtle-like contraption powered by horses and topped off with a statue of Liberty. Of course these wild and crazy subjects were entirely imaginary, but they played on the feeling of foreboding with which the general populace viewed the possibility of a French invasion.

Despite the fears of the populace, a remarkable number of humorous pamphlets appeared lampooning Napoleon. One flyer for a fictitious theatre show declared:

> Some dark, foggy, Night, about November next, will be attempted by a strolling Company of French Vagrants, an old Pantomimic Farce, called HARLEQUIN'S INVASION, or THE DISAPPOINTED BANDITTI. Harlequin Butcher, [played by] Mr BONAPARTE, from Corsica (who performed that Character in Egypt, Italy, Switzerland, Holland).

Another offered a 'Twenty Thousand Pounds Reward' for the capture of: 'a certain ill-disposed Vagrant and common Disturber, commonly called or known by the name of NAPOLEON BONAPARTE'.[20]

Despite the fears of the country, informed opinion was that invasion was highly unlikely due to the strategic deployment of the Royal Navy and the difficulties inherent in amphibious warfare. As early as August 1803 Colonel Robert Crawfurd declared: 'The distance is considerable. The management of a fleet of three or four hundred vessels is extremely difficult, even without being disturbed by an enemy.' Moreover, the problems caused by the weather could not be overcome; the necessary wind direction would bring the enemy onto a lee shore in heavy surf while anything more than a moderate wind would throw the invasion force into utter confusion.[21] St. Vincent himself had stated to the House of Lords: 'I do not say they cannot come; I merely say they cannot come by sea.' A speech made to the House of Commons by Sir Edward Pellew in response to William Pitt's calls for increased numbers of

Extract from a speech by Sir Edward Pellew Parliamentary Debates,
March 15 1804

As I very seldom trouble the House, I hope I may be permitted to make a few observations on a subject of which, from the professional experience I have had, I may be presumed to have some knowledge. From the debate of this night, there is one piece of information I have acquired, that the French have got upwards of a thousand vessels at Boulogne. I am glad to find they are shut up there; we have one advantage in it, we know where they are; but I wish we had any means of knowing when they intended to come out. I know thus much, however, that they cannot all get out in one day, or in one night either; and when they do come out, I trust that our 500 cockle-shells alone, as an Honourable Admiral has called a very manageable and very active part of our force, will be able to give a good account of them. Sir, I do not really see in the arrangement of our naval defence anything to excite the apprehensions even of the most timid among us; on the contrary, I see everything that may be expected from activity and perseverance, to inspire us with confidence. I see a triple naval bulwark, composed of one fleet acting on the enemy's coast, of another consisting of heavier ships stationed in the Downs, ready to act at a moment's notice, and a third close to the beach, capable of destroying any part of the enemy's flotilla that should escape the vigilance of the other two branches of our defence…

   As to gun-boats, they are the most contemptible force that can be employed; gun-brigs, indeed, are of some use, but between a gun-brig and a gun-boat there is almost as much difference as between a man-of-war and a frigate. I have lately seen half a dozen of them lying wrecked upon the rocks. As to the possibility of the enemy being able, in a narrow sea, to pass through our blockading and protecting squadrons, with all that secrecy and dexterity, and by those hidden means that some worthy people expect, I really, from anything that I have seen in the course of my professional experience, am not much disposed to concur in it. I know, Sir, and can assert with confidence that our navy was never better found, that it was never better supplied, and that our men were never better fed or better clothed. Have we not all the enemy's ports blockaded from Toulon to Flushing? Are we not able to cope, anywhere, with any force that the enemy dares to send out against us? And do we not even outnumber them at every one of those ports we have blockaded? It would smack a little of egotism, I fear, were I to speak of myself; but, as a person lately having the command of six ships, I hope I may be allowed to state to the House how I have been supported in that command. Sir, during the time that I was stationed off Ferrol, I had ships passing from the fleet to me every three weeks or month, and so much was the French commander shut up in that port deceived by these appearances, that he was persuaded, and I believe is to this very hour, that I had twelve ships under my command, and that I had two squadrons to relieve each other, one of six inside, and another of six outside…

Source: Hodges and Hughes, pp. 210–11.

smaller craft has been presented here in an abridged form. Naval officers knew that the large French invasion force of gun boats, prames and other small vessels would

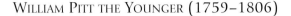

WILLIAM PITT THE YOUNGER (1759–1806)

The British Prime Minister at the time of Trafalgar was the second son of William Pitt, 1st Earl of Chatham. The Younger Pitt entered the House of Commons in 1780. A remarkable orator, his talents were obvious and led to his rapid rise to Cabinet rank as Chancellor of the Exchequer in 1782. At the 1784 election he became the head of government, concerning himself with securing financial stability for the country. During the wars with France Pitt was continually striving to organise European coalitions to fight France on the continent while Britain could fight France at sea, where her inherent advantages could be used to maximum effect. His support for Catholic Emancipation led to his resignation in 1801, but he was back in government in 1804.

During the vital year of 1805 Pitt made a major contribution to the Trafalgar campaign by appointing Sir Charles Middleton, Baron Barham, as First Lord of the Admiralty. Also acting as Foreign Secretary, Pitt attempted to organise another European Coalition. This entailed Royal Naval co-operation with Russia in the Mediterranean, leading to French efforts to frustrate these plans with Villeneuve's fleet in Cadiz. At a speech two days after Trafalgar he stated: 'Let us hope that England, having saved herself by her energy, may save Europe by her example.' Increasingly ill, Pitt's hope was crushed by the French victories on land. He died on 23 January 1806.

William Pitt the Younger in earlier times. By the time of Trafalgar Pitt was worn out by his work and lifestyle. His death in 1806 would leave a huge vacuum in British political life. (CPL)

be no match for the Royal Naval Squadron in the Downs. Without the protection of a battlefleet the invasion flotilla, and with it Napoleon's dreams of conquering Britain, would be sent to the bottom of the Channel. But Napoleon's plans to concentrate a large naval force in the Channel would be defeated by the blockade and, if the enemy did come out, by a large concentration of Royal Naval force.

Despite all the defensive measures undertaken and the difficulties encountered by the French, Nelson for one did not believe that Napoleon would ever give up the idea of a projected invasion. In the days before Trafalgar he wrote to William Stewart: 'Some day or other, that Buonaparte, if he lives, will attempt the invasion and conquest of Great Britain. The making of our Volunteers and Militia, Soldiers, was a wise plan, and we were very near having occasion to use them.'[22] The one sure way to prevent the French from ever being able to invade Britain was to annihilate their naval forces, a measure Nelson would be more than happy to undertake.

Blockading enemy fleets was a defensive measure, but the British defence against invasion was not entirely passive. A constant war was waged in the Channel during these years of threat, mainly small-scale raids and actions by the Royal Navy but with the occasional larger attack. The means were to harass the French invasion preparations by bombardment, landings, cutting out or destroying vulnerable

Lady Bessborough to Granville Leveson Gower, *Aug 14 1805*

The reports of invasion are so strong that no officer is allow'd to leave his post for twenty and four hours together. Genl Moore has been practising his men to fight breast high in the water – at the suggestion of Mr Pitt, he says, and that he is determin'd to attack before they land. But not withstanding all the hustle that is made – the Volunteers call'd out (and, by the by, behaving with great spirit and receiving the order of permanent duty with Shouts which now the novelty is over is really meritorious), every thing driven from the coast and preparations in every corner – I cannot perceive that it is much believ'd in…

Source: Leveson Gower, II, p. 102.

vessels. The object was to keep the French on the back foot, lower their morale and gather intelligence as to the invasion vessels and enemy plans.

One way to prevent an invasion was to negate the threat at source by attacking the flotilla while it was still in port. With a concentration of force in the well-protected harbour of Boulogne, it naturally became the centre of attention. Despite the employment of a variety of wild and wonderful technical devices, bomb vessels, rockets, explosive carcasses and fire ships, none of the major attacks caused any long-lasting material damage to the invasion flotilla or the ports. Of particular note was an attack on the night of 3 October using clockwork fused explosive devices, said to resemble a floating coffin, towed in by boats and then left to drift into the French flotilla. Anxiously watched by Pitt and Lord Harrowby in Walmer Castle and by Melville with the fleet, it was certainly spectacular as the whole of the coast seemed to take fire and explosions sent columns of flame into the night sky. But like many such attacks, it had little material success. Keith observed the affair aboard the *Monarch* with the man charged with this unconventional warfare, Sir Home Riggs Popham. After the attack Keith informed the Admiralty that 'no extensive injury seems to have been sustained' to the enemy, though he noted that 'it is evident that there has been very considerable confusion among them'.[23] According to Popham the major success of the operation was that the French were becoming very wary about stationing ships in the roadstead outside Boulogne harbour, a not inconsiderable effect as the flotilla would take several days to launch from inside the harbour leaving those outside extremely exposed to another attack.[24]

Captain Sidney Smith, in command of the inshore flotilla, wrote to Keith in September 1805 pleading for afurther attempts on Boulogne, but Keith tried to cool him off, pointing to the great expense for little material gain of the 1804 attack.[25] Undeterred, Smith approached the Government in October. It is interesting to note that even after the Battle of Trafalgar had been fought and won, Smith was still keen to attack the flotilla. After much wrangling and letter writing, including pleas by an American calling himself Mr Francis (in fact no less a person than Robert Fulton!), in December he was sent orders to implement an attack with Congreve rockets but it was not to be as Smith, now a Rear Admiral, was sent to the Mediterranean to operate under the command of Collingwood.[26]

BRITISH AND FRANCO-SPANISH FLEET OPERATIONS

To understand the battle of Trafalgar it is necessary to understand the activities of the various naval forces that were to determine whether Napoleon could mount a successful invasion of the British Isles. Particular attention must be concentrated on those under the command of Admirals Nelson and Villeneuve, for as Mahan has succinctly noted 'upon the opposing Mediterranean fleets turns the chief strategic interest of the intended invasion of England and of the Campaign which issues in Trafalgar'.[27]

Napoleon's re-assessment of his grand naval plans during October 1804 had called for fleet manoeuvres on a global scale. On 26 October he wrote to Admiral Missiessy instructing him to sail for the West Indies, seize Santo Domingo and St. Lucia and then drop off reinforcements at Martinique and Guadaloupe. When the Spaniards joined the war, Missiessy's orders were re-drafted on 23 December. After leaving Rochefort he was to head directly for Martinique and then take St. Lucia and Santo Domingo while awaiting the arrival of Villeneuve. Missiessy sailed on 10 January with six battleships and two frigates, reaching Martinique on 20 February. He had been observed the day after he left port, but the pursuit of his fleet by Rear Admiral Cochrane, who was stationed off Ferrol, was delayed until 24 February. Cochrane's blockade of Ferrol was taken over by a detachment from Cornwallis' fleet. In a classic example of the near impossibility of directing far-flung naval operations, Missiessy received orders in March 1805 to return to Rochefort, but on his way back to Europe he received contradictory orders from Napoleon instructing him to remain in the West Indies.

On 16 January the next part of Napoleon's plan was to be implemented. Villeneuve was ordered to sail for Cayenne, Surinam, Berbice and then Demerara.

After this he was to head for the West Indies and join with Missiessy, reinforce Santo Domingo and then return to Europe to pick up the Ferrol squadron before sailing to Rochefort. Villeneuve left Toulon on 18 January with ten battleships and seven frigates, but several of his ships lost masts in strong winds and the fleet had to put back into Toulon.

At Brest, Ganteaume's fleet awaited the results of Villeneuve and Missiessy's sorties until 2 March 1805 when he was ordered to sail for Ferrol with 21 ships-of-the-line. There he was to take nine Spanish and four French vessels into his fleet and then sail to the West Indies, making landfall at Martinique where he would find Villeneuve and Missiessy. This huge fleet of 40 ships-of-the-line would then return to Europe and sail up the Channel to cover the invasion, scheduled for sometime between 10 June and 10 July. But from the outset the plan started to fall apart. On 23 March Ganteaume's fleet was preparing to sail when from over the horizon the British blockading fleet of 28 ships appeared. Napoleon himself had informed Ganteaume that 'a naval victory at this juncture would lead to nothing. Have but one aim, that of accomplishing your mission. Leave port without an action.' But unable to evade the British fleet and unwilling to force the issue, on 30 March Ganteaume put back into Brest.[28]

In Toulon Villeneuve was preparing for his second attempt to head out into the Atlantic. His orders had now been trimmed to entail a direct voyage to the West Indies, where the French naval forces would concentrate, picking up the ships at Cadiz en route. He was to wait for Ganteaume at Martinique for 40 days. If the latter failed to appear he was directed to a second rendezvous in the Canary Islands, where he could wait 20 days for Ganteaume. On the same day that Ganteaume put back into Brest, Villeneuve's fleet, now comprising eleven ships-of-the-line and six frigates carrying 3,000 troops, made sail for Martinique. On 7 April Villeneuve arrived off the port of Cartagena, but the Spanish ships there would not join his fleet. Two days later he arrived off Cadiz. Waiting just long enough for the French Aigle and the six Spanish battleships and a frigate to weigh anchor, he set course for the Atlantic. The fleet made landfall at Martinique on 13 May.

Where was the Royal Navy while Villeneuve was seemingly cruising at will? During Villeneuve's first abortive cruise Nelson had been at his winter station off Sardinia. On learning that Villeneuve was out of Toulon, he scoured the Mediterranean. Fearing another French invasion of Egypt, he sailed to Alexandria but found no trace of Villeneuve. Sailing for Malta on 19 February, he learned that Villeneuve had in fact put back into Toulon and Nelson arrived off that port on 13 March. He did not want to blockade Toulon too closely, instead he preferred a loose blockade with a couple of frigates keeping watch while the battlefleet remained out to sea. He hoped this would tempt the French out and give him what he desired more than anything – another chance to destroy an enemy fleet. He had informed the Lord Mayor of London of his plans in August 1804: 'I beg to inform your Lordship that the port of Toulon has never been blockaded by me; quite the reverse; every opportunity has been offered the enemy to put to sea, for it is there that we hope to realise the hopes and expectations of our country…'.[29] Now, still fearing for the safety of Egypt, Nelson stationed his fleet to the west, hoping to pursue Villeneuve if he did indeed come out and head eastwards.

A major problem for Nelson was his chronic lack of frigates, 'the eyes of a Fleet' he called them, a situation he had been complaining about during the previous year.[30] Without sufficient frigates it was difficult to gather intelligence regarding the movements of the enemy. This had hampered his response to Villeneuve's first sortie and now, once again, caused problems. Nelson returned to Sardinia to take on supplies during March. Then, on 4 April, he learned that Villeneuve had embarked on a second cruise. Nelson's first thought was for the safety of Sicily, but he did not find the French fleet there. On 18 April he learned that Villeneuve had in fact passed Gibraltar and was heading west. Unsure of Villeneuve's ultimate destination, he followed in pursuit. After a tortuous struggle with contrary winds, Nelson arrived off Gibraltar on 6 May.

Nelson had left only two frigates to watch over Toulon and they had lost contact with Villeneuve's fleet. However, the French had been observed passing Gibraltar by frigates from Orde's command stationed off Cadiz. Outnumbered, Orde decided to fall back on Cornwallis' Channel Fleet leaving a frigate to shadow Villeneuve. Severely criticised for following orthodox policy, instead of the more dynamic pursuit as Nelson would do, Orde was ordered to strike his flag on arriving back in England. Off Ferrol, Calder was also preparing to fall back on the Channel Fleet. This was the

---

ADMIRAL CHARLES MIDDLETON, LORD BARHAM (1726–1813)

Barham is perhaps the forgotten man of the Trafalgar campaign. This is not surprising because he saw little action at sea during his career, was not present at the battle and his influence on events is heavily overshadowed by the looming presence of Nelson. Yet he was a remarkable administrator and as First Lord of the Admiralty was responsible for the grand strategic planning behind the Trafalgar campaign. Born in Leith in 1726, he gained immense experience in naval administration as Comptroller of the Navy for twelve years, 1778–90. In his seventy-ninth year, he came back to the centre of naval affairs on 2 May 1805 when he stepped into the breach after the resignation of the then First Lord, Melville. Ennobled as Baron Barham, he took operational control of the Royal Navy at a crucial moment.

His tenure was criticised by St. Vincent who thought he lacked service experience and the capacity for anything other than minor tasks. Historians have been more considered; Corbett remarked that he was 'the man who, for ripe experience in the direction of naval war in all its breadth and detail, had not a rival in the service or in Europe'. Handling the immense amount of naval correspondence was a daunting task; Barham was often writing solidly from 8 a.m. to 6 p.m. yet still finding there was more work to do. In this capacity he was responsible for deploying the Royal Navy's resources to frustrate Bonaparte's invasion plans, ordering Cornwallis to detach a squadron to prevent Admiral Villeneuve's Combined Fleet from entering the Channel in July 1805. He also gave Nelson, as the man on the spot, the freedom of command to deal with the Franco-Spanish fleet in Cadiz during the autumn of 1805. Barham, perhaps more than any other, can be considered as the architect of the Trafalgar campaign.

key element of British anti-invasion strategy. Once the enemy were at sea in large numbers, the British forces were to avoid taking on overwhelming odds and fall back on Cornwallis, thereby achieving a concentration of force in the decisive theatre. The French and Spanish fleets might damage trade in the West Indies, seize lucrative sugar islands, raid British possessions along the African coast or land troops in Egypt. But none of these would have had an immediate and decisive effect. What would have been disastrous for Britain was if the French naval forces could gain command of the English Channel, thereby allowing the invasion to begin.

Yet Nelson did not head for Cornwallis' fleet. Hearing no news of Villeneuve in European waters, he believed that the Franco-Spanish Fleet must have passed into the Atlantic. The key piece of intelligence that convinced Nelson came from Rear Admiral Donald Campbell, a British officer serving in the Portuguese Navy. He had crossed Nelson's path before. As a Commodore in the Portuguese service, he had caused controversy while acting with the Royal Navy at Naples in early 1799. Apparently he had burnt several Neapolitan ships in anticipation of a French advance on Naples, an act in direct contradiction to orders that Nelson had sent to the Marquis de Niza, commander of the Portuguese naval forces. Nelson was certainly annoyed that the ships might have been burnt prematurely and that his orders had been ignored. He wrote to Campbell: '[I] entirely disapprove of your destroying the Ships of his Sicilian Majesty…destroying them is in direct disobedience to my orders to the Marquis de Niza'. Writing to Sir John Acton, he remarked that had Campbell been an English officer he would have had him court-martialled for his conduct.[31] However, once the initial storm subsided, the Sicilian court decided not to implement proceedings against Campbell. Nelson wrote to Niza on 27 February informing him that Campbell could raise his broad pendant again 'without any thought of what has passed. I am sure of his good intentions'.[32]

Campbell now made up for his earlier indiscretion by assuring Nelson that Villeneuve was indeed heading for the West Indies. Leaving Rear Admiral Richard Bickerton in command of the Mediterranean, Nelson set off after Villeneuve with ten ships-of-the-line on 11 May 1805. Without orders from the Admiralty to leave his station Nelson realised he was taking an immense risk, but it was a calculated risk. He was sure that the remaining British ships in Europe were enough to handle Villeneuve's fleet. His own squadron could make the trip to the Caribbean and back in two months. He was not lured away from Europe by Napoleon's plan; his reason for following Villeneuve was clear, for as he himself admitted: 'I cannot forgo the desire of getting, if possible, at the Enemy.'[33]

The West Indies

To the uninitiated the chase to the West Indies seems a rather bizarre incident in the Trafalgar campaign. What did Napoleon hope to achieve and why was Nelson so keen to pursue Villeneuve to that part of the world when the threat of invasion at home was so evident? The key to understanding these moves is not just the importance of the West Indies to British trade, but also in the national psyche.

> ### Nelson to Marsden, Victory,
> 14 May 1805, 38 leagues from Madeira
>
> *My dear Sir,*
> *I am very much obliged by your friendly*
> *letter of April 17th. Under the most serious*
> *consideration which I can give from all I*
> *hear, I rather think that the West Indies*
> *must be the destination of the Combined*
> *Squadrons. A trip to England would have*
> *been far more agreeable, and more necessary*
> *for my state of health; but I put self out of*
> *the question upon these occasions. And,*
> *although it may be said I am unlucky, it*
> *shall never be said that I am inactive, or*
> *sparing of myself; and surely it will not be*
> *fancied I am on a party of pleasure, running*
> *after eighteen Sail of the Line with ten, and*
> *that to the West Indies. However, I know*
> *that patience and perseverance will do*
> *much; and if they are not there, the*
> *Squadron will be again off Cadiz by the end*
> *of June – in short, before the Enemy can*
> *know where I am gone to; and then I shall*
> *proceed immediately to England, leaving*
> *such a force as the Service requires; and as*
> *the Board will know where the enemy are, I*
> *shall hope to receive their orders off Cape*
> *St. Vincent, should I return, from their not*
> *being in the West Indies.*
>
> *Source: Nicolas, VI, pp. 436–7.*

During the French Revolutionary and Napoleonic wars Britain was not a European country, but was at the centre of an Atlantic Empire[34] encompassing possessions in the West Indies, East Indies and Canada that were vital to the well-being of the British economy, and therefore the war effort against Napoleon. This Atlantic Empire was based on maritime commerce and was protected by the Royal Navy. It was only natural that in fighting France Britain should rely on those advantages granted to her by an insular strategic position at the centre of a trading empire. For Britain the successful outcome of the wars was largely built on her maritime and naval strength, *vis-à-vis* her two main rivals, Spain and France. Despite a succession of continental setbacks from 1793 onwards leading to the collapse of anti-French coalitions, Britain would not accept defeat. The loss of overseas commercial possessions, in particular the West Indian colonies, would have had a catastrophic effect on the British war effort.[35]

The West Indies were vital for the long-term financial strength of Britain and were 'almost universally regarded as still the most desirable facet of empire'.[36] By the 1790s the West Indian trade was of such value that British administrations feared that here 'a war for maritime supremacy might be lost' but also 'where they hoped to achieve the ultimate victory'.[37] The area had a massive influence on the British economy, supplying cocoa, sugar, coffee, cotton and rum. The West Indies provided four-fifths of the income from British overseas investments,[38] while during the period 1802-8 the value of British export trade to the region doubled to just under £7 million.[39] Imports into Britain from the region totalled just over £7 million, with sugar accounting for more than half of this amount.[40]

A number of groups had vested interests in the region, such as shipping agents, sugar plantations owners, cotton manufacturers, financiers and insurers. West

Indian merchants had 'wealth and influence, votes and pocket-boroughs'.[41] Investing in the West Indies was an expensive affair, so the merchants had formed two powerful organisations, the Society of West India Merchants and the Meeting of West India Planters and Merchants, to remind government of the vulnerability of the Islands. This provided them with a strong voice in domestic politics and strategy, for instance through direct access to the President of the Board of Trade.[42]

Contemporaries understood the value of the British possessions in the West Indies and the threat from France. None more so than Napoleon: when he wanted British fleets distracted from intercepting a possible invasion attempt, he directed Villeneuve to sail for the West Indies. Collingwood himself recognised this: 'I believe their object in the West Indies to be less conquest, than to draw our force from home'.[43] But Nelson was not decoyed away from European waters because he fell for Napoleon's ruse, rather he was concerned at the havoc the French might cause in the Caribbean and hoped to catch and defeat Villeneuve. He mentioned his anxiety about French ambitions in the islands several times during May and June 1805. He was particularly fraught about Jamaica:

> I was in a thousand fears for Jamaica, for that is a blow which Buonaparte would be happy to give us. I flew to the West Indies without any orders, but I think the Ministry cannot be displeased…kind Providence, may some happy day, bless my endeavours to serve the public weal, of which the West India colonies form so prominent and interesting a part. I ever have been, and shall die, a firm friend to our present colonial system. I was bred, as you know, in the good old school, and taught to appreciate the value of our West India possessions.[44]

His fears for Jamaica were well-founded because the island accounted for half of all British investments in the region.[45]

The Chase to the West Indies
Before he could be certain where Nelson actually was (he did not receive confirmation that Nelson had sailed for the Caribbean until 5 June), Barham had deduced that Villeneuve would in fact sail for the West Indies and had begun to react to the new French naval movements. Barham thought if Nelson did not follow Villeneuve, he would either stay in the Mediterranean or fall back on Cornwallis and on 9 May he forwarded instructions along these lines to Nelson. If Nelson had decided on either of these options, Collingwood would be the one sent in pursuit of Villeneuve. Orders to that effect were sent out on 10 May.

Collingwood was preparing to sail for Lisbon when the new orders arrived from Barham. If Collingwood could be sure that Villeneuve had gone to the West Indies and Nelson was in pursuit, he was to dispatch enough ships to ensure that Nelson had twelve ships-of-the-line if the enemy force numbered no more than eighteen. If Villeneuve did have more than eighteen battleships, Collingwood was to reinforce Nelson with as many as the enemy had above that figure. If in the unlikely event that

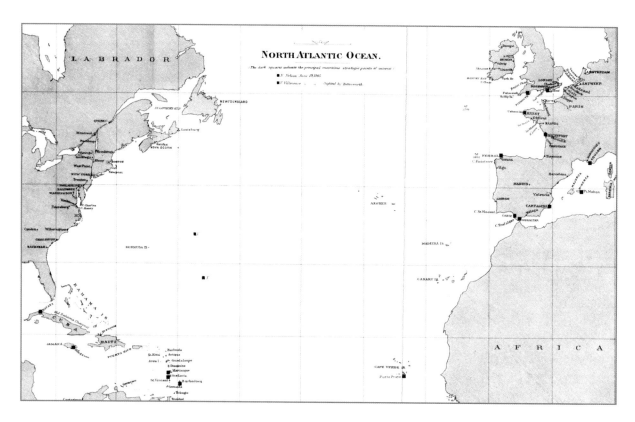

Chart of the Atlantic
and the West Indies.
(CPL)

Nelson had not sailed for the West Indies, Barham instructed Collingwood himself to head for Barbados with twelve ships-of-the-line, adding additional ships to his command if Villeneuve had more than eighteen battleships.

On 13 May Villeneuve arrived off Martinique, where he was joined by the Spanish and a straggling French ship-of-the-line two days later. On 30 May two ships from the Rochefort squadron bolstered his numbers to 20 ships-of-the-line. With Napoleon's orders instructing him to wait for 40 days for the arrival of Ganteaume from Brest, Villeneuve decided to put his force to some good.

In one of the strangest events in naval history, a small 600ft high rocky island off the coast of Martinique had been seized by British forces early in 1804 and commissioned into the Royal Navy as HM Sloop of War *Diamond Rock*, under Commander James Maurice. Substantial efforts were made to defend the position and make it habitable, including building a 3,000-gallon water tank for the 107 man garrison and landing two 24pdr guns (weighing 2 tons apiece). By late February two long 18pdrs had been hauled to the pinnacle of the rock and placed on gun platforms, giving them a range of two miles. This remarkable achievement was successful, as Fort-de-France, the capital of Martinique, remained under a virtual blockade for eighteen months. This was the target Villeneuve, whose fleet had been fired upon from *Diamond Rock*, chose to attack.

He detached two 74-gun ships, *Berwick* and *Pluton*, the frigate *Sirène* and the schooner *Argus*, all under the command of Commodore Julien Marie Cosmao-Kerjulien. At 8 a.m. on 31 May the French attack began. With suitable provisions and ammunition the defenders could have held out for a very long time, but, an earth tremor having cracked the cistern which was the island's only supply of fresh water, the end was inevitable. In soaring temperatures, Maurice was left with no alternative but to surrender the rock. His casualties were two killed and a single man wounded as against the 50 killed or wounded in the ranks of the attackers.

In the meantime Villeneuve had been apprised of yet another change of plan. On 30 May he received orders from Napoleon instructing him to return to European waters. On arrival he was to pick up the fifteen French and Spanish battleships in Ferrol, then join with Ganteaume's 21 ships, which had failed to get out of Brest. The entire fleet was then to enter the Channel giving Napoleon a force of 50 battleships, sufficient to drive off Cornwallis and Keith and allow the invasion to proceed. Villeneuve now embarked additional soldiers from Martinique and Guadeloupe, making his forces up to 8,600 men. He left the West Indies on 5 June and three days later seized a British convoy from which he may have learned that Nelson was hot on his tail.

On 11 May Nelson had set sail for the West Indies, 31 days after Villeneuve had left Cadiz. He arrived in Carlisle Bay, Barbados at noon on 4 June, where he found Rear Admiral Cochrane in the *Northumberland*. Receiving information that Villeneuve had indeed arrived in the West Indies, proving he was right, Nelson embarked 2,000 soldiers and prepared to sail. Leaving Barbados on the morning of 5 June, the fleet was made ready for battle that afternoon and headed south, acting on intelligence from Brigadier General Brereton that the Combined Fleet had been seen heading for Trinidad. Receiving further intelligence from the brig *Curieux* that a large fleet was in the area, seemingly confirming Brereton's information, Nelson approached Trinidad. But upon reaching the island on 7 June there was no news of Villeneuve. Next morning intelligence arrived that the enemy had been operating 100 miles to the north-west at Martinique and had seized Diamond Rock. Weighing anchor, Nelson's fleet was at Grenada by 9 June and Antigua on the 12th, but there was still no sign of Villeneuve. Here Nelson did receive some useful intelligence from an American citizen who had heard that Villeneuve had disembarked all the troops and stores he had taken on at Guadeloupe and had been seen heading northwards. 'I must be satisfied,' he wrote to the Admiralty Secretary William Marsden, 'they have bent their course for Europe.'[49] By 8 p.m. on 12 June he was so sure Villeneuve was headed back to Europe that he sent Captain Bettesworth's *Curieux* ahead with dispatches to warn the Admiralty. The *Curieux*, an incredibly fast vessel, actually sighted Villeneuve's fleet on 19 June, but instead of turning to inform Nelson, Bettesworth made all speed for England.

Meanwhile Nelson's fleet was in hot pursuit. Both fleets passed the Azores at about the same time in early July. Nelson sailed south of the islands, believing that the enemy were headed for the Mediterranean. On 15 June he wrote to Robert

VICE ADMIRAL LORD CUTHBERT COLLINGWOOD (1750–1810)

Collingwood has been described by some as inattentive to the needs of his officers and aloof. George Elliot called him 'a selfish old bear... In body and mind he was iron, and very cold iron.'[46] In fact Collingwood was one of a special group of individuals regarded by the Admiralty as a safe pair of hands. An extremely competent seaman and an excellent naval commander, his personality may have appeared cold from the outside but in private company he could unwind, displaying immense kindness and humour. For instance, on meeting Collingwood to complain about the wants of the squadron, Codrington found that Collingwood was surprised to hear of them, and found too that the Admiral was 'good humoured, chatty and communicative'. After Trafalgar Codrington saw Collingwood on deck in public view and his opinion of him changed; though admitting he was brave and a 'good man', he complained that 'he has none of the dignity an admiral should have', remaining aloof from those around him.[47] His public reserve may have stemmed from the conflict between his dedication to duty (he died aboard his flagship in 1810, not having returned to England for many years) and his longing to return home. He, like many other competent naval officers, has had his contribution to the war effort eclipsed by the figure of Nelson.

Collingwood was born in Newcastle-upon-Tyne in 1750 and began a career at sea by joining HMS *Shannon* at the age of eleven. Like many of the men who made their name during the wars with France, he saw active service in the War of American Independence, during which he was promoted to lieutenant. Joining Captain William Locker's *Lowestoffe* as first lieutenant in 1778, his career became entwined with Nelson, who had just moved from Locker's ship into the *Bristol*. After the war both captained frigates in the West Indies, attempting to prevent a contraband trade between the islands and America, in the process cementing their life-long friendship. Collingwood spent the majority of his time ashore on half pay from 1786 until 1793 in his beloved Northumberland. When out walking he carried a handful of acorns, planting them in suitable locations so that future generations would always have oak with which to build warships. Later in 1805 he complained that country gentlemen were not planting enough oaks, wishing that they would follow his example.[48] When war broke out with Revolutionary France Collingwood was quickly back at sea. His service was now confined to ships-of-the-line, commanding HMS *Barfleur* at the Glorious First of June in 1794 before transferring to *Excellent* in 1795 where, as part of the Mediterranean Fleet, he again came into contact with Nelson. In *Excellent* Collingwood secured two Spanish prizes at the battle of Cape St. Vincent in 1797, as well as providing assistance to Nelson's battered *Captain*. He was with St. Vincent's blockade of Cadiz until returning to England in 1799, when he was promoted to flag rank in February of that year. Collingwood then served with the Channel Fleet in *Triumph* and then

Fitzgerald, the British Minister at Lisbon: 'I do not yet despair of getting up with them before they arrive at Cadiz or Toulon, to which ports I think they are bound.'[50] Villeneuve, instructed to head for the Channel, actually sailed to the north of the islands, the distance between the fleets now being about 200 miles. On 30 June Nelson, desperate for news, sent Captain Parker's *Amazon* ahead to Cadiz in an attempt to locate Villeneuve's fleet. By 18 July Nelson's fleet was approaching the Straits of Gibraltar, and the next day his ships anchored in the bay 'without having obtained the smallest intelligence of the Enemy's fleet'.[51]

Barfleur until the peace of 1802. Collingwood was back with the Channel Fleet after the war resumed in 1803, then in 1805 was detached to blockade Cadiz where he again met Nelson before Trafalgar. Nelson always had great confidence in 'Dear Col', as he himself affectionately called Collingwood, sending him his plan of attack before the battle.

With his record of service in the Mediterranean and his position within the fleet, it was with little surprise that Collingwood was appointed Nelson's successor as commander of that fleet. He spent the next four extremely difficult and stressful years aboard ship, promoting British diplomacy and overseeing naval operations in the Mediterranean. In March 1810 he was succeeded by Rear Admiral Martin and finally received permission to go home. But he was never to see England again; he began his passage home from Minorca in the *Ville de Paris* on 6 March 1810, but next day at about 6 p.m. he died aged 59, worn out by his dedication to duty over 44 years of active naval service.

Admiral Cuthbert Collingwood. Second in Command at Trafalgar, Collingwood was a close friend of Nelson and led the Lee Line during the battle of Trafalgar. (CPL)

SIR ROBERT CALDER'S ACTION

On the morning of 22 July the fleet of Vice Admiral Sir Robert Calder with fifteen ships-of-the-line was waiting off the Spanish coast for the arrival of the Combined Fleet under Villeneuve. The next few hours were to have a major impact on the future of not only Calder's career but also the entire war at sea.

Calder had been purposely stationed 100 miles to the west of Cape Finisterre by Barham. The First Lord had already surmised that Villeneuve's passage to the West Indies was a decoy. On the morning of 9 July the Admiralty received Nelson's dispatch warning of the likely arrival of the Franco-Spanish fleet back in European waters. The dispatch had arrived just before midnight on the 8th, Barham had already retired to bed and no one had been willing to wake him. Next morning Barham, in his nightgown and absolutely livid at the precious hours lost, organised the fleet dispositions to await Villeneuve's arrival. It was a master class in maritime grand strategy.

What were Villeneuve's intentions, and where to position an appropriate force to intercept him wherever he appeared? Nelson and Barham had both thought that the Mediterranean was Villeneuve's objective, but here providence assisted the elderly First Lord. The *Curieux* had actually shadowed the enemy fleet as it was heading northwards, not to the south. Recognising that the most important consideration was the Royal Navy's continued superiority in the Channel, Barham decided to intercept Villeneuve off the north-west coast of Spain. He scrapped an initial idea to draw reinforcements from the fleet stationed off Brest and instead directed Cornwallis to abandon the blockade of Rochefort and use those five ships-of-the-line under Rear Admiral Charles Stirling to link up with Calder, who had been blockading Ferrol since 1 March. Calder's enlarged fleet, now comprising fifteen ships-of-the-line, would take up station off Cape Finisterre. Cornwallis was then to position the Channel Fleet to cover the sector from Ushant down to Finisterre, thereby blocking Villeneuve's approach to the invasion ports. The enemy ships in Cadiz could be handled by the returning Nelson. Cornwallis complied on the 11th, detaching Stirling and the five battleships to join Calder.

Nelson arrived at Gibraltar on 19 July 1805 but there was still no sign of Villeneuve. Off Cape Finisterre the weather on 22 July was foggy, hampering visibility and making recognition difficult. At about 11 a.m. several ships-of-the-line began to emerge from the gloom. Calder, with his own ships from the blockade of Ferrol and Stirling's five, now had fifteen ships-of-the-line. He had expected the enemy fleet to number seventeen. Instead, 20 French and Spanish battleships accompanied by seven frigates came into view.

Calder's Action

Despite being outnumbered, Calder could draw confidence from the fact that his fleet had a marked superiority in terms of heavy ships. The 2nd rate three-decked 98-gun ships provided a powerful core to his fleet, giving him a distinct advantage at close quarters. It was considered naval opinion that a three-decker could hold its own against two lighter 74-gun ships, and Calder had four of these heavy battleships as opposed to the single enemy three-decker.

At about midday Calder cleared for action, and at 1 p.m. ordered his fleet into line of battle. With the frigate *Sirius* ahead informing him of the enemy's movements, on the quarterdeck of the *Prince-of-Wales* Calder could see little through the fog as the British fleet stood towards the enemy. With visibility so poor, both fleets manoeuvred for position, Calder tacking to prevent Villeneuve escaping while the Combined Fleet ensured that the rear of their closely ordered line was not exposed. Ahead of the British fleet *Sirius* almost fell upon Admiral Federico Gravina's 90-gun *Argonauta*, leading the van of the combined squadron. Taking evasive action, *Sirius* bore to the leeward, passing the *Argonauta*, *Terrible* and *America*. Following the understood but unwritten convention, none of the enemy line-of-battle fired upon the vastly outgunned British frigate until she came to the *España* at about 5.15 p.m. At this point the leading British ship, Captain Alan Hyde Gardner's 74-gun *Hero*, emerged from fog and was fired upon by the *Argonauta*, with the *España* opening up against the retreating *Sirius*.

Recognising that the van of the combined fleet had in fact come round on to the starboard tack, *Hero* followed suit to open up her starboard guns and commenced firing at about 5.20 p.m. This manoeuvre was made on Gardner's initiative without any signal from the *Prince-of-Wales*. In fact at 5.09 p.m. Calder had made the signal to engage as closely as possible, presuming the enemy to be on their original tack. Next in line after *Hero* was Captain William Brown's 74-gun *Ajax*, who bore his ship round to inform Calder of the change in the enemy's direction, then resumed a position as the twelfth ship in the line, astern of Admiral Stirling's 98-gun *Glory*.

With *Ajax* bearing away from the van, at the moment Gardner had tacked the *Hero*, the sixth British ship in the line, Captain Charles Boyles' three-decked 98-gun

BRITISH FLEET
Vice Admiral Sir Robert Calder
Order of sailing at about 3pm

Ship	Guns	Commander
Hero	74	Capt. Alan Hyde Gardner
Ajax	74	Capt. William Brown
Triumph	74	Capt. Henry Inman
Barfleur	98	Capt. George Martin
Agamemnon	64	Capt. John Harvey
Windsor-Castle	98	Capt. Charles Boyles
Defiance	74	Capt. Philip Charles Durham
Prince-of-Wales	98	Vice Admiral Sir Robert Calder
		Capt. William Cuming
Repulse	74	Capt. Arthur Kaye Legge
Raisonnable	64	Capt. Josias Rowley
Dragon	74	Capt. Edward Griffiths
Glory	98	Rear Admiral Charles Stirling
		Capt. Samuel Warren
Warrior	74	Capt. Samuel Hood Linzee
Thunderer	74	Capt. William Lechmere
Malta	80	Capt. Edward Buller
Other vessels		
Egyptienne brig		Capt. Charles Elphinstone
Sirius	36	Capt. William Prowse
Nile lugger	12	Lieut. John Fennel
Frisk cutter		Lieut. James Nicholson

Source: James, IV, p. 2

Windsor-Castle had made her port tack in the wake of the preceding five vessels. Informed of the change in position of the Combined Fleet at 5.50 p.m., Calder signalled to tack in succession to bring the fleet alongside the enemy. In fact, before the signal was even raised the ships following in *Hero's* wake, *Triumph* (74), *Barfleur* (98), *Agamemnon* (64), *Windsor-Castle* and *Defiance* (74) had already followed Gardner's lead in tacking without orders. With the engagement becoming general, all the British fleet had tacked to starboard by about 6 p.m., except Captain Edward Griffiths' 74-gun *Dragon*, which was working up from the leeward. Most of Calder's ships now lay alongside an opposite number. With thick gun smoke adding to the already heavy fog, the poor visibility became almost impenetrable and the battle degenerated into a number of confused and individual combats.

FRANCO-SPANISH FLEET
Vice Admiral P. C. J-B. S. Villeneuve
Order of Sailing at about 3pm

Ship	Guns	Commander
Argonauta (Sp)	90	Admiral Don Federico de Gravina
		Rear Admiral Don Antoñio Escano
Terrible (Sp)	74	Capt. Don Francisco Mondragon
America (Sp)	64	Capt. Don Francisco Darrac
España (Sp)	64	Capt. Don Francisco Monios
San-Rafaël (Sp)	80	Comm. Don Franciso Montez
Firme (Sp)	74	Capt. Don Rafaël Villavicencio
Pluton	74	Comm. Jean Marie Cosmao Kerjulien
Mont-Blanc	74	Comm. Jean Noel La Villegris
Atlas	74	Capt. Pierre Nicolas Rolland
Berwick	74	Capt. Jean Giles Filhol-Camas
Neptune	80	Comm. Esprit Tranquille Maistral
Bucentaure	80	Vice Admiral P C J B S Villeneuve
		Capt. Jean-Jacques Magendie
Formidable	80	Rear Admiral P R M E Dumanoir de Pelley
		Capt. Jean Marie Letellier
Intrépide	74	Capt. Léonore Deperonne
Scipion	74	Capt. Charles Bérenger
Swiftsure	74	Capt. C E L'Hôpitalier-Villemadrin
Indomptable	80	Capt. Jean-Joseph Hubert
Aigle	74	Capt. Pierre Paul Gourrége
Achille	74	Capt. G Deniéport
Algéciras	74	Rear Admiral Charles Magon de Médine
		Capt. Gabriel Auguste Brouard

Other vessels

Cornélie	40	Rhin	40	Uranie	38
Hortense	40	Sirène	36	Furet brig	18
Incorruptible	38	Thémis	40	Naïade	16

Sources: James, III, pp. 323, 330, IV, p. 2–3

Some of Calder's ships found themselves engaged with multiple opponents. Illustrative is the experience of the *Windsor-Castle*. After tacking on to the starboard tack the fog lifted a little, revealing two French line-of-battle, a frigate and a brig, at which point the *Windsor-Castle* opened a furious cannonade. The enemy were shortly joined by a Spanish ship-of-the-line and then Calder's own *Prince-of-Wales*

Sir Robert Calder (1745–1818)

Sir Robert Calder remains a controversial character. He joined the navy in 1759 and three years later while serving as a lieutenant he participated in the capture of a Spanish treasure ship, which brought him a windfall of £13,000. Made Captain in 1780, by the time of the battle of St. Vincent he was Jervis' captain of the fleet, though he received criticism from the formidable Jervis for his cautious outlook. After this his main service was in the monotonous task of blockade and home defence with the Channel Fleet, which perhaps better suited his temperament. He achieved flag rank as rear admiral in 1799 and vice admiral in 1804. When, on 22 July 1805, he intercepted the numerically superior Villeneuve off the coast of Spain in heavy fog, Calder failed to capitalise on his initial success in capturing two Spanish ships. He was severely and publicly criticised in London for failing to do his utmost to defeat the enemy (a very moot point in the Royal Navy; a similar charge had led to Admiral John Byng's execution on his own quarterdeck in 1757). The Admiralty reacted by ordering a court-martial, a procedure Calder had already demanded in an attempt to clear his name. Nelson was sympathetic towards Calder, granting him the courtesy of returning to England in his flagship *Prince of Wales*, a magnanimous gesture which removed a three-decked ship from his already outnumbered fleet. In December 1805 Calder was cleared of cowardice, but severely reprimanded by the Admiralty. Although the verdict effectively ended his sea career, it did not signal the end of his naval life; he was created a full admiral in 1810 and was appointed commander at Portsmouth in 1815.

His actions in July 1805 often form a footnote to the great battle of 21 October, yet facing a numerically superior fleet in tricky conditions Calder had actually prevented Villeneuve from entering the Channel. But, accustomed to the more decisive nature of Nelsonic battles, perhaps the public and the Admiralty had been too expectant of Calder. With a little more luck and more fighting spirit he might have won a famous victory and Trafalgar might never have taken place.

came up and joined the fray. *Windsor-Castle* suffered greatly in this engagement, losing most of her standing and running rigging and receiving damage to her masts, so much so that after the battle *Dragon* was ordered to remain with the disabled ship and take her in tow if necessary.

Although some British ships suffered – in addition to *Windsor-Castle* the *Malta* and *Ajax* were badly damaged – the Combined Fleet took heavier losses. Dropping to leeward during the battle, and hence closer to the British ships, *Firme* (74), *San-Rafaël* (80) and *España* (64) received heavy punishment. Despite brave attempts by Cosmao-Kerjulien's 74-gun *Pluton* to shield the *Firme* from British fire, the latter ship struck at about 8 p.m. Cosmao-Kerjulien did manage to save the *España* with the assistance of *Mont-Blanc* and *Atlas*, but the latter was so heavily battered in the attempt that she too needed rescuing. *San-Rafaël* was almost as badly damaged as the *Firme* and struck not long after her compatriot.

At 8.25 p.m. with night falling, his fleet in a confused and disjointed state in the fog and with the Combined Fleet still within cannon shot, Calder, perhaps prudently, signalled his ships to cease the action. Due to the poor visibility the signal was not acted upon by all ships and fire punctuated the gloom for more than an hour until about 9.30 p.m. when the combat ended. Losses in the two captured

Admiral Sir Robert Calder. The much-criticised Calder, perhaps like many, suffered from operating in Nelson's shadow. Calder's action on 22 July 1805 was the decisive moment of the campaign, preventing the enemy Combined Fleet from entering the Channel. (National Maritime Museum)

Spanish vessels were heavy, 53 killed and 114 wounded in the *San-Rafaël* and 41 killed and 97 wounded in the *Firme*. Total killed and wounded for the Combined Fleet were 476, including Captain Deperrone of the *Intrépide* and Captain Rolland of the *Atlas*.[52] In the British ships losses were proportionate to their place in battle. The *Windsor-Castle* and the *Malta*, which had been in the thick of the fighting, suffered ten and five killed, 35 and 40 wounded respectively. Total losses in the British fleet amounted to 39 officers and men killed, and 159 wounded.[53]

Calder's own ship spent the night repairing damage and he directed the *Frisk* and *Nile* to ascertain the condition of the rest of the fleet. Next morning the main fleets were about seventeen miles apart, with heavy fog again hampering visibility. *Barfleur, Hero, Triumph* and *Agamemnon* were lying five miles to windward of the main British position, six miles away from Villeneuve's advanced squadron of four ships-of-the-line. Having received worse than expected damage reports from the fleet, Calder decided to concentrate his ships. Placing his disabled vessels *Windsor-Castle* (towed by *Dragon*), *Malta* and *Thunderer*, and the prizes to the leeward, at 9 a.m. he set a north-easterly course on the larboard tack. At his court-martial Calder later maintained that not one of his ships was 'in a state to carry sufficient sail to take them to windward' and therefore it was impossible to renew the attack.[54]

Catching the occasional glimpse of the British moves to concentrate the fleet, Villeneuve, believing that they were in fact withdrawing in some disorder, determined to renew the action. As the weather deteriorated with a heavy swell coming from the north, the wind, also from that direction, fell. Just after midday Villeneuve had formed his fleet into order of battle and began bearing up for the British fleet. It was not until 3.10 p.m. that this slow advance was noticed by Calder, who responded by hauling to the wind in readiness for an attack. At about 4 p.m. Villeneuve hauled on to the same tack as Calder's fleet, therefore apparently declining to come within engagement range. Both fleets now followed a similar course until they had to respond to changes in the wind during the night of 23 July, leading to the Combined Fleet lying astern of Calder, who was now to windward, by 8 a.m. on the 24th. With almost no wind, Calder declined the opportunity to engage and continued on his course, taking his damaged ships and prizes towards Cornwallis off Ushant. Villeneuve headed south towards Vigo and by early evening both fleets were out of touch.

Certainly Calder's action had a major influence on the outcome of the campaign. His number one priority was to prevent Villeneuve from entering the Channel and joining with the Brest fleet, an object which he clearly achieved. This more than

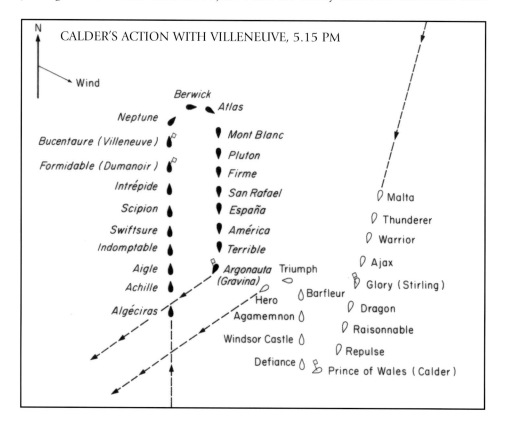

ADMIRAL DON FEDERICO GRAVINA (1757–1806)

Perhaps because of his crushing defeat at Trafalgar, Gravina's name is all but forgotten today. Even in Spain his memory has faded into obscurity. Yet he was in fact one of the most experienced and capable Spanish admirals to serve during the wars.

Gravina was born on the then Spanish island of Sicily to an aristocratic family with links to the Spanish monarchy. He joined the Spanish Navy at the age of twelve and rapid promotion followed. This was not due to his influential patrons, but rather to his ability and determination. During the Spanish blockade of Gibraltar (1779–82) Gravina gained his first taste of combat and commanded one of the specially-built ships designed to batter the fortifications. At Cape Spartel, when Admiral Howe fought the Spanish fleet, Gravina commanded the *Santíssima Trinidad*. Promoted commodore in 1789 at the age of thirty-three, his incredibly fast passage from Cadiz to Cartagena de Indias that year showed his excellent seamanship. The following year his administrative and organisational talents helped to mobilise the Spanish Navy in response to the Nootka Sound crisis with Britain. Second in command of the Spanish fleet that was with Admiral Hood at Toulon in 1793, he was promoted Vice Admiral the following year. During this period of Anglo-Spanish naval co-operation he visited Portsmouth, where he was urged to introduce lime juice into the Spanish Navy to combat scurvy, something which Gravina viewed with indifference to the great cost of Spanish sailors.

With Spain committed to France after 1796, he commanded the joint Franco-Spanish 'Ocean Squadron' operating out of Brest. Unlike many of his fellow countrymen, Gravina had excellent personal relations with the French and Napoleon in particular, leading to his posting as Ambassador in Paris in 1803–4. He returned to sea in 1805 to command the Spanish fleet at Cadiz, and participated in the controversial action with Calder on 22 July. Arguing for delay and unconvinced by Villeneuve's plans for the Combined Fleet after the action, he none the less went along with his allies' wishes. Villeneuve's change of direction at Trafalgar left Gravina's squadron at the rear of the combined fleet. Gravina, in the three-decked 112-gun *Principe de Asturias*, was severely wounded in the left arm during the fight with Collingwood's division. With Villeneuve captured, command fell to Gravina and he ordered the survivors to head for Cadiz. His wound failed to heal and he died (remarking that he hoped he was going to join Nelson) in March 1806.

Admiral Frederico Gravina commanded the Spanish ships operating with Villeneuve. (CPL)

anything put an end to Napoleon's invasion plans. Yet Calder's fight remains controversial. Despite the fact that the enemy outnumbered him in very difficult conditions, he was criticised for not building on the success of 22 July and making the combat decisive in a Nelsonic style. The British press, perhaps expecting a Nile or St. Vincent, lambasted Calder for a lack of fighting spirit. The mood was encapsulated by Lady Bessborough, writing on 20 August:

> Nothing is talk'd of but bringing Sir Robert Calder to a Trial: *fusiller un amiral pour encourager les autres* [to shoot an admiral to encourage the others – an allusion to Voltaire's famous remark concerning the fate of Admiral Sir John Byng], but indeed his conduct does seem extraordinary. The combined fleets were all the time in Vigo close to him, and publish every where that they repeatedly offer'd to renew the fight, and we declin'd.[55]

Sir Robert Calder's Action, 22 July 1805. (From Jenkins' Naval Achievements reprinted by Sim Comfort Associates)

Instrumental in the criticism was the Admiralty's decision not to publish the whole of Calder's dispatches – that part omitted detailed his reasons for not engaging the enemy after 22 July. When Calder received news of the furore at home he immediately demanded a court-martial to investigate his conduct, pre-empting the arrival of news from the Admiralty on 30 September that he would indeed stand trial for his conduct.[56]

TYPES OF SHOT

Ships' guns were smoothbore and hence could fire several different types of projectile. Most common was round shot, a solid cast iron ball, the weight of which denoted the gun from which it was fired, 32pdr, 24pdr and so on. Their role was to smash into the hull of a ship, punching a hole through timbers. Three types of shot were designed to damage rigging and sails to slow down an enemy ship. All three would spin in flight, cutting through rope, sail and flesh. Bar shot was like a dumbbell, two cast iron hemispheres or circular iron discs connected by a bar. Chain shot was just that, two spheres of iron linked by a chain. Expanding shot had two hemispheres joined by two pieces of metal, so positioned that they would slide apart in flight. The equivalent of canister shot on land, grape shot consisted of a number of 1in–2in round iron balls, enclosed in a cartridge or canvas bag. They would spread out on firing, creating a hail of shot. They were particularly effective against personnel.

While the majority of guns were of a standard pattern, one type reflected the close-in nature of sea battles in the age of sail: the carronade. Named after the Carron Company Ironworks in Scotland, after 1800 most ships in the Royal Navy carried them, while variants were also used by foreign navies. Carronades had a short barrel, compared to normal guns, which made them useless at long range. But they were designed for close-quarter work. It was a particularly deadly weapon. Firing a large ball at a low muzzle velocity, their shot smashed into timbers, creating a shower of splinters and causing horrific wounds. They usually came in 32 and 24pdr variants, though at Trafalgar *Victory* carried two monster 68pdr carronades on her forecastle. The first round fired from her port 68pdr, consisting of a 68lb ball and a large keg of 500 musket balls, completely wrecked the stern of the French flagship *Bucentaure*.

The Naval Chronicle recognised this:

We cannot but consider, that the disappointment of the public mind in not hearing of any farther success of Sir Robert Calder, was chiefly excited by that very reprehensible practice, which we have so frequently had occasion to condemn, of mutilating the *letters on service*. Had the official dispatch of Sir Robert Calder, to Admiral Cornwallis, appeared in the gazette, as it was addressed to the commander-in-chief the disappointment could not have been material: as it was, expectations were excited at home, which were never warranted, or even felt, by Sir Robert Calder.

Nelson, himself once a victim of the popular press, initially felt some sympathy for Calder. Writing to his close friend Captain Fremantle, who had forwarded him a packet of English newspapers, he declared: 'I was in truth bewildered by the account of Sir Robert Calder's Victory, and the joy of the event; together with the hearing that *John Bull* was not content, which I am sorry for.' Nelson himself was feeling the pressure of his own success and realised the effect it had on other, less gifted, naval officers: 'Who can, my dear Fremantle, command all the success which our Country may wish? We have fought together, and therefore well know what it is. I have had

Two images
showing the
difference between
a long gun (right)
and a carronade
(below). (CPL)

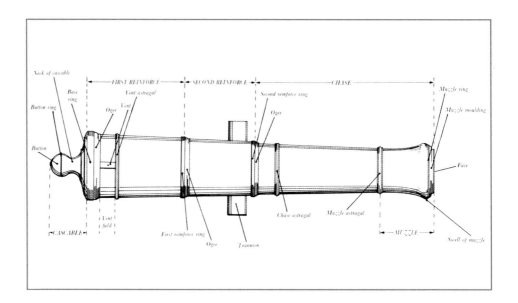

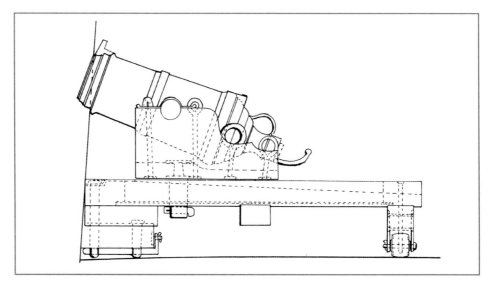

the best disposed Fleet of friends, but who can say what will be the event of a battle? And it most sincerely grieves me, that in any of the papers it should be insinuated, that Lord Nelson could have done better. I should have fought the Enemy, and so did my friend Calder; but who can say that he will be more successful than another?'[57] Once ashore in September he confided to Charles Rose Ellis that Calder 'had great difficulties, and I hope all this will be forgotten amidst the huzzas and illuminations for a glorious Victory'.[58]

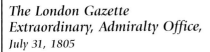

The London Gazette Extraordinary, Admiralty Office, July 31, 1805

Vice-Admiral Sir Robert Calder to Admiral Cornwallis, Prince of Wales, July 23, 1805

Sir, Yesterday, at noon, lat.43° 30′N, long. 11° 17′W, I was favoured with a view of the combined Squadrons of France and Spain, consisting of 20 sail of the line, also three large ships armed en flute, of about 50 guns each, with five frigates, and three brigs: the force under my directions at this time consisted of 15 sail of the line, two frigates, a cutter and a lugger, I immediately stood towards the enemy with the squadron, making the needful signals for battle in the closest order; and on closing with them, I made the signal for attacking their centre. When I had reached their rear, I tacked the squadron in succession; this brought us close under their lee, and when our headmost ships reached their centre, the enemy were tacking in succession; this obliged me to make again the same manoeuvre, by which I brought on an action which lasted upwards of four hours, when I found it necessary to bring-to the squadron to cover the two captured ships, whose names are in the margin [San-Rafaël and Firme]. I have to observe, they had every advantage of wind and weather during the whole day. The weather had been foggy at times, a great part of the morning; and very soon after we had brought them to action, the fog was so very thick at intervals, that we could with great difficulty see the ship a-head or a-stern of us; this rendered it impossible to take the advantages of the enemy by signals I could have wished to have done. Had the weather been more favourable, I am led to believe the victory would have been more complete. I have very great pleasure in saying, every ship was conducted in the most masterly style; and I beg leave here publicly to return every captain, officer, and man, whom I had the honour to command on that day, my most grateful thanks, for their conspicuously gallant and very judicious good conduct.

The Honourable Captain Gardner, of the Hero, led the Van Squadron in a most masterly and officer-like manner, to whom I feel myself particularly indebted; as also to Captain Cuming, for his assistance during the action.

Enclosed is a list of the killed and wounded on board the different ships. If I may judge from the great slaughter on board the captured ships, the enemy must have suffered greatly. They are now in sight to windward; and when I have secured the captured ships, and put the squadron to rights, I shall endeavour myself of any opportunity that may offer to give you some further account of these combined squadrons…

Source: Naval Chronicle, III, pp. 157–8.

The Admiralty initially wanted Calder turned out of his flagship the *Prince-of-Wales* into the *Dreadnought*, also a 2nd rate but a notoriously slow vessel. Calder, who was also unwilling to serve under Nelson, now bombarded him with heartfelt appeals against this indignity. Perhaps showing signs of mental stress, he also requested the presence of Rear Admiral Stirling and all the captains present at the action to be released for attendance at his court-martial! Captain Durham of the *Defiance* flatly refused to go unless specifically ordered, preferring to remain

---

Extract from Calder's Defence at his court-martial

25 December 1805

I felt that the manner of publishing the account of the victory in the Gazette might have given occasion for the aspersions against me; for you will observe, that instead of being published as an extract of my dispatch, it was published as a copy, and concluded with the passage, 'When I have put this squadron to rights, I shall endeavour to renew the action,' omitting altogether the subsequent part of the letter. Here I must protest against the slightest censure on the Admiralty. They, doubtless, were anxious to give the public the earliest intimation of the victory, and did not think it necessary to give any account of the Rochefort and Ferrol squadrons. If they had done so, the public would not have drawn the conclusions they did, nor would the public have been so sanguine in their expectations, if the letter had been published as an extract, because they would have imagined there was something else in the letter which the Admiralty thought proper to conceal…

I think it can be attended with no bad consequences to state that passage in my letter, the omission of which I complain. It is this – 'At the same time it will behove me to be on my guard against the combined squadrons in Ferrol and Rochefort; therefore I may find it necessary to make a conjunction with the Commander-in-Chief off Ushant.' Had this part of my letter been published, I beg leave to ask whether the public would have been so sanguine as they have been? – Assuredly they would not; nor should I have had occasion to give you this trouble.

Source: *Naval Chronicle*, III, pp. 167–8.

---

with the fleet and the possibility of engaging the enemy. In the end only Captains Brown of the *Ajax* and Lechmere of *Thunderer* attended and therefore missed the battle of Trafalgar.[59]

Nelson, perhaps fearing that Sir Robert's continued presence was casting a shadow over his fleet, wrote to Emma: 'I have been, as you may believe, made very uneasy or rather uncomfortable by the situation of Sir Robert Calder. He was to have gone home in another Ship and a vast lumber. However, I have given way to his misery, and directed the *Prince-of-Wales* to carry him to Spithead; for whatever the result of the inquiry may be, I think he has a right to be treated with respect.' Calder was therefore allowed to return home in his flagship, thereby depriving Nelson's fleet of a powerful three-decker. A broken man, Calder left the fleet on 13 October. After his departure Nelson confided to Collingwood: 'I am glad Sir Robert Calder is gone; and from my heart I hope he will get home safe, and end his inquiry well. I endeavoured to give him all the caution in my power respecting the cry against him; but he seemed *too wise*.'[60]

At Calder's court-martial, held in late December after the battle of Trafalgar had been fought and won, the admiral was charged with 'not having done his utmost to renew the said engagement [22 July], and to take or destroy every ship of the enemy, which it was his duty to engage accordingly'. On Christmas Day 1805 Calder detailed his defence (the statement was actually read out by his adviser, a Mr

Gazelee). Due to the damage sustained to his own fleet, his fear that his own damaged vessels and the two prizes might be re-captured, the numerical superiority of the enemy, and the possibility that the Ferrol and Rochefort squadrons might appear on the horizon with an additional 21 ships-of-the-line, he maintained that he had followed the 'most proper course to be adopted'.[61] Calder was aware that 'by renewing the action I should run too great a hazard, and put my fleet in a state of danger… I thought it best to keep my squadron together, and not to force the enemy to a second engagement, till a more favourable opportunity'. Instead he determined to keep the fleet between Villeneuve and Ferrol, preventing a junction with the enemy fleet stationed there.[62]

Calder's summing-up was a little gauche, stating that by chasing Villeneuve into Cadiz he had 'laid the foundation of that splendid victory which engages the attention of the country'. By demanding the court-martial Calder was 'prevented from sharing in the glories of that day; and, believe me, that has been no small part of my sufferings', to which *The Naval Chronicle* added that 'the gallant Admiral turned round, and wiped a tear from his eye'. The judgement of the court was that although Calder was to be cleared of cowardice, the charge of 'not having done his utmost to renew the said engagement, and to take or destroy every ship of the enemy, has been proved'. This 'error in judgement' was the reason the court found him 'severely reprimanded'.[63]

Historians have been split over Calder's action. Oliver Warner called it 'little more than a creditable brush in the old style… a poor result for being directed to be in the right place at the right time', concluding that it had wrecked Barham's plans as the Combined Fleet 'was still together… the crisis of the campaign had not yet been resolved'.[64] The over-emphasis on the battle of Trafalgar itself has been a cause of confusion between tactical success and strategic success. Historical writing after Trafalgar has traditionally placed too much emphasis on the concept of decisive battle. A decisive battle was preferable, but an obsession with it could be stifling to the wider debate regarding British strategy. With this in view, modern historians are a little kinder, Nicholas Tracy noting how Calder's action 'was a skilful manoeuvre carried out in foggy conditions. With an inferior force he engaged the enemy line, and captured two of them'.[65] For David Lyon the tactical outcome was secondary. 'Strategically,' he argues, 'Calder's action was a thundering success; it was this confrontation and not Trafalgar which put the stopper on Napoleon's over-ingenious invasion plans'. The credit for this does not belong to Calder himself, but to 'the elderly nightshirted figure of Charles Middleton, Lord Barham, writing the orders which swung the far-flung squadrons of the Royal Navy into action to block Villeneuve'.[66] Yet if the threat of invasion had passed, albeit perhaps temporarily, there were still unresolved strategic considerations.

THE SITUATION AFTER CALDER'S ACTION

Napoleon's rethink of his invasion plans came just after Villeneuve had arrived back in port following his cruise of early 1805. It was an overcomplicated plan to achieve domination of the Channel that had little actual chance of success. The Rochefort and Toulon squadrons were to meet up in the West Indies, and then head back to Brest. After Calder's action, Villeneuve had to put into Vigo, but because it could not be adequately defended he set sail for Ferrol. While trying to work his fleet into Ferrol, orders arrived from Napoleon directing him to head for Brest. Although the French ships were still outside the port, Gravina's Spanish vessels had already entered and could not leave because of contrary winds. On 13 August Napoleon learned that Villeneuve had put into Ferrol. There were nine Spanish ships there, but they were ill prepared for a meeting with the Royal Navy. With news arriving of Villeneuve's sailing on 22 August, Napoleon assumed that he was heading for Brest to cover the invasion. In accordance with his plans he ordered Ganteaume's Brest fleet to put to sea.

In fact Villeneuve had gone south. After crossing the Atlantic to the West Indies and back, then fighting a close-range action against the Royal Navy, his fleet was in a poor state. With limited supplies and the failure to introduce antiscorbutics into the seamen's diet, unlike the Royal Navy, many on board the ships were desperately sick. Even before Calder's action the Combined Fleet had more than 1,700 men ill.[67] Now two Spanish and one French ship had to be left at Vigo with the wounded and sick aboard. With his ships suffering natural wear and tear after the long voyage as well as battle damage inflicted on 22 July, there was only one place where Villeneuve could refit and re-supply – the Spanish base at Cadiz. He

> **Napoleon to Ganteaume, Boulogne Camp,** *22 August 1805*
>
> *Vice-Admiral Villeneuve got under way from Ferrol on August 10th, but did not actually leave until the 14th, in order to join you at Brest. From what I can gather from his dispatches, it seems to me that he means to go through the Raz. It also seems to me that he is doubtful if, after his junction with you, he will not spend several days revictualling at Brest. I have already informed you, by telegraph, of my intention that you should not allow him to lose a single day, in order that, profiting by the superiority which 50 ships of the line give me, you should immediately put to sea to reach your destination and to enter the Channel with all your forces. I count upon your talents, your firmness, and your character at this all-important juncture. Set out and come here. We shall have avenged six centuries of insults and shame. Never will my sailors and soldiers have exposed their lives for a grander object.*
> Source: Hodges and Hughes, p. 208.

arrived off that port on 22 August, drove off the Royal Naval blockading force and entered the safety of the harbour.[68]

Despite its great natural harbour, Villeneuve was disappointed in Cadiz. Napoleon had gone to great lengths to ensure that provisions had been stored at Brest, Rochefort and Ferrol in anticipation of his fleet revictualling in those ports, but none had been collected at Cadiz. Moreover, disease had ravaged the surrounding countryside, food was in short supply because the coastal trade on which the city depended for importing food was strangled by the British blockade, naval stores were almost non-existent and there was little chance of receiving fresh seamen to replace those sick. It is not surprising that the French and Spanish were in low spirits and soon marked divisions were opening up in the fleet. The Spaniards were mistrusting of French intentions; it particularly galled them that the two ships lost in action with Calder were both Spanish. Villeneuve himself drew criticism for his cautious and pessimistic outlook, specifically for not being more vigorous in an action against a numerically inferior fleet.

Frustrated in his plans by Calder's blocking action, on 25 August Napoleon informed his principal minister Talleyrand that he had decided against an invasion attempt. Instead he would strike at a more accessible target, Britain's ally Austria. The very next day, a full two months before the battle of Trafalgar, Napoleon's Chief of Staff, Louis Berthier, received orders to break up the Boulogne Camp and *La Grande Armée* began to march east. On 3 September Napoleon himself left the invasion camps for war with Austria. After 22 July the chance for any invasion attempt had gone, at least until 1806. Napoleon now decided that Villeneuve's force could be utilised elsewhere, so on 15 September he sent orders for him to convoy French troops to Naples. There they would attack a British force under General Craig operating in support of a Russian army arriving from Corfu. These orders were received by Villeneuve on 28 September.

By 1 October Villeneuve's fleet was making the final preparations for sea. During the next 24 hours 4,000 French soldiers were embarked in the French ships of the fleet. Destined for Southern Italy, these troops would provide small-arms fire from

the ships' tops and upper decks in case of a fleet action. The next day Admiral
Gravina came aboard *Bucentaure*. He had received credible intelligence from Lisbon
that Nelson was on his way to take up command of the British fleet and that it was
highly likely that he would try an incendiary attack to burn the Combined Fleet in
the harbour of Cadiz.[69] With the fleet ready for sea on 2 October, Villeneuve, anxious
to get underway, prepared a memorandum for the fleet. He hoped the captains
would 'see with satisfaction the opportunity that is offered to us to display that
resolution and daring which will ensure success, revenge the insults offered to its
flag, and lay low the tyrannical domination of the English upon the seas'.[70]

There now followed a frustrating few weeks for Villeneuve as contrary winds
prevented the fleet from sailing. In order to put the views of the fleet on record, he
arranged a Council of War on 8 October. All the senior officers from both fleets were
present. Villeneuve began this feisty meeting by outlining his sailing orders and his
belief that they should put to sea at the first opportunity. The Spaniards, familiar
with the probable weather conditions should the fleet put to sea during the autumn,
opposed this course of action. They argued for a delay, hoping that the British would
be forced off station by the winter storms or to search for supplies. Moreover, they
stressed that the Spanish ships needed at least another two weeks in order to be
ready. At this juncture Admiral Magon made a sarcastic comment calling into doubt
the honour of the Spanish officers, causing Commodore Galiano to leap to his feet
in a fury, placing his hand on the hilt of his sword ready to challenge the French
admiral to a duel. Fortunately for the Combined Fleet the situation was defused by
the intervention of his brother officers.

In this volatile situation Villeneuve compounded matters by upsetting the Spaniards
once more by insisting that the fleet should sail, to which Gravina took great
exception, remarking that it was madness to put to sea in the present conditions. As
the factious Council rumbled on, Commodore Churruca questioned the whole
concept of the French and Spanish fleets operating in concert. Pointing to a lack of
support from French ships on 22 July, he accused them of being 'passive spectators'
while the two Spanish ships had been captured. Once again tempers flared as the
French responded to this insult. After emotions had been calmed once more,
Villeneuve settled on a middling course of action. The fleet would be positioned at the
mouth of the harbour ready to sail when the weather cleared and, as they believed
would certainly happen, the British detached part of their fleet to procure victuals and
water. Villeneuve then wrote to Decrès informing him of the outcome of the meeting
and declaring that the Council had agreed that the fleet was in no state to implement
the orders received from Paris, thereby placing this statement on the record.[71] On 9
October the fleet began to move down to the roadstead, but gales that picked up next
day lasted for an entire week and locked the fleet up in port. More worrisome for
Villeneuve, on about 15 October, he received news that Admiral Rosily was on the way
to supersede his command. Keen to rescue his reputation, which had been in question
ever since the battle of Aboukir Bay, he resolved to sail.

Villeneuve had used the time in Cadiz to try to explain to his captains how he
intended to fight the British fleet. To his great credit, he had in part anticipated what

tactics Nelson would employ. His experience of the Battle of the Nile was vital here; he knew that Nelson wanted to cut the line and engage from the leeward side:

> The enemy will not confine himself to forming on a line of battle parallel with our own and with engaging us in an artillery duel... he will endeavour to envelope our rear, to break through our line and to direct his ships in groups upon such as ours as he shall have cut off, so as to surround them and defeat them.[72]

However, he did not come up with a firm plan to counter Nelson's expected tactics. All he could do was to follow orthodox convention which all his captains would understand. If he found Nelson to leeward Villeneuve resolved to attack, each ship picking out an opponent. If his own fleet was to leeward they would close up in line ahead and try to fend off the inevitable attack. Once the battle had begun there would be little else he could do. Instead Villeneuve placed a degree of trust in his captains, explaining to them that:

> 'All your efforts must be to assist one another, and, as far as possible, follow the movements of your admiral. You must be careful not to waste ammunition by

---

Lady Bessborough to Granville Leveson Gower, Thursday, 12 September 1805

The best thing I can do is write you an account of a dinner with Ld. Nelson; Bess [Lady Elizabeth Foster] and Ca. [The Duke of Devonshire] din'd at Crawford's Tuesday [10 September] to meet him. Both she and he say that so far from appearing vain and full of himself, as one had always heard, he was perfectly unassuming and natural. Talking of Popular Applause and his having been Mobb'd and Huzza'd in the city, Ly. Hamilton wanted to give an account of it, but he stopp'd her. 'Why,' said she, 'you like to be applauded – you cannot deny it.' 'I own it,' he answer'd; 'popular applause is very acceptable and grateful to me, but no Man ought to be too much elated by it; it is too precarious to be depended upon, and it may be my turn to feel the tide set as strong against me as ever it did for me.' Every body
join'd in saying they did not believe that could happen to him, but he seem'd persuaded it might, but added: 'Whilst I live I shall do what I think right and best; the Country has a right to that from me, but every man is liable to err in judgement.'
...He was very kind to Bess, and in taking a letter from her to Clifford [Lady Foster's son serving with the fleet] said: 'Now kiss it, and I will carry him the letter and the kiss.' He says nothing short of the annihilation of the Enemy's fleet will do any good. 'When we meet, God be with us, for we must not part again till one fleet or the other is totally destroy'd.' He hopes to be return'd by Christmas, and has the whole command of the Mediterranean, Cadiz included, and near 30 Ships of the Line; the Enemy, he says, have 100 [in total], and on being ask'd how many we had in all, he answer'd: 'Oh, I do not count our Ships.'
Source: Granville, vol. II, p. 112.

long-range firing: wait and fight only at close quarters. At the same time you must, each captain, rely rather on your own courage and ardour for glory than on the admiral's signals. In the smoke and turmoil of battle an admiral can see very little himself; often he cannot make any signals at all.'[73]

On 18 October Villeneuve learned that Rosily had reached Madrid, and he gave the order to sail. Perhaps more importantly for this decision was a report that a detachment from the British fleet blockading Cadiz had been spotted making for Gibraltar, leaving, he thought, only 22 ships-of-the-line. The Combined Fleet weighed anchor on 19 October with twelve ships-of-the-line, the remainder following at 8 a.m. the next day.

Nelson Ashore

On 19 July Nelson arrived at Gibraltar after chasing Villeneuve to and from the West Indies. There was still no news of Villeneuve's whereabouts, though Nelson remained convinced that his destination had been the Mediterranean. Spending four days at Gibraltar, Nelson became increasingly depressed over the false information obtained from Brereton. To Alexander Davison he lamented: 'But for General Brereton's damned information, Nelson would have been, living or dead, the greatest man in his Profession that England ever saw. Now, alas! I am nothing – perhaps shall incur censure for misfortunes which may happen, and have happened.'[74] The day after writing this letter Nelson's black mood lifted; at 4 a.m. on 25 July, HMS *Termagant* arrived at Gibraltar with news that *Curieux* had seen the enemy fleet heading northwards on 19 July. He immediately made ready to head northwards with eleven ships-of-the-line for a junction with the Channel Fleet off Ushant.

Once again Nelson thought he was on Villeneuve's tail – it was becoming an obsession. His long, mentally and physically exhausting watch over Toulon, followed by the chase to and from the West Indies, had taken up more than two years. He wrote to Cornwallis on 25 July: 'I shall only hope, after all my long pursuit of my Enemy, that I may arrive at the moment they are meeting you.'[75] Struggling against contrary winds, he did not come up with the Channel Fleet until the afternoon of 15 August. But again he was frustrated in his search for the elusive Villeneuve. He left his squadron under the command of Cornwallis, having been ordered to take *Victory* and *Superb* to Spithead. Hearing of Calder's action while at sea on the 16 August, he arrived at Spithead on 18 August and at 9 p.m. the following night his flag was lowered and he stepped ashore. Travelling overnight, he arrived at his home in Merton at 6 a.m. on the 20th.

Nelson was ashore out of the *Victory* for 25 days. He was tired, ill and unsure of the reception he would receive after having failed to intercept and destroy the Combined Fleet. After spending the night of 20 August at Merton, he went to London. His first official call was on Lord Barham at the Admiralty to discuss the strategic naval situation. He then visited his prize agents and the Navy Board, before heading back to the Admiralty and then on to see Pitt, returning to Merton at 4 p.m.

On 23 August he had a meeting with Viscount Castlereagh, Secretary of State for War. The same day the West India Merchants agreed to offer Nelson their thanks for his concerns for the safety of the West Indies possessions. All the time he was in London Nelson was shadowed by newspaper reporters and crowds of people, all keen to catch a glimpse of the naval hero. Sir Gilbert Elliot, Lord Minto, spent a number of days with Nelson at this time; on one occasion he told his wife:

> I met Nelson to-day in a mob in Piccadilly, and got hold of his arm, so that I was mobbed too. It is really quite affecting to see the wonder and admiration and love and respect of the whole world; and the genuine expression of all these sentiments at once, from the gentle and simple the moment he is seen. It is beyond anything represented in a play or a poem of fame.[76]

Captain Sir Henry Blackwood. A recent entry into Nelson's inner circle, Blackwood was an immensely skilled frigate captain, commanding the inshore squadron which kept watch over the enemy fleet at Cadiz. (CPL)

SIR HENRY BLACKWOOD (1770–1832)

An excellent, aggressive frigate commander and one of Nelson's inner circle of comrades, Blackwood played an important role in the Trafalgar campaign. Born in December 1770, accounts vary as to the date he joined the navy, but it is certain that he became a lieutenant in 1790 and served at the Glorious First of June in 1794. The following year he was promoted to captain, beginning his dashing career as a frigate commander. In the 36-gun *Penelope* he engaged the superior French ship-of-the-line *Guillaume Tell* of 80 guns, forcing her to slow and leading to her capture by the approaching British fleet. In *Euryalus* during 1805, he served as the eyes of Nelson's fleet, close inshore at Cadiz reporting on the enemy fleet. On the morning of 21 October Blackwood, together with Hardy, witnessed the codicil to Nelson's will. Fearing for the Admiral's safety, he tried in vain to persuade Nelson to retire to the *Euryalus* for the duration of the battle. Upon Blackwoood's leaving the *Victory* as the battle began, Nelson uttered the words which have convinced many that the great Admiral had a fateful premonition: 'God bless you Blackwood. I shall never speak to you again.' Having taken *Euryalus* into the battle to provide assistance to the heavily engaged ships-of-the-line, Blackwood's ship served as the flagship after Collingwood moved into the frigate from the badly damaged *Royal Sovereign*. After the battle Blackwood escorted Villeneuve into captivity and took part in Nelson's state funeral.

At the Dardanelles in 1807 he was captain of the *Ajax*, a ship-of-the-line, and was lucky to survive when she was engulfed by fire. Moved to *Warspite*, another ship-of-the-line, for the remainder of the war, he served as Captain of the Fleet during the victory review at Spithead in 1815, was raised to the peerage with a baronetcy and achieved flag rank as rear admiral, with the next step to vice admiral occurring in 1821.

Carrying news that the Combined Fleet had been found at Cadiz, Captain Henry Blackwood, on his way to the Admiralty, stopped off at Merton at 5 a.m. on 2 September. Already up and dressed, Nelson remarked, 'I am sure you bring me news of the French and Spanish fleets, and I think I shall yet have to beat them.' He then followed Blackwood to London, where upon meeting him again he declared, 'Depend on it, Blackwood, I shall yet give Mr. Villeneuve a drubbing.'[77] Nelson then had meetings with Pitt and Castlereagh, as well as Barham. Back with Barham on 4 September, he received his orders to take command of the fleet off Cadiz. Before heading back to the *Victory*, he picked up 50 copies of a revised version of Sir Home Riggs Popham's telegraphic code, an extremely useful tool for fleet signalling.

On 12 September Nelson's intriguing meeting with Sir Arthur Wellesley took place outside Castlereagh's office. According to the Duke of Wellington's recollection thirty years after the event, Nelson 'entered at once into a conversation with me, if I can call it conversation, for it was almost all on his side, and all about himself, and, really, in a style so vain and silly as to surprise and almost disgust me'. After briefly leaving Wellesley alone to inquire whom exactly he was conversing with, Nelson returned:

All that I thought a charlatan style had vanished, and he talked… with a good sense, and a knowledge of subjects both at home and abroad, that surprised me equally and more agreeably than the first part of our interview had done; in fact, he talked like an officer and a statesman… I don't know that I ever had a conversation that interested me more.

Wellington later suspected that Castlereagh had engineered the meeting:

…if the Secretary of State had been punctual & admitted Lord Nelson in the first quarter of an hour, I should have had the same impression of a light and trivial character that other people have had, but luckily I saw enough to be satisfied that he really was a very superior person…[78]

Nelson arrived back at Merton that day and spent the evening with Emma, Minto and his neighbours.

After spending the next day with Emma, Nelson visited his daughter Horatia, prayed for her, and left Merton for the last time at 10.30 p.m. on Friday 13 September. By 6 a.m. next morning he was back in Portsmouth making preparations to embark for the *Victory*. He attempted to evade the large numbers of spectators who had gathered to see him off, by embarking from the beach where the bathing machines were located. It was no use for, according to Southey, the scenes that day took on a religious intensity:

> …a crowd collected in his train, and many knelt down before him, and blessed him as he passed. England has had many heroes, but never one who so entirely possessed the love of his fellow-countrymen as Nelson… they love him as truly and fervently as he loved England. They pressed upon the parapet to gaze after him when his barge was pushed off, and he was returning their cheers waving his hat.

Nelson, reportedly turned to Captain Hardy and declared, 'I had their huzzas before – I have their hearts now!'[79] Nelson was back aboard *Victory*, with his flag raised at 11.30 a.m. He entertained George Rose and George Canning in *Victory*'s Great Cabin, before they went ashore. In company with Blackwood's *Euryalus* the *Victory* weighed anchor at 8 a.m. on 15 September.

Cadiz Blockaded

On 17 July the naval situation had become more complicated for Cornwallis when Commodore Zachaire Allemand had escaped from Rochefort. His intention had been to join Villeneuve and although this never took place, the prospect weighed heavily on Cornwallis' mind. On 17 August, Cornwallis, clearly aware that the

Nelson's day cabin aboard HMS *Victory*. (CPL)

> **Nelson's Private Diary**
> **Friday Night,**
> *13th September*
> At half-past ten drove from dear dear
> Merton, where I left all which I hold dear
> in this world, to go to serve my King and
> Country. May the Great God whom I adore
> enable me to fulfil the expectations of my
> Country; and if it is His good pleasure that
>
> I should return, my thanks will never cease
> being offered up to the Throne of His Mercy.
> If it is his good providence to cut short my
> days upon earth, I bow with the greatest
> submission, relying that He will protect
> those so dear to me, that I may leave
> behind. – His will be done: Amen, Amen,
> Amen.
> Source: Nicolas, VII, pp. 33–5.

enemy fleet movements were part of a wider strategy involving the huge French army camped around Boulogne, sent Calder with 20 ships-of-the-line to watch over Ferrol. Once it was confirmed that Villeneuve had left that port and headed south, Cornwallis directed Calder to join the fleet watching Cadiz under the command of Collingwood. He was now left with seventeen ships-of-the-line keeping watch over the 21 enemy ships in Brest.

Despite the problems farther north, Nelson arrived off Cadiz in the evening of 28 September and, for the final time, took command of a British fleet. He had sent Blackwood ahead to inform Collingwood that he wanted no salutes or recognition signals, lest the enemy be informed of his presence and remain in port. Nelson now received news that a British force under General Craig's force had been successfully landed at Malta and the Anglo-Russian armies were ready to operate in Southern Italy. He surmised that Villeneuve, unable to head north, would be required to enter the Mediterranean. As during his long watch at Toulon, Nelson

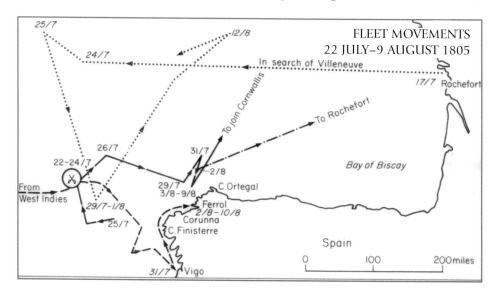

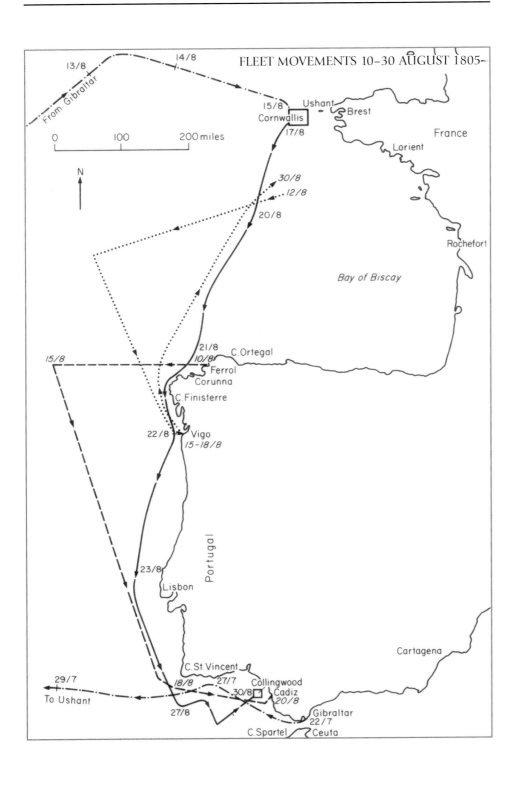

13/8

14/8

From Gibraltar

0   100   200 miles

N

15/8
Cornwallis

17/8

Ushant

Brest

France

Lorient

30/8

12/8

20/8

Rochefort

Bay of Biscay

21/8   C.Ortegal

10/8

15/8

Ferrol

Corunna

C.Finisterre

22/8   Vigo

15-18/8

Portugal

23/8

Lisbon

Cartagena

C.St.Vincent

29/7

Collingwood

18/8   27/7

To Ushant

30/8   Cadiz

20/8

27/8

Gibraltar

22/7

C.Spartel   Ceuta

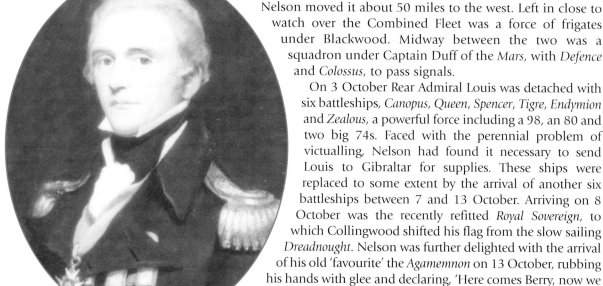

Captain Edward
Berry, one of
Nelson's beloved
'Band of Brothers'.
He had served at the
battles of Cape St.
Vincent and Aboukir
Bay, where he had
been Nelson's flag
captain aboard HMS
Vanguard. He was
now in command of
HMS *Agamemnon*,
Nelson's favourite
ship. (National
Maritime Museum)

wanted to give the enemy every opportunity to come out. Collingwood had based the fleet fifteen miles off Cadiz; now Nelson moved it about 50 miles to the west. Left in close to watch over the Combined Fleet was a force of frigates under Blackwood. Midway between the two was a squadron under Captain Duff of the *Mars*, with *Defence* and *Colossus*, to pass signals.

On 3 October Rear Admiral Louis was detached with six battleships, *Canopus*, *Queen*, *Spencer*, *Tigre*, *Endymion* and *Zealous*, a powerful force including a 98, an 80 and two big 74s. Faced with the perennial problem of victualling, Nelson had found it necessary to send Louis to Gibraltar for supplies. These ships were replaced to some extent by the arrival of another six battleships between 7 and 13 October. Arriving on 8 October was the recently refitted *Royal Sovereign*, to which Collingwood shifted his flag from the slow sailing *Dreadnought*. Nelson was further delighted with the arrival of his old 'favourite' the *Agamemnon* on 13 October, rubbing his hands with glee and declaring, 'Here comes Berry, now we shall have a Battle'. Berry had just made a skilful escape from Allemand's squadron while passing to the west of Cape Finisterre.[80]

Nelson was concerned that the Combined Fleet would refuse to come out, especially if they determined his exact strength; he even wrote to the publisher of the *Gibraltar Gazette*, requesting him to refrain from stating the strength of his fleet. Yet he held out the hope that Villeneuve would have to put to sea. This opinion was shared by Collingwood, who was certain that the Combined Fleet could not stay in Cadiz. 'We shall have these fellows out at last, my dear Lord,' he told Nelson. 'I firmly believe they have discovered that they cannot be subsisted in Cadiz: their supply from France is completely cut off.'[81]

Nelson was also worried that if they did come out they might shake him off again. The lack of frigates was crucial, as it had been earlier in the year. On 5 October he wrote to complain to the Admiralty and also to Castlereagh: 'I have only two frigates to watch them, and not one with the Fleet. I am most exceedingly anxious for more eyes, and hope the Admiralty are hastening them to me. The last Fleet was lost to me for want of Frigates; God forbid this should.'[82] On 14 October Nelson's fleet was further weakened by the loss of a powerful three-decker, as he allowed Calder to go home in his flagship *Prince-of-Wales*. A further loss occurred on 16 October when the *Donegal* was sent to Gibraltar, leaving Nelson with 27 battleships, including two small 64s, to face 33 enemy ships. Maintaining his fleet off a hostile shore, re-supplying at sea from Gibraltar and keeping a close eye on the enemy fleet while at the same time providing them with every chance of escape, Nelson was watching and waiting for his opportunity to strike and annihilate. The mode of his attack would decide the outcome of the battle.

'THE NELSON TOUCH'

Some mention has already been made regarding the tactics employed by the Combined Franco-Spanish fleet at Trafalgar. Villeneuve based his battle plan on an orthodox line of battle with a squadron on observation to windward to provide timely relief to the centre during the course of an engagement. Drawing on his experience of the battle of Aboukir Bay, he, in part, second-guessed what Nelson would try to do.

The way in which the two commanders' tactics were implemented will be found in the next chapters concerning the battle itself. The question here is what exactly were Nelson's intended tactics to bring about the annihilation of the enemy fleet? His death in the battle denied Nelson the opportunity to examine the results of his most famous engagement and compare the course of the fight with his pre-battle plans. What we are left with are several documents and a couple of reported conversations, which allow us to build a picture of how he intended to fight. For many years the tactics Nelson employed at the battle of Trafalgar were a controversial and misunderstood subject among historians. So much so that during the centennial celebrations in 1905, the Institute of Naval Architects held an in-depth discussion and many of the important naval theorists of the day had their say about the controversy. As late as 1913 the Admiralty published the findings of an inquiry into the battle to determine what exactly had taken place.[83]

The idea that Nelson's tactics were revolutionary and new, partly founded on Nelson's own writings before the battle, has now been largely disproved. Instead it is now accepted that his tactics were evolutionary, building on the foundations of his predecessors and his own particular battle experiences, rather than revolutionary. Moreover, it was not necessarily the tactics that were the key to the 'Nelson touch' but

'The Nelson Touch'. Nelson explains his intentions to the admiral and captains in his fleet, prior to Trafalgar. A heavily stylised illustration, it none the less captures the personal, face-to-face, verbal briefings that Nelson so favoured for instructing his subordinates of his battle plans. Such camaraderie built strong bonds of professional and personal loyalty to him and to one another, a factor which would prove crucial in the battle of Trafalgar. (CPL)

rather the way he instilled into his captains the kind of battle he wished to bring about and how they should act within this remit.

The Line of Battle

During the eighteenth century naval tactics underwent some significant changes. The very design of the sailing warship presented naval tacticians with a conundrum. Wind power filled the sails to propel the ship forward, but the main armament was positioned on the sides of the hull. The answer was the line of battle, where a fleet would form in line ahead presenting their broadsides to an enemy fleet. It was an effective formation for fleets wishing to defend against attack by allowing the fleet to retain cohesion, it required less seamanship than more complicated manoeuvres and it protected the vulnerable stern and bow of all but the lead and rear ships. It was also easier for an Admiral to exercise a degree of control over his ships. The defending force typically took up a position to leeward of the attacker, giving them the option of escape. The traditional response was to mirror the enemy formation on a slowly converging tack, thereby bringing about an engagement, which would be decided by attrition caused by gunfire. This brought limited results and posed a problem for the aggressive naval doctrine that the Royal Navy favoured.

The options and directives a British admiral had to follow were contained in the Admiralty Fighting Instructions, which provided a basic doctrine for fleet handling. But they also caused problems; in the heat of battle masts were shot away, smoke obscured visibility and signals could be misunderstood. At Minorca in 1756 Admiral Byng signalled for his lead ship to bear down on the enemy's course. The signal was misunderstood and Byng, unable to see what was happening at the front of the fleet, ordered the entire fleet to bear down in line abreast. Suffering much damage to his ships from the French broadsides, Byng broke off the action and retired to Gibraltar to repair. Minorca surrendered and Byng was shot for not doing his utmost to engage the enemy. Three years later a more dynamic and intelligent man overcame the problems with orthodox doctrine at Quiberon Bay. Chasing the French fleet inshore in a full-blown gale, Admiral Hawke simply ordered his ships to form line abreast, make all sail and bear down on the French fleet, his van forming a line as they came up with the enemy rear. While naval theorists and admirals struggled to improve the effectiveness of fleet signalling, and therefore tactics, the last naval battle of the War of American Independence highlighted a different solution. At the Battle of the Saintes in 1782, Admiral Rodney cut the enemy line of battle for the first time in over a hundred years. It is still debated whether Rodney exercised control, and it was certainly not a premeditated manoeuvre, but the effects were important. Ships cutting a line could rake the vulnerable stern and bows of enemy ships as they passed through. But it was also dangerous, as the unengaged lee side of the enemy line could now fire on the sterns of the ships after they had passed through. At the Saintes the French fleet had lost cohesion and the British, to leeward of the enemy, seized the opportunity. At the Glorious First of June in 1794, Lord Howe, after trying to give battle from the leeward position, manoeuvred and attacked from windward, closed quickly with the French and, cutting their line, engaged from leeward to prevent their escape.

To the above developments, Nelson added personal experience; in essence a combination of aggressive action to close and bring the enemy to battle at close quarters coupled with the freedom for well-briefed and tactically astute captains to take the initiative. Nelson displayed his own tactical awareness at the battle of Cape St. Vincent in 1797, when he wore out of the loose line of battle formed by Admiral Sir John Jervis, possibly in accordance with Jervis' instructions, to assist the British van in its fight with the Spanish rear. He saw it in action at the Nile when Captain Foley, instead of laying alongside the lead French ship, rounded the head of the enemy line to engage from leeward, catching the van in a crossfire.

Therefore by the time of Trafalgar Nelson was ready to build on the tactical developments and his personal experience to bring about the battle of annihilation he so desired. Writing to George Rose on 6 October 1805 he declared:

The first page of Nelson's memorandum of 9 October 1805. A mission statement for the fleet, in this memorandum he refined and simplified his tactical ideas to the point where he declared 'no captain can do very wrong if he places his ship alongside that of his enemy'. (CPL)

I have not the very smallest doubt but that a very few days, almost hours, will put us in battle; the success no man can ensure, but as to fighting them, if they are to be got at, I pledge myself… it is, as Mr. Pitt knows, annihilation that the Country wants, and not merely a splendid Victory of twenty-three to thirty-six, – honourable to the parties concerned, but absolutely useless in the extended scale to bring Buonaparte to his marrow bones: numbers can only annihilate.[84]

Nelson's plans for annihilation of the enemy were not clear 'tactical doctrines' but more a collection of ideas that he instilled into those under his command through their trust and faith in him as the commander. They were based on a number of assumptions. First, as Nicholas Tracy has argued, 'close mutual support, efficient ship handling and good gunnery were more important than good station keeping and fleet manoeuvre'.[85] Therefore Nelson wanted his fleet to ram into the enemy to get in close and use superior British gunnery and discipline to overwhelm them. This in turn was based on the belief, from his own experiences of seeing Spanish and French fleets in action, that the enemy would be suffering from poor morale and would be unwilling to stand up and fight. His major tactical concern

Nelson's Plan of Attack

The business of an English commander-in-chief being first to bring the Enemy's fleet to battle on the most advantageous terms to himself (I mean that of laying his ships close on board the enemy as expeditiously as possible and secondly to continue them there without separating until the business is decided), I am sensible beyond this object it is not necessary that I should say a word, being fully sensible that the admirals and captains of the fleet I have the honour to command will, knowing my precise object, that of a close and decisive battle, supply any deficiency in my not making signals, which may, if extended beyond those objects, either be misunderstood, or if waited for very probably from various causes be impossible for the commander-in-chief to make. Therefore it will only be necessary for me to state in as few words as possible the various modes in which it may be necessary for me to obtain my object; on which depends not only the honour and glory of our country, but possibly its

safety, and with it that of all Europe, from French tyranny and oppression.

If the two fleets are both willing to fight, but little manoeuvring is necessary, the less the better. A day is soon lost in that business. Therefore I will only suppose that the enemy's fleet being to leeward standing close upon a wind on the starboard tack and that I am nearly ahead of them standing on the larboard tack. Of course I should weather them. The weather must be supposed to be moderate, for if it be a gale of wind the manoeuvring of both fleets is but of little avail, and probably no decisive action would take place with the whole fleet.

Two modes present themselves, one to stand on just out of gun-shot, until the van ship of my line would be about the centre ship of the enemy; then make the signal to wear together; then bear up engage with all our force the six or five van ships of the enemy, passing, certainly if opportunity offered, through their line. This would prevent their bearing up, and the action, from the known bravery and conduct of the

during October 1805, right up until the first shots were fired, was that the enemy would make a run for it.

During the chase to the West Indies, Nelson took the opportunity of circulating a plan of attack to the fleet, directing Captain William Parker's *Amazon* for this duty. Writing to Sir John Laughton in 1891, Vice Admiral Augustus Phillimore recalled: 'I believe in Sir W[illiam] P[arker]'s journal or log it is mentioned that the *Amazon* delivered Lord Nelson's plan of attack to each ship while at sea. The manner of doing this was described to me by Sir Wm. Parker himself.'[86]

In Nelson's first plan there are several key points. The captains of the fleet knew Nelson wanted a decisive close quarters battle, but it would not be governed by signals; to keep everything simple all the manoeuvring was to be done ahead of the actual combat. By attacking in such a way Nelson could choose where to cut the line giving him the opportunity to sail for the flagship, pass close under her stern and rake with double shot then engage on the leeward side. He was aiming to cut off the van and destroy it before support could arrive from the rear. It was a high-risk tactic which would expose his ships to the fire of the enemy van, and his own van to the enemy rear. Once the enemy fleet was engaged: 'The great object is for us to support each

---

admirals' captains, would certainly be decisive. The second or third rear ships of the enemy would act as they please, and our ships would give a good account of them, should they persist in mixing with our ships.

The other mode would be to stand under an easy but commanding sail directly for their headmost ship, so as to prevent the enemy from knowing whether I should pass to leeward or to windward of him. In that situation I would make the signal to engage the enemy to leeward, and cut through their fleet about the sixth ship from the van, passing very close. They being on a wind and you going large could cut their line when you please. The van ships of the enemy would, by the time our rear came abreast of the van ships, be severely cut up, and our van could not expect to escape damage. I would then have our rear ship and every ship in succession wear and continue the action with either the van ship or the second as it might appear most eligible from her crippled state; and this mode pursued I see nothing to prevent the capture of

five or six ships of the enemy's van. The two or three ships of the enemy's rear must either bear up or wear; and in either case, although they would be in a better plight probably than our two van ships (now the rear), yet they would be separated and at a distance to leeward, so as to give our ships time to refit. And by that time I believe the battle would, from the judgement of the admiral and captains, be over with the rest of them. Signals from these moments are useless when every man is disposed to do his duty. The great object is for us to support each other, and to keep close to the enemy and to leeward of him.

If the enemy are running away, then the only signals necessary will be to engage the enemy on arriving up with them; and to the other ships to pass on for the second, third &c., giving if possible a close fire into the enemy on passing, taking care to give our ships engaged notice of your intention.

Source: BL Add MS 36,747 f.55. See also Tracy, (1996), p. 207, James, III, pp. 371–2, Nicolas, VI, pp. 443–4.

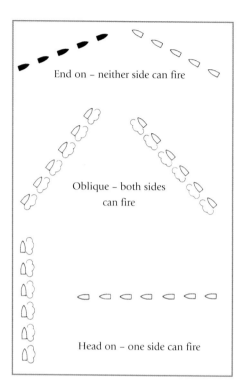

End on – neither side can fire

Oblique – both sides can fire

Head on – one side can fire

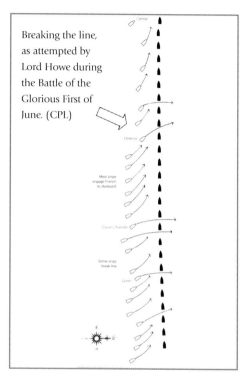

Breaking the line, as attempted by Lord Howe during the Battle of the Glorious First of June. (CPL)

other', as the ships' captains would be in the best position to know how to use their ship, either to 'lay themselves alongside' an enemy or to help comrades already in action. Again, the key to his plan was the superior ship handling, gunnery and morale of the Royal Navy.

While ashore he had refined his ideas even more. In a conversation with Sir Richard Keats of HMS *Superb*, Nelson made clear what he wanted. Gone was the rigid and ordered formation based around line of battle which took too long to manoeuvre for his battle of annihilation. Instead he wanted a close-quarter 'pell-mell' battle. A force of fast two-decked ships would be placed to windward, which he would use to seize the initiative and surprise the enemy. This fast division could pin the enemy while the remainder of the fleet, deployed in two columns, struck the decisive blow at the enemy van. Shortly before leaving England Nelson explained to Lord Sidmouth exactly how he intended the attack to form, drawing it out in wine on a tablecloth: 'I will attack in two lines, led by myself and Collingwood, and I am confident I shall capture either their Van and Centre, or their Centre and Rear.'[87]

Such a mode of attack was reliant on a high degree of professionalism in seamanship, bravery, discipline, and the captains' trust, in the admiral and one another. The leading ships would suffer damage without being able to fight back, they would then find themselves in the heart of the enemy line 'where they either had to fight with a skill and courage based on confidence in Nelson and themselves, or perish'.[88] It was here that the much-vaunted 'Nelson touch' would be vital. Nelson used his remarkable interpersonal skills to inspire his subordinates with complete confidence in his plans and in one another. This was not something that could be propagated by paper talk, but by personal contact. It is a fallacy to believe that Nelson's famous 'Band of Brothers' were at Trafalgar. He had coined the phrase, lifted from *Henry V*, to describe those captains with whom he had a very close bond and relates specifically to those present at Aboukir Bay. They were a remarkable professional élite who, as contemporaries, had moved up through the navy at about the same time, exposed to the same core ideas from St. Vincent and Nelson. At Trafalgar there were 22 ships from the Channel Fleet that had not been part of his Mediterranean Fleet. From the 27 captains, eight had previously served under him, but of these only Hardy had been present at all Nelson's battles. It was therefore imperative that he immediately transmited his message across to the unfamiliar captains in a lucid and simple fashion.

The medium was informal dinner meetings with his captains and junior admirals, to impress upon them his confidence and his plans. On the way back from the West Indies Nelson had called several ships' captains to dine aboard *Victory*, and on 1 July it was the turn of Rear Admiral Louis and Captain Hargood of *Belleisle*.[89] Off Cadiz he held a dinner to celebrate his 47th birthday on 29 September 1805 for the senior officers, and

---

Memorandum of a conversation between Lord Nelson and Admiral Sir Richard Keats [HMS Superb], the last time he was in England, before the battle of Trafalgar:

One morning, walking with Lord Nelson in the grounds at Merton, talking on Naval matters, he said to me, 'No day can be long enough to arrange a couple of fleets, and fight a decisive Battle, according to the old system. When we meet them,' (I was to have been with him), 'for meet them we shall, I'll tell you how I shall fight them. I shall form the Fleet into three Divisions in three Lines. One Division shall be composed of twelve or fourteen of the fastest two-decked Ships, which I shall keep always to windward, or in a situation of advantage; and I shall put them under an Officer who, I am sure, will employ them in the manner I wish, if possible. I consider it will always

be in my power to throw them into Battle in any part I may choose; but if circumstances prevent their being carried against the Enemy where I desire, I shall feel certain he will employ them effectually, and, perhaps, in a more advantageous manner than if he could have followed my orders.' (He never mentioned, or gave any hint by which I could understand who it was he intended for this distinguished service.) He continued – 'With the remaining part of the Fleet formed in two Lines, I shall go at them at once, if I can, about one-third of their formed Line from their leading Ship.' He then said, 'What do you think of it?' Such a question I felt required consideration. I paused. Seeing it, he said, 'But I'll tell you what I think of it. I think it will surprise and confound the Enemy. They won't know what I am about. It will bring forward a pell-mell Battle, and that is what I want.'

Source: Nicolas, VII, p. 241.

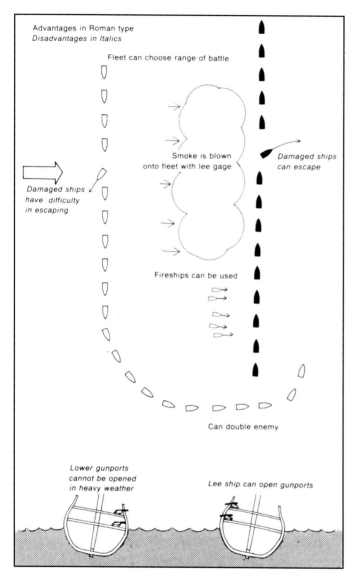

Advantages in Roman type
Disadvantages in Italics

Fleet can choose range of battle

Smoke is blown
onto fleet with lee gage

Damaged ships
can escape

Damaged ships
have difficulty
in escaping

Fireships can be used

Can double enemy

Lower gunports
cannot be opened
in heavy weather

Lee ship can open gunports

A diagram depicting
the advantages and
disadvantages of the
weather gauge. (CPL)

another for the junior captains on 30 September. Fremantle attended both, and Captain Duff of the *Mars* told his wife on 1 October: 'I dined with his Lordship yesterday, and had a very merry dinner; he certainly is the pleasantest admiral I ever served under.' After entertaining them he wrote to Collingwood: 'If the weather is fine perhaps you will come on board to-morrow. If the weather suits I will ask you to dinner: our party will not be so numerous as yesterday and to-day. Captain Rotherham of course.'[90]

It was during these meetings, he informed Emma on 1 October, that he explained the 'Nelson touch': 'It was like an electric shock. Some shed tears, all approved — It was new — it was singular — it was simple!'; and, from Admirals downwards, it was repeated — It must succeed, if ever they will allow us to get at them!' He wrote again to an unnamed correspondent on 3 October:

The Officers who came on board to welcome my return, forgot my rank as Commander-in-Chief in the enthusiasm with which they greeted me. As soon as these emotions were past, I laid before them the Plan I had previously arranged for attacking the Enemy; and it was not only my pleasure to find it generally approved, but clearly perceived and understood.

Creating a feeling of confidence and mutual support among the fleet was not limited to culinary occasions. On 9 October Captain Moorsom of the *Revenge* began to paint his ship with the famous 'Nelson chequer', two or three broad bands of yellow paint around the hull with the lids of the gun ports painted black to create the chequerboard pattern. On 10 October Captain Duff wrote again to his wife:

I am sorry the rain has begun to night, as it will spoil my fine work, having been employed for this week past to paint the ship *à la Nelson*, which most of the Fleet are doing. He is so good and pleasant a man, that we all wish to do what he likes, without any kind of orders.[91]

> ### The Nelson Touch
> ### Victory,
> #### October 1st, 1805.
>
> *My dearest Emma,*
>
> *It is a relief to me, to take up the pen, and write you a line; for I have had, about four o'clock this morning, one of my dreadful spasms, which has almost enervated me. It is very odd; I was hardly ever better than yesterday. Fremantle stayed with me till eight o'clock, and I slept uncommonly well; but was awoke with this disorder. My Opinion of its effect, some one day, has never altered. However, it is entirely gone off, and I am only quite weak. The good people of England will not believe that rest of body and mind is necessary for me! But perhaps this spasm may not come again these six months. I had been writing seven hours yesterday; perhaps that had some hand in bringing it upon me.*
>
> *I joined the Fleet on the evening of the 28th of September, but could not communicate with them until the next morning. I believe my arrival was most welcome, not only to the Commander of the Fleet, but also to every individual in it, and, when I came to explain to them the 'Nelson touch' it was like an electric shock. Some shed tears, all approved — 'It was new — it was singular — it was simple!'; and, from Admirals downwards, it was repeated— 'It must succeed, if ever they will allow us to get at them! You are, my Lord, surrounded by friends whom you inspire with confidence.' Some may be Judas's; but the majority are certainly much pleased with my commanding them.*
>
> *The Enemy's fleet is 35 or 36 sail of the line in Cadiz, the French have given the dons an old 74 to repair and taken possession of the Santa Anna of 112 guns. [Admiral] Louis is going into Gibraltar and Teutan to get supplies of which the fleet is much in want and Admiral Knight as I am told has almost made us quarrel with the Moors of Barbary however I am sending Mr Ford and money to put us right again.*
> *God bless you Amen Amen Amen*
> Source: White, (2002), p. 271, original BL, Eg 1614; Nicolas, VII, p. 60 misses off the last paragraph.

While off Cadiz Nelson amended his earlier memorandum, incorporating all his ideas into one mission statement for the fleet. More an outline of intentions than a battle plan, it was an exercise in simplification. The order of sailing in the fleet was to be the order of battle, thereby avoiding any fleet manoeuvres that would waste valuable time. The order of battle would form up on the flagships, which would then move farther back in the lines to protect them. The attack from windward head on against the enemy's broadsides was dangerous, perhaps foolhardy, but it was worth the calculated risk. The attack was to be made under full sail: the slower sailing vessels would naturally fall behind which would increase the risk of collisions, but the speed would reduce the time the ships had to spend passing through the enemy's field of fire, reducing damage and casualties. The key to success would be the delivery of a heavy blow at the decisive points, one of which was the enemy commander's ship, by having his powerful three-deckers concentrated at the head of the attacks:

Nelson to…
Victory off Cadiz,
3 October 1805
The reception I met with on joining the
Fleet caused the sweetest sensation of my
life. The Officers who came on board to
welcome my return, forgot my rank as
Commander-in-Chief in the enthusiasm
with which they greeted me. As soon as
these emotions were past, I laid before them
the Plan had previously arranged for
attacking the Enemy; and it was not only

my pleasure to find it generally approved,
but clearly perceived and understood. The
Enemy are still in Port, but something must
be immediately done to provoke or lure them
to a Battle. My duty to my Country
demands it, and the hopes centred in me, I
hope in God, will be realised. In less than a
fortnight expect to hear from me, or of me,
for who can foresee the fate of Battle? Put
up your prayers for my success, and may
God protect all my friends!
Source: Nicolas, VII, pp. 66–7.

Téméraire 98, *Superb* 74, *Victory* 100, *Neptune* 98
Prince 98, *Mars* 74, *Royal Sovereign* 100, *Tonnant* 80

To increase the shock of the attack he envisaged three columns engaging more of the enemy, isolating and destroying a section of the enemy line and thereby making the outcome more decisive. But like many of the paper ideas, in practice at Trafalgar Nelson simply did not have enough ships to implement his ideas in full. In the confusion of battle, if the plan or signals were misunderstood, the course of action was a simple one: 'no Captain can do very wrong if he places his Ship alongside that of an Enemy.'

Interpretations of Nelson's tactics at Trafalgar have been given a new twist by the discovery of a pre-battle plan drawn up sometime in 1805, perhaps during his time ashore. The discovery by Colin White of this drawing among the Nelson papers in the National Maritime Museum is intriguing on several counts. It is the only drawing that has come to light where Nelson explained his tactics before a battle. Moreover, it seems to highlight the ideas that Nelson discussed with Sir Richard Keats on his final visit ashore, the latter recording the conversation in 1829. The plan clearly shows the British fleet organised in three separate divisions, presumably to windward of the enemy fleet, as Nelson intended in his various memoranda. The enemy are shown as taking up a conventional line of battle. Two divisions of the British fleet attack in line ahead, cutting the line near the centre and at one end, perhaps the rear, one of the lines is hooked, as if to suggest ranging alongside the enemy on the leeward side to prevent their escaping, a major worry for Nelson during the campaign. The third British squadron takes up a position alongside the unengaged section of the enemy line, presumably the van, to prevent them assisting their colleagues. As Colin White has noted: 'It is even possible to catch an echo of the excitement with which Nelson has demonstrated the cutting of the enemy line – his pen had dug deeply into the paper and the ink has flowed freely'. Above this diagram is another, a little more unclear. Perhaps it shows how an enemy might respond to the British attack to catch them in a cross fire, or perhaps it shows the tactics employed at the Nile of rounding and doubling the enemy van to destroy it.[93]

With his aggressive tactics clearly defined and instilled into the fleet by conversation and memoranda, Nelson remained 50 miles off Cadiz, desperate for the chance to implement them. He would not have long to wait.

Nelson's Theoretical Order of Battle

1	*Téméraire**		1	*Prince**
2	*Superb*		2	*Mars**
3	*Victory**		3	*Royal Sovereign**
4	*Neptune**		4	*Tonnant**
5	*Tigre*		5	*Bellerophon**
6	*Canopus*		6	*Colossus**
7	*Conqueror**		7	*Achilles**
8	*Agamemnon**		8	*Polyphemus**
9	*Leviathan**		9	*Revenge**
10	*Prince-of-Wales*		10	*Britannia**
11	*Ajax**		11	*Swiftsure**
12	*Minotaur**		12	*Defence**
13	*Queen*		13	*Orion**
14	*Donegal*		14	*Zealous*
15	*Spencer*		15	*Thunderer**
16	*Spartiate**		16	*Defiance**
			17	*Dreadnought**

*Present at Trafalgar.

Sources: Nicolas, vol. VII, p. 94; Tracy (1996), p. 177; BL Ad MS 33,963 also lists the above, but with *Belleisle* (joined the fleet on 10 October) following *Tonnant* and *Africa* (joined the fleet on 14 October) following *Swiftsure* in the second column, making that up to 19 ships-of-the-line.

Nelson to Collingwood
Victory,

October 9th, 1805

I send you my Plan of Attack, as far as a man dare venture to guess at the very uncertain position the Enemy may be found in. But, my dear friend, it is to place you perfectly at ease respecting my intentions, and to give full scope to your judgement for carrying them into effect. We can, my dear Coll., have no little jealousies. We have only one great object in view, that of annihilating our Enemies, and getting a glorious Peace for our Country. No man has more confidence in another than I have in you: and no man will render your services more justice than your very old friend.

Source: Nicolas, VII, p. 95.

Nelson's Cadiz Memorandum

From the original holograph draft in the
British Museum. Interlineations are shown
in square brackets, deletions in roman, as in
the Blue Book on the Tactics of Trafalgar,
Cd. 7120
Memn.

Victory, off Cadiz,

9th October, 1805.

Thinking it almost impossible to bring a
Fleet of forty Sail of the Line into a Line of
Battle in variable winds, thick weather, and
other circumstances which must occur,
without such a loss of time that the
opportunity would probably be lost of
bringing the Enemy to Battle in such a
manner as to make the business decisive.

I have [therefore] made up my mind to
keep the Fleet in that position of sailing
(with the exception of the First and
Second in Command) that the Order of
Sailing is to be the Order of Battle,
placing the Fleet in two Lines of sixteen
Ships each, with an Advanced Squadron
of eight of the fasting [sic] sailing Two-
decked Ships, [which] will always make if
wanted a Line of twenty-four Sail, on
whichever Line the Commander-in-Chief
may direct.

The Second in Command will in fact
Command [his line] and after my
intentions are made known to him will have
the entire direction of His Line to make the
attack upon the Enemy and to follow up the
Blow until they are captur'd or destroy'd.

If the Enemy's Fleet should be seen to
windward [in Line of Battle] but [and] in
that position that the Two Lines and the
Advanced Squadron can fetch them (I shall
suppose them forty Six Sail [in] of the
Line of Battle) they will probably be so

extended that their Van could not succour
their Rear.

I should therefore probably make your the
2nd in Commds signal to lead through about
their Twelfth Ship from their Rear, (or
wherever you [He] could fetch if not able to
get so far advanced) My Line would lead
through about their Centre and the Advanced
Squadron to cut two or three or four Ships
Ahead of their Centre, so as to ensure getting
at their Commander-in-Chief, on whom every
Effort must be made to capture.

The whole impression of the British [fleet]
must be, to overpower from two or three Ships
ahead of their Commander-in-Chief, supposed
to be in the centre, to the Rear of their Fleet. [I
will suppose] twenty Sail of the [Enemys] Line
to be untouched, it must be some time before
they could perform a Manœuvre to bring their
force compact to attack any part of the British
Fleet engaged, or to succour their own Ships,
which indeed would be impossible, without
mixing with the Ships engaged.[92] Something
must be left to chance, nothing is sure in a Sea
Fight beyond all others, shot will carry away
the masts and yards of friends as well as foes,
but I look with confidence to a Victory before
the Van of the Enemy could succour their
friends [Rear], and then that the British Fleet
would most of them be ready to receive their
twenty Sail of the Line or to pursue them
should they endeavour to make off.

If the Van of the Enemy tacks the Captured
Ships must run to leeward of the British Fleet,
if the Enemy wears the British must place
themselves between the Enemy and the
Captured & disabled British Ships and should
the Enemy close I have no fears as to the
result.

The Second in Command will in all
possible things direct the Movements of his
Line by keeping them as compact as the

nature of the circumstances will admit and Captains are to look to their particular Line as their rallying point. But in case Signals can neither be seen or perfectly understood no Captain can do very wrong if he places his Ship alongside that of an Enemy.

Of the intended attack from to Windward, the Enemy in Line of Battle ready to receive an attack: [see diaram below]

The Divisions of the British Fleet will be brought nearly within gun shot of the Enemy's Centre. The signal will most probably [then] be made for the Lee Line to bear up together to set all their sails even steering sails in order to get as quickly as possible to the Enemy's Line and to cut through beginning from the 12 Ship from the Enemies rear some Ships may not get through their exact place, but they will always be at hand to assist their friends and if any are thrown round the Rear of the Enemy they will effectually compleat the business of Twelve Sail of the Enemy. Should the Enemy wear together or bear up and sail

Large still the Twelve Ships composing in the first position the Enemys rear are to be [the] Object of attack of the Lee Line unless otherwise directed from the Commander-in-Chief which is scarcely to be expected as the entire management of the Lee Line after the intentions of the Commander-in-Chief is [are] signified is intended to be left to the judgment of the Admiral commanding that Line.

The remainder of the Enemy's Fleet 34 Sail are to be left to the management of the Commander-in-Chief who will endeavour to take care that the Movements of the Second in Command are as little interrupted as is possible.

Source: Hodges and Hughes, pp. 219–23. See also Nicolas, VII, pp. 89–92; Tracy, (1996), p. 208.
[The document is here reproduced as the draft document printed in Hodges and Hughes, Select Naval Documents as that version contains the passages deleted out of the document as published in Nicolas.]

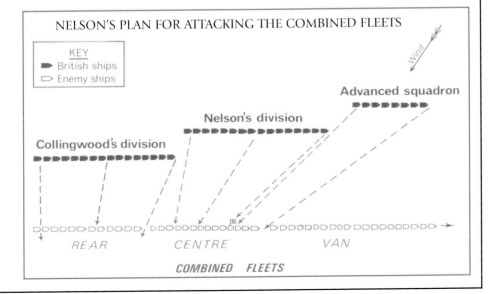

NELSON'S PLAN FOR ATTACKING THE COMBINED FLEETS

PREPARING FOR BATTLE

At 6 a.m. on 19 October 1805, Captain William Prowse's *Sirius*, in the inshore squadron under Captain Henry Blackwood watching over Cadiz harbour, hoisted the signal 'Enemy have their topsail yards hoisted'. Signal number 370 followed about an hour later: 'The enemy is coming out or under sail'. In the advance squadron, located between Cadiz and the main fleet, Captain Duff's *Mars* relayed the signal to the *Victory* which was with the main fleet stationed 50 miles out to sea. *Victory* acknowledged receipt at 9.30 with an excited Nelson ordering the signals 'General Chase' and then 'Prepare for Battle' to be hoisted. He then formed up his Advanced Squadron and the remainder of the fleet into order of sailing and set a course for the Straits of Gibraltar, believing that Villeneuve was headed into the Mediterranean. But in heavy rain, fog and squalls, on the morning of 20 October there was no sign of the enemy.

In fact the Combined Fleet had been very slow in getting to sea as a consequence of a combination of poor seamanship, lack of co-operation between the French and Spaniards and the prevailing light winds. It was not until 20 October that the fleet, with the exception of the Spanish *Rayo*, were drawn up outside the harbour in a thoroughly chaotic manner. Finally, at about 3 p.m. the ships had managed to achieve an orthodox formation of a kind, with Villeneuve in the centre flanked to port by Vice Admiral Alava and to starboard by Gravina's Observation Squadron. Between 6 p.m. and 7.30 p.m., with the fleet eight to ten miles out from Cadiz, *Aigle*, in Gravina's squadron, signalled that she had seen a British fleet of eighteen vessels shadowing their movements to the south. Villeneuve signalled 'prepare for battle', wore round to the north-west and at 11 p.m. ordered the three squadrons to form up into one line of battle.

VICE ADMIRAL IGNACIO MARÍA DE ALAVA (1750-1817)

Alava, the Spanish second in command at Trafalgar, engaged in a friendly correspondence concerning the care and exchange of British and Spanish prisoners with Collingwood after the battle. He was born in 1750 to an upper class family in Vitoria. With Gravina, he had fought with the Royal Navy at the start of the wars with France, operating with Lord Hood at the capture of Toulon in 1793. An excellent seaman with great experience, he had served in the Spanish Philippines, saving the *Montañes* from foundering in a hurricane during April 1797. During Gravina's foray to the West Indies in 1805, Alava had remained at Cadiz to re-organise the great naval base. At Trafalgar Alava's ship *Santa Ana* was engaged by Collingwood's *Royal Sovereign* and he received a severe wound to the head. In March 1806 he was appointed commander of the Spanish squadron in Cadiz. Ordered to Havana in 1810, he encountered Hercules Robinson and discussed the battle with him over dinner. Returning to Cadiz as Captain General in 1812, after the end of the Napoleonic Wars, he was promoted to Captain General of the Fleet three months before his death in 1817. Alava's nephew, General Miguel Ricardo, had the remarkable distinction of being present at both Trafalgar, aboard the *Principe de Asturias*, and at the battle of Waterloo in 1815 as part of Wellington's headquarters staff.

Admiral Ignacio Alava was an expert sailor and the Spanish Second-in-Command at Trafalgar where his ship the *Santa Ana* took a terrible battering from Collingwood's *Royal Sovereign*. (Warwick Leadlay Gallery)

With the winds increasing during the early hours of the 20th, at 7 a.m. the British frigate *Phoebe* confirmed that the Combined Fleet was heading for the Straits. Heading to cut them off, Nelson did not want to sail too far east as the winds and currents would blow his large ships into the Mediterranean. While Nelson was about 25 miles south-west of Cadiz, news came from Blackwood's *Euryalus* that the enemy had been seen through a clearing in the weather heading west by north-west.[94]

Nelson again signalled the order of sailing, hove to and summoned Collingwood aboard. At this discussion Collingwood expressed his desire to attack straight away. But Nelson wanted to wait. Perhaps, with Calder's action in mind, it was too late in the day for a fully decisive battle and with the enemy still close to Cadiz he did not want them to be able to run into the safety of that harbour. Nelson was still unsure of Villeneuve's intentions and if he would stand and fight. In fact Villeneuve did want to get into the Mediterranean but the south-westerly winds forced him to stand on. To bring him closer to the enemy, at 8.40 p.m. Nelson wore to the south-west, then at 4 a.m. on the morning of 21 October, with the fleets converging too quickly, headed north by west, then brought the fleet round in an arc to bring him once again on a collision course with the Combined Fleet. As dawn broke the two fleets were about eleven miles apart, somewhat to the west of the treacherous coast of Cape Trafalgar.

The Morning of 21 October 1805, the Experience of the Combined Fleet

At 6.30 a.m. the French frigate *Hermione* sighted Nelson's fleet to windward. Villeneuve's fleet was now heading south in a chaotic rough line about nine miles in length located twelve miles to the west of Cape Trafalgar. Half an hour later

Villeneuve repeated the signals of the previous night to form line of battle and to clear for action. At 7.10–7.15 a.m. *Hermione* signalled that the British fleet numbered 27 ships-of-the-line. Aboard *Bucentaure*, Villeneuve now realised that the British were stronger than he had expected, and moreover they were to windward and thus could launch an attack. He ignored his plan of battle, instructing the fleet to form a single line and head south-west. Again the inexperience of some French and Spanish crews led to gaps opening up in the fleet as their ships struggled to form a coherent line. At 7.20 a.m. Villeneuve ordered the fleet to close up to a cable's length between ships. The fleet, now led by Gravina's *Principe de Asturias*, was only a few miles off the Straits of Gibraltar leading into the Mediterranean.

But in the light winds Villeneuve concluded that his fleet could never reach the Straits without engaging in a running fight with the British fleet. Making the fateful decision to abandon his attempt to gain the Mediterranean, at 8.00 a.m. *Bucentaure* ran up the signal for the entire fleet to reverse course, with each ship wearing round in station, bringing them on a virtual collision course with Nelson's fleet. It was clear that an attack by the British was now probable and Villeneuve was keen to keep Cadiz on his lee, which would enable the fleet to run for the safety of the port. Again, the poor ship handling in the fleet was compounded by the light winds and strong ground swell, causing widespread confusion.

It was not until after 10 a.m. that the *volte face* was completed, with Rear Admiral Dumanoir's squadron now forming the van of an irregular crescent, with the centre a little to leeward of the wings. Moreover, many of the ships were not in their proper stations, and in places the line was becoming bunched, with two or three ships abreast of one another, whereas in other places gaps were opening up. Gravina's Observation Squadron, which was supposed to act to windward of the fleet, now joined the line towards the rear, in effect lengthening the line of battle. In this disordered state the Combined fleet headed north led by the *Neptuno*, while Nelson slowly approached from windward.

Realising that the line had not formed as he desired and with the British fleet now visibly bearing down on him, Villeneuve attempted to instruct Gravina to form up in his allotted station. Flag Captain Jean Prigny stated in his official report:

> At 11.30 the breeze being light, a signal was made to the Squadron of Observation, which was then in the rear, and bearing away to take station in the wake of the fleet, to keep its luff, in order to be able to proceed to reinforce the centre of the line against the attack of the enemy who was bearing down on it in two columns.[95]

Villeneuve's plan to have a compact and powerful reserve force to windward was now impossible to achieve. By ordering Gravina to reinforce the centre of his fleet, which was now becoming seriously strung out, Villeneuve was clearly attempting a tactical response to the two-pronged British attack, in the realisation that if the enemy intended to cut his line and engage from the leeward side, the best defence was increased depth. But Gravina's decision to join the tail rather than reinforce the centre relegated several powerful ships to the rear.

The slow advance of Nelson's fleet was met with an eagerness to test the old enemy from the officers and men of the Combined Fleet. Some French accounts suggest that the depression that had engulfed the fleet since the battle with Calder on 22 July lifted as spirits rose. Nevertheless, there must have been many who witnessed the slow approach with dread. At 11.30 Villeneuve ordered the fleet to open fire when the first British ships came within range. When the first ranging shots were fired by the *Fougueux*, the ships of the Combined Fleet ran up their colours, and aboard the *Redoutable* the drum beats rolled out as the crews cheered seven times *'Vive l'Empereur!'*

The experience of the British Fleet

With his ships heading for the Combined fleet at 6.40 a.m. on 21 October, Nelson hoisted signal 72 to 'Form order of sailing in two columns' and then number 13 'Prepare for battle'. This was followed ten minutes later by 'bear up'. *Victory* then set all sail and cleared for quarters. With the ship now ready and making three knots, around walking pace, there was a long and tedious wait ahead for the crews of the British fleet. It seemed as if a battle was now inevitable, though Nelson remained unsure whether Villeneuve would fight or run for the Mediterranean.

A little after 6 a.m. Nelson had a conference with the frigate captains, instructing them as to their role in the action. Meaning to 'bleed the Captains of the Frigates', Nelson informed Blackwood that their task would not be the usual subordinate one.

Extract from Surgeon Beatty's Narrative

Soon after daylight, Lord Nelson came upon deck: he was dressed as usual in his Admiral's frock-coat, bearing on the left breast four stars of different Orders which he always wore with his common apparel. He did not wear his sword in the Battle of Trafalgar; it had been taken from the place where it hung up in his cabin, and was laid ready on the table; but it is supposed he forgot to call for it. This was the only action in which he ever appeared without a sword. He displayed excellent spirits, and, expressed his pleasure at the prospect of giving a fatal blow to the Naval power of France and Spain; and spoke with confidence of obtaining a signal Victory notwithstanding the inferiority of the British Fleet, declaring to Captain Hardy that 'he would not be contented with capturing less than twenty

Sail of the Line.' He afterwards pleasantly observed, that 'the 21st of October was the happiest day in the year among his family'; but did not assign the reason of this.* His Lordship had previously entertained a strong presentiment that this would prove the auspicious day; and had several times said to Captain Hardy and Doctor Scott (Chaplain of the Ship, and Foreign Secretary to the Commander-in-Chief, whose intimate friendship he enjoyed), 'The 21st of October will be our day.' The wind was now from the West; but the breezes were very light, with a long heavy swell running.

*Nelson was referring to his maternal uncle, Captain Maurice Suckling's action of 21 October 1757. Suckling, in the Dreadnought, and two other battleships attacked a superior French squadron of four battleships and three frigates, forcing them to withdraw.

Source: Nicolas, VII, pp. 137–8.

Recollection of Captain Blackwood

At six o'clock on the morning of the 21st my signal was made to repair on board the Victory. In a few minutes I went on board, and had the satisfaction to find the Admiral in good, but very calm spirits. After receiving my congratulations at the approach of the moment he so often and so long had wished for, he replied, 'I mean to-day to bleed the Captains of the Frigates, as I shall keep you on board until the very last minute.' His mind seemed entirely directed to the strength and formation of the Enemy's Line, as well as to the effects which his novel mode of attack was likely to produce. He seemed very much to regret, and with reason, that the Enemy tacked to the Northward, and formed their Line on the larboard, instead of the starboard tack,

which the latter line of bearing would have kept the Straits' Mouth open; instead of which, by forming to the Northward, they brought the shoals of Trafalgar and St. Pedro under our lee; and also, with the existing wind, kept open the Port of Cadiz, which was of infinite consequence to them. This movement was in a great degree the cause of Lord Nelson's making the signal 'Prepare to Anchor', the necessity of which was impressed on his mind to the last moment of his life; and so much did he think of the possibility of the Enemy's escape into Cadiz, that he desired me to employ the Frigates, as much as I could, to complete the destruction of the Enemy, whether at anchor or not; and not to think of saving Ships or men, for annihilation to both was his first object, and capture but a secondary one.
Source: Nicolas, VII, pp. 138–9.

It was common practice for frigates to remain out of the main fleet actions. Much smaller, not as stoutly built and lighter armed than the big line-of-battle ships, they were extremely vulnerable to the heavy guns; a single broadside from a battleship could wreck a frigate. Instead their main roles were to relay signals from the flagship, assist damaged battleships by towing them out of the line, saving crews or to take in tow enemy prizes. In return for this passive role it was the unwritten rule that battleships would not fire on enemy frigates unless fired on by them first. Nelson now had a different concept of how to employ his frigates: to assist in the utter annihilation of the enemy fleet he so desired.[96]

Aboard his flagship *Royal Sovereign* Collingwood had also been preparing for the coming fight. With his instructions to form a column on line of bearing about a mile to the south of Nelson's, Collingwood remained under the direct command of his chief until firing started and signals would become obscured by smoke. He would then have independence of action. Yet, the distance between the divisions would soon provide him with the opportunity to bend the rules somewhat as he and Nelson both raced for the honour of being the first to cut the enemy's line. Like his friend in *Victory*, Collingwood was also excited at the prospect of battle, but remained impressively calm in the presence of his servant Mr Smith:

I entered the Admiral's cabin about daylight, and found him already up and dressing. He asked if I had seen the French fleet; and on my replying that I had

CAPTAIN THOMAS MASTERMAN HARDY (1769–1839)

Nelson's great friend and his Flag Captain at Trafalgar was born in Dorset in 1769. He joined the navy in 1781, returned to his schooling and then re-joined the navy as a midshipman in 1790. As a lieutenant in the 38-gun frigate *La Minerve* Hardy served under the then Commodore Nelson. Captured by the Spaniards while commanding a prize ship in 1796, a prisoner exchange saw Hardy back with Nelson in *La Minerve* during the run up to the battle of Cape St. Vincent, 14 February 1797. Two days before the battle a famous incident had occurred, which highlights the affection with which Nelson regarded Hardy. On the morning of Sunday 12 February, while heading for the fleet of Sir John Jervis, *La Minerve* was hotly pursued by two Spanish ships. When seaman William Barnes fell overboard, a jolly boat, commanded by Hardy, was lowered to rescue him. As the Spaniards closed Barnes could not be found and the jolly boat was in great danger of being captured. With the Spaniards nearing engagement range, Nelson was faced with the prospect of sacrificing Hardy but saving his ship or risking the lives of all onboard *La Minerve* to rescue the boat. Nelson did not waste a moment, shouting, 'By God, I'll not lose Hardy – back that Mizzen topsail,' and as *La Minerve* slowed Hardy and the jolly boat were saved. It was Nelson's good fortune that the pursuing Spaniards thought *La Minerve* was signalling a British fleet, invisible over the horizon, and so stood off.[97]

Captain Thomas Masterman Hardy, Nelson's Flag Captain at Trafalgar. Hardy was the only member of the 'Band of Brothers', present at all of Nelson's major battles, and was his closest friend in the service. (CPL)

Hardy was promoted to Commander in 1797, and commanded the *Mutine* at the Battle of the Nile the following year. Promoted to Captain in the *Vanguard* after the battle, he was in the *Foudroyant* with Nelson during 1798-9 at Naples and Sicily. He commanded the *St. George* at Copenhagen in 1801 before joining the *Victory* in 1803, and was Nelson's Flag Captain for the blockade of Toulon, the chase to the West Indies and of course for Trafalgar. On the morning of 21 October 1805 Hardy, together with Henry Blackwood, witnessed a codicil to Nelson's will. As the *Victory* sailed into battle, Hardy paced the quarterdeck with Nelson, was beside him when the Admiral was mortally wounded, twice visited the dying Nelson in the cockpit of the *Victory* and of course kissed his friend in his final moments.

After Trafalgar Hardy received the thanks of Parliament and was created a baronet. During the Peninsular War he commanded the Royal Naval forces off Lisbon until the war with America in 1812 when he was moved to the North American Station until 1813. After the Napoleonic Wars he commanded the Royal Navy's South American squadron from 1819 to 1824. Hardy was promoted Rear Admiral in 1825 and Vice Admiral in 1837. He also served as First Sea Lord of the Admiralty from 1830 until 1834 when appointed Governor of Greenwich Hospital. Hardy died on 20 September 1839 and, with his coffin containing a miniature of Nelson, was buried at Greenwich. Throughout his naval career Hardy proved to be a cool-headed, capable and reliable officer – the perfect companion for the more precocious Nelson. He was the only member of the famous 'Band of Brothers' who was present at all of Nelson's battles and was perhaps the great admiral's closest friend.

not, he told me to look out at them, adding that, in a very short time, we should see a great deal more of them. I then observed a crowd of ships to leeward; but I could not help looking with still greater interest at the Admiral, who, during all this time, was shaving himself with a composure that astonished me.

After finishing dressing with particular care Collingwood then gave some sound advice to Lieutenant Clavell 'You had better put on silk stockings, as I have done: for if one should get a shot in the leg, they would be so much more manageable for the surgeon.' He then went up on deck to encourage the men before addressing the officers: 'Now, gentlemen, let us do something to-day which the world may talk of hereafter.'[98]

Nelson's attack in two divisions was now well under way, Collingwood aiming to cut off the enemy van while Nelson destroyed the rear. As the fleets converged Nelson must have rued the missing six ships under Admiral Louis, still not returned from Gibraltar. Their arrival would have enabled him to form the 'Advance Squadron' and fully implement his plan of attack as outlined in his various conversations and memorandum.

But at 8.30 a.m., in full view of the British fleet, Villeneuve began his about turn. On Victory's quarterdeck Nelson was astounded by this course of action and completely unsure as to what the intentions of the enemy really were: to give battle or, unable to make the Mediterranean, were they running for Cadiz? It was perhaps this unease that forced Nelson and Collingwood into the headlong dash towards the Combined Fleet, to bring about an engagement before the enemy had a chance to flee.

A number of signals were issued from Nelson's flagship directing ships to 'keep in close order', but at the same time to 'make more sail'. Both Royal Sovereign and Victory ordered slower sailing vessels to allow their speedier comrades to pass. This had the effect of slightly disorganising the order of attack, as ships jockeyed for position and may have helped to create the impression that there was no plan of attack. Moreover, two ships, Africa and Orion, destined for the Weather Column, were in fact nowhere near Nelson's advancing ships. Separated during the night, the 64-gun Africa was supposed to be the sixth ship in the attack, but was too far to northward. Captain Codrington's Orion was a little south, half-way between the two divisions. There was also the very visible slow sailing of Rear Admiral the Earl of Northesk's three-decked Britannia, supposedly part of Nelson's initial heavy punch.

The actual attacks were delivered at a slow pace, 2½ knots, because of the light winds. In the meantime there was much to do to prepare the British ships for battle: breaking up the captains' and officers' cabins, sails and prepared as emergency stretchers to carry the wounded below, the surgeons would begin their grisly day by laying out their bandages and operating tools. In order to pass some of the anxious wait for action, in Bellerophon the crew were piped to dinner at 11 a.m. 'thinking that Englishmen would fight all the better for having a comfortable meal'. With all the mess tables moved below to clear the decks for action 'Captain Cooke joined us in partaking of some cold meat &c on the rudder head'. In Victory, after beating to quarters at 11a.m. to make the final preparations, the crew were served a dinner of pork and wine.[99]

Clearing for action, William Robinson, HMS Revenge

During this time [the slow advance] each ship was making the usual preparations, such as breaking away the captain's and officers' cabins and sending all the lumber below – the doctors, parson, purser and loblolly men, were also busy, getting the medicine chests and bandages out; and sails prepared for the wounded to be placed on, that they might be dressed in rotation as they were taken down to the after cock-pit.

In such a bustling, and it may be said, trying as well as serious time, it is curious to note the different dispositions of the British sailor. Some would be offering a guinea for a glass of grog, whilst others were making a sort of mutual verbal will, such as, if one of Johnny Crapeau's shots (a term given to the French), knocks my head off, you will take all my effects; and if you are killed, and I am not, why, I will have yours, and this is generally agreed to.
Source: King, p. 160.

Some of the senior officers voiced concern for the safety of Nelson if *Victory* continued to lead the column. Particular attention was directed at his dress with the four embroidered decorations clearly visible on his chest, but there was no time to change it, he retorted. Blackwood suggested that he move his flag into *Euryalus* from which he could have some control over the action and where he would be much safer. Naturally, Nelson refused. It was also suggested that *Victory* could slow a little and take up a position behind the second or third in the attack. Again this was refused, though again Hardy requested that *Téméraire*, astern of *Victory* in the column, should overtake to lead the column. Nelson initially agreed, but perhaps never intending to move aside, when *Téméraire* began to close up to *Victory*'s stern Nelson hailed her: 'I'll thank you Captain Harvey to keep your proper station which is astern of the *Victory*!'

At about 11 a.m. only three miles separated the two fleets. It was about this time that John Pascoe, the signals Lieutenant in *Victory*, discovered Nelson on his knees writing in his cabin. He was making a last diary entry in the form of a prayer. He then penned a codicil to his Will, noting that the services Emma had provided to the British fleet through her influence with the Queen of Naples had been un-rewarded. Unable himself to provide for Emma, he declared: 'I leave Emma Lady Hamilton, therefore, a Legacy to my King and Country, that they will give her an ample provision to maintain her rank in life'. The codicil was witnessed by Captains Blackwood and Hardy.

After the brief solitude of his cabin, Nelson returned on deck. He now decided to 'amuse the fleet' with a signal. It is possible that he thought to begin with 'Nelson confides…' but soon settled on 'England confides…' Instructing Pascoe to send it to the fleet, Pascoe suggested switching 'expects' for 'confides' as the latter was not included in Sir Home Riggs Popham's code and would have to be spelled out. Nelson agreed and at about 11.25 a.m. the most famous signal ever given at sea was hoisted: 'England expects that every man will do his duty'.

For a man who viewed duty as a fundamental part of his make-up, it was typically Nelsonic in tone. In some instances it may not have initially struck the right note;

Nelson on the
quarterdeck of HMS
Victory while the
signal 'England
Expects that Every
Man Will Do His
Duty' is hoisted.
(National Maritime
Museum)

Collingwood himself declared 'What is Nelson signalling about? We all know what
we have to do.' As Colin White has pointed out, as the signal would have taken a
number of separate hoists to transmit, Collingwood's remark may have stemmed
from a little impatience. When informed of the entire signal he 'expressed great
delight and admiration and made it known to the officers and ship's company'.[100]
Certainly, once the significance of the message was comprehended it was met with
loud cheering throughout the fleet.

Another instruction came from the flagship, this time a telegraphic message
directly for Collingwood: 'I intend to pass through the enemy's line to prevent them
getting into Cadiz'. This was followed by the signal to anchor at the close of the
action. While this might seem a little bizarre, Nelson was utilising the final few
minutes before action when a commander had the last chance to communicate
directly with the fleet as a whole. Nelson, ever the consummate seamen, knew the
waters around Cape Trafalgar well. A darkening sky and the increasingly heavy swell
could only mean one thing – a very heavy storm was approaching from the west,
threatening to drive damaged ships on to the treacherous lee shore. Nearing the
enemy line, *Victory* hoisted a typical Nelsonic last instruction to the fleet.
Throughout his conversations and memoranda on tactics, Nelson had always
espoused a clear and simple aggressive doctrine aptly summed up by the signal now
flying from *Victory*: 'Engage the enemy more closely'.

With Marine bands playing 'Hearts of Oak', 'Britons Strike Home', 'Rule Britannia'
and other patriotic songs, the two British columns progressed on their slow but
determined attack. With Collingwood's division more advanced than Nelson's, at
about midday the first shots were fired from the French *Fougueux* at Collingwood's
Royal Sovereign. The British ships responded by hoisting Union Flags, the White
Ensign and battle flags. As the first shots rang out from *Fougueux*, Nelson sent
Blackwood from the *Victory*. Leaving his commander, Blackwood said good-bye with
the words, 'I trust, my Lord, that on my return to the *Victory*, which will be as soon

as possible, I shall find your Lordship well and in possession of twenty prizes.' With perhaps a sense of the danger *Victory* would shortly be exposed to, Nelson replied, 'God bless you Blackwood. I shall never speak to you again.'[101]

Did Nelson have a premonition of death? His comment to Blackwood seems to suggest so. During his 25 days ashore, Nelson had called in to see the coffin sent to him by Captain Ben Hallowell and fashioned from the mainmast of the doomed French flagship *L'Orient* at the Nile. Nelson now asked for the lid to be engraved with the coffin's unusual history, remarking 'I think it highly that I may want it on my return'.[102] On 6 October he had informed Rose that: 'I verily believe the Country will soon be put to some expense for my account, either a Monument, or a new Pensions and Honours.'[103] But a few days later he was writing to William Stewart that he was anxious to get a battle over and done with: 'The sooner the better, I don't like to have these things upon my mind; and if I see my way through the fiery ordeal, I shall go home and rest for the winter.'[104] It seems as if Nelson, always a little mischievous, was perhaps indulging in the black humour that was part of a seaman's psyche rather than suffering from premonitions of his own impending death. He knew his plan to attack the enemy was dangerous, not just for the fleet but for himself. He was willing to risk his life to achieve the decisive results he wanted. He was not the only one who approached the battle with determination, grim humour and a sense of duty.

The British Fleet
At the start of the action
27 ships of the line, 2,148 guns, 17,000 men
Command Vice Admiral Lord Horatio Nelson

Ship	Guns	Commander	Casualties (killed/wounded)	Fate
WEATHER COLUMN – Vice Admiral Lord Horatio Nelson				
Victory	100	Vice Ad. Lord Horatio Nelson Capt. Thomas Masterman Hardy	57 / 102	
Téméraire	98	Capt. Eliab Harvey	47 / 76	
Neptune	98	Capt. Thomas Francis Fremantle	10 / 34	
Leviathan	74	Capt. Henry William Bayntun	4 / 22	
Britannia	100	Rear Admiral Earl of Northesk Capt. Charles Bullen	10 / 42	
Conqueror	74	Capt. Israel Pellew	3 / 9	
Africa	64	Capt. Henry Digby	18 / 44	
Agamemnon	64	Capt. Sir Edward Berry	2 / 8	
Ajax	74	Lieut. John Pilford*	2 / 9	
Orion	74	Capt. Edward Codrington	1 / 23	
Minotaur	74	Capt. Charles John Moore Mansfield	3 / 22	
Spartiate	74	Capt. Sir Francis Laforey	3 / 20	

Ship	Guns	Commander	Casualties (killed/wounded)	Fate
LEE COLUMN – Vice Admiral Cuthbert Collingwood				
Royal Sovereign	100	Vice Admiral Cuthbert Collingwood / Capt. Edward Rotherham	47 / 94	
Belleisle	74	Capt. William Hargood	33 / 93	
Mars	74	Capt. George Duff	29 / 69	
Tonnant	80	Capt. Charles Tyler	26 / 50	
Bellerophon	74	Capt. John Cooke	27 / 123	
Colossus	74	Capt. James Nicoll Morris	40 / 160	
Achilles	74	Capt. Richard King	13 / 59	
Dreadnought	98	Capt. John Conn	7 / 26	
Polyphemus	64	Capt. Robert Redmill	2 / 4	
Revenge	74	Capt. Robert Moorsom	28 / 51	
Swiftsure	74	Capt. William G Rutherford	9 / 8	
Defiance	74	Capt. Philip Charles Durham	17 / 53	
Thunderer	74	Lieut. John Stockham*	4 / 12	
Defence	74	Capt. George Hope	7 / 29	
Prince	98	Capt. Richard Grindall	none	

OTHER VESSELS

Ship	Guns	Commander
Euryalus	36	Capt. Henry Blackwood
Naiad	38	Capt. Thomas Dundas
Phoebe	36	Capt. Thomas Bladen Capell
Sirius	36	Capt. William Prowse
Pickle, schooner	10	Lieut. John Richards Lapenotière
Entreprenante, cutter	8	Lieut. Robert Benjamin Young

*acting, Captains William Brown and William Lechmere having departed for England as witnesses at Calder's court-martial.

Sources: Clowes, Vol. V p. 131; James, Vol. IV, p. 26, Gardiner, p. 134.

The Franco-Spanish Combined Fleet
33 ships of the line, 2,568 guns, 30,000 men
Command Vice Admiral P. C. J-B. S. Villeneuve

Ship	Guns	Commander	Casualties (killed/wounded)	Fate
REAR - Rear Admiral P. R. M. E. Dumanoir de Pelley				
Neptuno (Sp)	80	Comm. Don Cayetano Valdés	42 / 47	Captured by *Minotaur*; retaken 23 Oct, wrecked, burnt 31 Oct
Scipion	74	Capt. Charles Bérenger	none	Escaped, captured 4 Nov by Strachan

Ship	Guns	Commander	Casualties (killed/wounded)	Fate
Rayo (Sp)	100	Comm. Don Enrique Macdonnell	18 total	Escaped; captured by *Donegal*, burnt 31 Oct
Formidable	80	Rear Admiral P. R. M. E. Dumanoir de Pelley Capt. Jean Marie Letellier	65 total	Escaped, captured 4 Nov by Strachan
Duguay-Trouin	74	Capt. Claude Touffet	minimal	Escaped, captured 4 Nov by Strachan
San Francisco de Asís (Sp)	74	Capt. Don Luis de Flores	17 total	Escaped, wrecked 23 Oct
Mont-Blanc	74	Comm. Jean Noel La Villegris	none	Escaped, captured 4 Nov by Strachan

CENTRE – Vice Admiral P. C. J-B. S. Villeneuve

Ship	Guns	Commander	Casualties (killed/wounded)	Fate
San Augustín (Sp)	74	Capt. Don Felipe X. Cagigal	180 / 200	Captured by *Leviathan*, burnt 30 Oct
Héros	74	Capt. Jean B. J. R. Poulain	minimal	Escaped to Cadiz
Santíssima Trinidad (Sp)	136	Rear Admiral Don B. Hidalgo de Cisneros Comm. Don Francisco de Uriate	heavy	Captured by *Prince*, sank 24 Oct
Bucentaure	80	Vice Admiral P. C. J-B. S. Villeneuve Capt. Jean-Jacques Magendie	209 total	Captured by *Conqueror*, wrecked 23 Oct
Neptune	84	Comm. Esprit Tranquille Maistral	none/ minimal	Escaped to Cadiz
San Leandro (Sp)	64	Capt. Don José Quevedo	30 total	Escaped to Cadiz
Redoutable	74	Capt. Jean J. E. Lucas	474 / 70	Captured by *Téméraire*, sank 22 Oct

VAN – Vice Admiral Don Ignosia Maria de Alava

Ship	Guns	Commander	Casualties (killed/wounded)	Fate
Intrépide	74	Comm. Louis A. C. Infernet	306 total	Captured by *Orion*, burnt 24 Oct
San Justo (Sp)	74	Capt. Don Miguel Gastón	– / 7	Escaped to Cadiz
Indomptable	80	Comm. Jean-Joseph Hubert	minimal	Escaped; wrecked 24 Oct
Santa Ana (Sp)	112	Vice Admiral Don Ignosia Maria de Alava Capt. Don José Guardoquí	97 / 141	Captured by *Royal Sovereign*; retaken 23 Oct; escaped to Cadiz
Fougueux	74	Capt. Louis Alexis Beaudouin	400 total	Captured by *Téméraire*, wrecked 22 Oct
Monarca (Sp)	74	Capt. Don Teodoro Argumosa	100 / 150	Captured by *Bellerophon*, wrecked 25 Oct
Pluton	74	Comm. Jean Marie Cosmao-Kerjulien	300 total	Escaped to Cadiz

Ship	Guns	Commander	Casualties (killed/wounded)	Fate
SQUADRON OF OBSERVATION – Admiral Don Federico de Gravina				
Algésiras	74	Rear Admiral Charles Magon de Médine Capt. Gabriel Auguste Brouard	216 total	Captured by *Tonant*; retaken, escaped to Cadiz
Bahama (Sp)	74	Comm. Don Dionisio Galiano	400 total	Captured by *Colossus*, taken into RN, BU 1814
Aigle	74	Capt. Pierre Paul Gourrége	270 total	Captured by *Defiance*, wrecked 5 Oct
Swiftsure	74	Capt. C. E. L'Hôpitalier-Villemadrin	250 total	Captured by *Colossus*, taken into RN, BU 1816
Argonaute	74	Capt. Jacques Epron	160 total	Escaped to Cadiz
Montañes (Sp)	74	Capt. Don José Alcedo	49 total	Escaped to Cadiz
Argonauta (Sp)	90	Comm. Don Antonio Pareja	100 / 200	Captured by *Belleisle*, scuttled 30 Oct
Berwick	74	Capt. Jean Giles Filhol-Camas	250 total	Captured by *Achille*, wrecked 27 Oct
San Juan Nepomuceno (Sp)	74	Capt. Don Cosmé Churruca	300 total	Captured by *Dreadnought*, taken into RN sold 1818
San Ildefonso (Sp)	74	Comm. Don José de Vargas	34 / 126	Captured by *Defence*, taken into RN, BU 1816
Achille	74	Capt. G. Deniéport	499 total	Engaged by *Prince*, caught fire, blew up 21 Oct
Principe de Asturias (Sp)	112	Admiral Don Federico de Gravina Rear Admiral Don Antoñio Escaño Capt. Rafael de Hore	41 / 107	Escaped to Cadiz

OTHER VESSELS – all French

Ship	Guns	Commander
Cornélie	40	Capt. de Martinenq
Hermione	40	Capt. Mahe
Hortense	40	Capt. La Marre La Meillerie
Rhin	40	Capt. Chesneau
Thémis	40	Capt. Jugan
Furet **brig**	18	Lieut Dumay
Argus **brig**	16	Lieut Taillard

Sources: James, Vol. IV, p. 28; Gardiner, pp. 134–5; Tracy, (1996), p. 179.

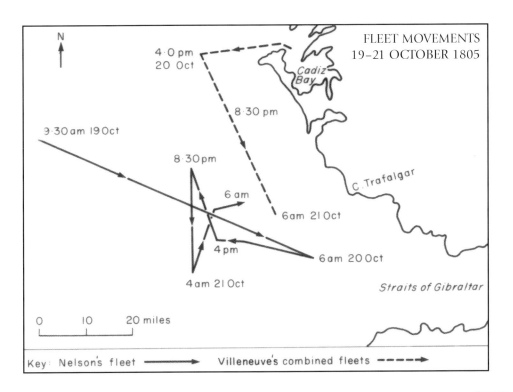

FLEET MOVEMENTS
19–21 OCTOBER 1805

N

4·0 pm
20 Oct

Cadiz
Bay

8·30 pm

9·30 am 19 Oct

8·30 pm

6 am

6am 21 Oct

C. Trafalgar

4 pm

6am 20 Oct

4am 21 Oct

Straits of Gibraltar

0   10   20 miles

Key: Nelson's fleet ————➤   Villeneuve's combined fleets ----➤

Victory's lower gun
deck. (CPL)

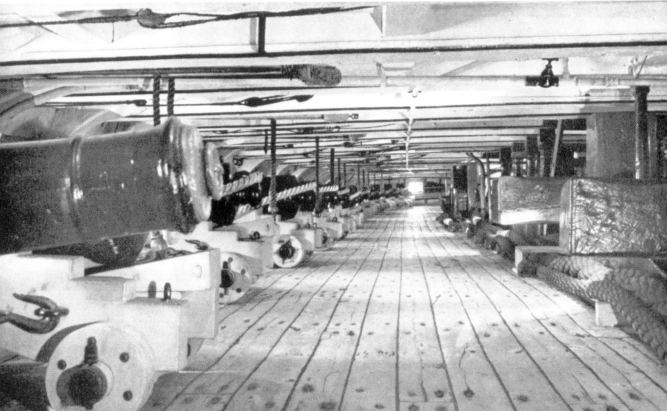

Nelson's Private Diary
Monday, *October 21st, 1805.*

At daylight saw the Enemy's Combined Fleet from East to E.S.E.; bore away; made the signal for Order of Sailing, and to Prepare for Battle; the Enemy with their heads to the Southward: at seven the Enemy wearing in succession. May the Great God, whom I worship, grant to my Country, and for the benefit of Europe in general, a great and glorious Victory; and may no misconduct in any one tarnish it; and may humanity after Victory be the predominant feature in the British Fleet. For myself, individually, I commit my life to Him who made me, and may his blessing light upon my endeavours for serving my Country faithfully. To Him I resign myself and the just cause which is entrusted to me to defend. Amen. Amen. Amen.
Source: Nicolas, VII, pp. 139–40.

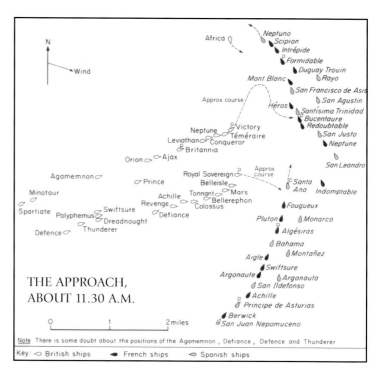

THE APPROACH,
ABOUT 11.30 A.M.

0   1   2 miles

<u>Note</u> There is some doubt about the positions of the Agamemnon, Defiance, Defence and Thunderer

Key: ◠ British ships   ● French ships   ◠ Spanish ships

The commencement of the battle. In the centre of the picture *Victory* and *Téméraire* lead the weather column; to the right Collingwood's *Royal Sovereign* is breaking the line. (CPL)

COLLINGWOOD'S LEE LINE

The two British divisions would deliver their attacks in markedly different ways. Instead of following in the wake of the lead ship, as was the order of sailing in the Weather column a little to the north, the ships following Collingwood's flagship, the powerful three-decked 100-gun *Royal Sovereign*, delivered their attack in a slanting line *en echelon*. Nelson had planned to penetrate the enemy line in several places to engage the whole of the rear, and thus increase the effectiveness of the blow, but there was little time for the attack to deploy as Nelson desired. The headlong advance of the attack, a direct consequence of his desire to prevent the Combined Fleet running for Cadiz, and the variable sailing qualities of the ships in the lee line, left the rear ships trailing a long way behind the head of the line. Instead of one heavy blow falling on the enemy rear, a succession of smaller blows were delivered by individual ships. This placed a heavy reliance on the initiative of individual captains to judge where their ships could have the greatest influence.

Collingwood's original ship had been the *Dreadnought*, whose crew he had trained to fire three well-directed broadsides in three and a half minutes, but she was a notoriously slow ship.[105] *Royal Sovereign* also had a reputation as a poor sailer, but crucially had recently been dry-docked to have her copper bottom repaired. The covering of ships' bottoms with copper sheathing had been introduced into the navy to prevent *teredo navalis* (ship worm) from burrowing into and hence weakening the hull. When newly cleaned it also produced a smooth underwater surface which reduced drag and increased the speed of a ship. *Royal Sovereign* now benefited from this, and with the White Ensign and the Union Flag flying from the fore top gallant, Collingwood's ship began to pull ahead of the other ships.[106]

In fact, Nelson was adamant that *Belleisle* should lead Collingwood's attack, and signalled his desire that *Royal Sovereign* should slow to let her take up this prestigious station. Perhaps Nelson was concerned that the punishment meted out to the two ships leading the attack, *Victory* and *Royal Sovereign*, could be so severe as to incapacitate both the Commander-in-Chief and his second in command when the leadership of at least one of them would be needed after the battle, especially with a storm brewing. Nelson himself was unwilling to let *Téméraire* pass him to lead the Weather Column, and it is not surprising that Collingwood followed suit, ignoring his superior officer and spearheading the advance. In any case, slowing *Royal Sovereign* would have delayed the advance for a precious few minutes, exposing the flagship and those following to a longer period of enemy fire.

With the first shots being fired at noon, *Royal Sovereign* endured a period of about 20 minutes when she received desultory fire from the enemy line, in particular from *Santa Ana*, *Indomptable* and *Fougueux*. But it was not until *Royal Sovereign* had closed to about 400 yards, when the enemy ships would open their full broadsides, that she was in real danger. It was a calculated risk, for this final part of the advance under heavy fire would take five to six minutes. But everyone in the British fleet knew that the French and Spanish would only be able to manage two or a maximum of three broadsides, before their line was penetrated and vengeance exacted. With Flag Captain Edward Rotherham responsible for the actual sailing of *Royal Sovereign*, there was little that Collingwood could do once within range of the enemy to direct the attack of his division:

> As the mode of our attack had been previously determined on, and communicated to the Flag-officers and Captains, few signals were necessary, and none were made, except to direct close order as the lines bore down.[107]

Collingwood, realising his would be the first British ship to break the enemy line, declared to Rotherham, 'What would Nelson give to be here!'. Nelson, watching from the *Victory* at about the same time, commented, 'See how that noble fellow, Collingwood, takes his ship into action. How I envy him!'.[108]

With the rest of the line trailing about a mile behind her, Collingwood's *Royal Sovereign* burst through the enemy line of battle at 12.20. It was Nelson's original intention that this should have occurred at the twelfth ship from the rear, but, as the man on the spot, Collingwood instead used his initiative. Seeing that there was a first rate ahead of the allotted ship, Collingwood made for the three-decker, cutting the line fifteen ships from the rear. This was Vice Admiral Alava's 112-gun *Santa Ana*. *Royal Sovereign* passed astern of her and across the bows of the 74-gun *Fougueux*. Raking the former with a devastating double-shotted broadside that inflicted many casualties, *Royal Sovereign* fired into *Fougueux* before taking up a position to engage *Santa Ana* from leeward. Almost immediately the two flagships became locked together in a deadly combat that would last the better part of two hours.

Santa Ana's first starboard broadside was delivered with such force that *Royal Sovereign* shuddered and heeled over a couple of feet. Moreover, the nature of the attack left Collingwood, now nonchalantly munching an apple while musing over the progress of the fight, in a very exposed position. Unsupported and in the midst of the enemy line of battle, *Royal Sovereign* was alone for nearly fifteen hellish minutes. The fire at this point was very hot; apart from *Santa Ana*, *Fougueux* raked her stern while *San Leandro*, *Indomptable* and *San Justo* all targeted the lone British ship. Collingwood ordered the marines, who were taking heavy casualties, to leave their exposed position on the poop deck. Despite the fire, Captain Rotherham continued to walk the decks in a large and very conspicuous cocked hat, and it is perhaps remarkable that both he and Collingwood, the latter receiving a slight leg wound caused by a splinter, survived the battle. Despite heavy

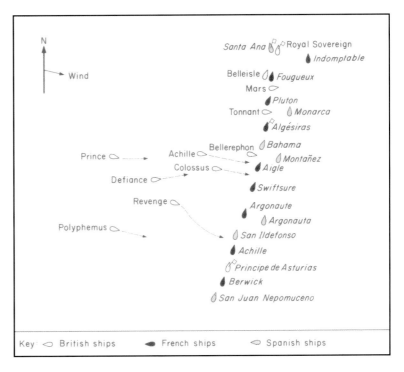

Key: ○ British ships ◖ French ships ○ Spanish ships

The action between Collingwood's division and Villeneuve's rear at about 12.30 pm.

casualties, and the fact that according to Collingwood *Santa Ana* 'towered over the *Royal Sovereign* like a castle', the British ship continued to pour broadside after broadside into the Spaniard.[109]

At 2.20 p.m. Collingwood's bloody battle with *Santa Ana* ended with the surrender of the Spaniard after two hours' hard fighting; she had been completely dismasted and her sides were 'almost entirely beat in'. Casualties in *Santa Ana* were heavy with 97 killed and 141 wounded, the latter including the seriously injured Alava. With such a concentration of enemy fire directed against *Royal Sovereign* it is surprising that her crew did not suffer higher casualties than 47 killed and 94 wounded. After the battle one midshipman recalled 'it is shocking to see many brave seamen mangled so, some with their heads half shot away, others with their entrails mashed lying panting on the deck, the greatest slaughter was on the quarterdeck and Poop'.[110] The material damage to *Royal Sovereign* had been severe: her mizzen mast had been blown away and the mainmast was about to go over the side. In a shattered state and unable to manoeuvre, she was taken in tow by Blackwood's *Euryalus*. It was at this time that Lieutenant Alexander Hill approached *Royal Sovereign* to inform Collingwood that Nelson was wounded. Collingwood asked Hill if the wound was serious: 'He hesitated; then said he hoped it was not; but I saw the fate of my friend in his eye; for his look told what his tongue could not utter.'[111]

Support had finally reached Collingwood in the form of Captain William Hargood's 74-gun *Belleisle*, which had originally been astern of the slower *Tonnant*,

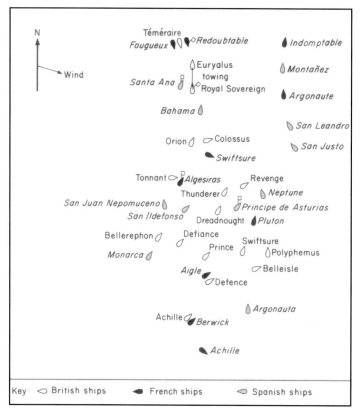

N

Wind

Téméraire
Fougueux · Redoubtable   Indomptable

Euryalus
towing   Montañez
Santa Ana   Royal Sovereign

Bahama   Argonaute

San Leandro

Orion   Colossus   San Justo

Swiftsure

Tonnant   Algesiras   Revenge
Thunderer   Neptune
San Juan Nepomuceno
San Ildefonso   Dreadnought   Principe de Asturias
Pluton
Bellerephon   Defiance
Monarca   Prince   Swiftsure
Aigle   Polyphemus
Defence   Belleisle

Argonauta
Achille   Berwick

Achille

Key: ○ British ships   ● French ships   ◐ Spanish ships

The action between
Collingwood's
division and
Villeneuve's rear at
about 2.30 pm.

but had overtaken her and *Mars* in the advance. A withering fire from perhaps eight to ten ships was already causing casualties, even though Hargood's crew were lying down between the guns, as his ship approached the enemy line in eerie silence. Hargood himself received several wounds, though none caused serious injury. Rejecting a suggestion from his First Lieutenant to bear up and deliver a broadside, Hargood remained faithful to Nelson's plan: 'we are ordered to go through the line, and go through we shall'. As her crew leapt to their feet and stood by their guns, *Belleisle* became the second ship to pass through the enemy line, astern of *Santa Ana* and ahead of *Fougueux* and *Indomptable*. As with Collingwood, Hargood's advance had been observed from the *Victory*. Despite the enemy fire Hargood had done well to hold his grape and double-shotted first broadside:

…until she had brought both broadsides… to bear upon ships on each side of her, and was within pistol shot, when her two broadsides were discharged spontaneously, and with the precision of a volley of musketry; upon seeing which Lord Nelson exclaimed, 'Nobly done Hargood'.[112]

After firing on *Santa Ana* and *Fougueux*, *Belleisle* turned to rake *Indomptable*, which wore away. Fired upon by the 74-gun *San Juan Nepomuceno*, *Belleisle* settled into a desperate struggle with *Fougueux*. The French *Achille* soon came up to support her compatriot, and took up a position off *Belleisle*'s quarter where she could engage Hargood's ship without suffering in reply. Soon after this, *Belleisle*'s mizzen mast and sails fell, covering a number of her guns. At about 2 p.m. *Belleisle*'s mainmast went over the side as the French *Neptune* came up to join the assault. Over the next ninety minutes *Belleisle* was turned into an unmanageable wreck. With her rigging and masts gone, a Union flag was fixed to a boarding pike and her colours literally nailed to the stump of the mizzen mast.

Relief for *Belleisle* finally came at about 3.15 p.m. as the British 74-gun *Swiftsure* and the 64-gun *Polyphemus* emerged from the smoke and drove off her assailants while *Defiance* arrived on the scene a few minutes later. Despite having lost all her masts and with her hull peppered with holes, *Belleisle* had continued firing until the arrival of her rescuers, at which point the crew was ordered to leave the guns and begin to clear up the decks. Engaged by a total of nine ships of the Combined Fleet, it is not surprising that Hargood's ship sustained 25 per cent casualties. With the battle around her subsiding, *Belleisle* managed to secure the Spanish *Argonauta*, which had been battered by and then had nominally surrendered to Captain King's *Achilles*. *Argonauta*'s deck was strewn with mangled bodies and wreckage, not a living soul could be seen according to *Belleisle*'s prize party, the remainder of the crew having moved below to gain some cover. With her Captain wounded, *Argonauta*'s second officer was rowed over to present his sword to Hargood, arriving in time to take tea with *Belleisle*'s officers.

Next in action after *Belleisle* was the 74-gun *Mars* commanded by Captain George Duff. Fired on by several ships during her advance, *Mars* had already sustained damage aloft. Seeing she was aiming to pass between the two-decked 74-gun ships *San Juan Nepomuceno* and *Pluton*, Commodore Cosmao-Kerjulien moved *Pluton* forward to close the gap. Manoeuvring to avoid being raked by *Pluton*, Duff tried to get his ship ahead of the pair, but suffered further damage to his rigging and sails as *Mars* collided with *Santa Ana*. Turning to avoid the Spanish three-decker, *Mars* exposed her stern to Rear Admiral Magon's *Algéciras* and the Spanish *Monarca*. With *Leviathan* now coming up to support *Mars*, Duff's ship was engaged by *Pluton* and the *Fougueux*, the latter still in combat with *Belleisle*. As *Mars* became increasingly unmanageable due to damage aloft, the officers, men and marines stationed on her upper decks suffered greatly: in total 29 men were killed and 69 wounded during the day. Among the former was Captain Duff, a shot from one of the French ships ripping his head from his shoulders. With many shots between wind and water and

Although highly exaggerated, this line drawing provides a clear demonstration of the crescent shape formed by the Franco-Spanish Combined Fleet. (Warwick Leadlay Gallery)

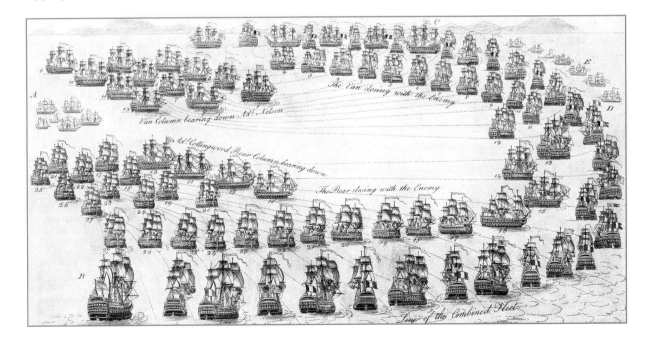

> ### Collingwood to Sir Thomas Pasley
> ### Queen, off Carthagena, 16th December, 1805
>
> *My Dear Sir Thomas,*
> *I am exceedingly obliged to you for your late letter of congratulation on the great events; a happy day it would have been indeed had my dear friend survived it; but I cannot separate from the glory of such a day the irreparable loss of such a hero. He possessed the zeal of an enthusiast, directed by the talents which Nature had very bountifully bestowed upon him, and everything seemed as, if by enchantment, to prosper under his direction. But it was the effect of system, and nice combination, not of chance. We must endeavour to follow his example, but that is the lot of very few to attain his perfection. We knew that, whenever they gave us a meeting, they would be very numerous. You know what time is required to form a regular Line of Battle. Lord Nelson determined to substitute for exact order an impetuous attack in two distinct bodies. The Weather Line he commanded, and left the Lee Line totally to my direction. He had assigned the points to be attacked. It was executed well, and succeeded admirably; probably its novelty was favourable to us, for the enemy looked for a time when we should form something like a Line. The light wind was unfavourable to us. I thought it a long time after I got through their Line before I found my friends around me. Duff, worthy Duff, was next me, but found a difficulty in getting through; for we had to make a kind of S to pass them in the manner they were formed; and had we to pass them from leeward, it would have been still more difficult, as it required nice steerage, and which was the cause of so many of our Ships getting on board them. Those dots will give you an idea*
>
>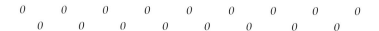
>
> *how they were formed, except that they did not make it a right Line, but the centre bent to leeward; but in half an hour there was nothing like order. The* Victory *got on board the* Redoutable, *the* Téméraire *boarded the* Fougueux *and another, and many of the ships astern of me were on board the Frenchmen. The* Defiance *boarded* L'Aigle, *and had the possession of her poop for some time, when the Frenchmen rallied and drove them back; and if I could tell you all the histories of all the Ships, you would find much to admire… P.S. – Truly sorry am I that Calder was not of the Party, that he might have settled his account with Villeneuve.*
> *Source: Nicolas, VII, pp. 241–2.*

much damage to her masts and rigging, *Mars* was effectually out of the battle and would drift for the next few hours, the occasional raking fire from passing ships compounding her misery.[113]

Further support for *Mars* had arrived in the form of Captain Charles Tyler's 80-gun *Tonnant*, which cut the increasingly confused line ahead of *Monarca* and astern of the *Pluton*. Delivering a fearsome broadside into *Algéciras*, she also engaged *Monarca*. After a few more broadsides *Monarca* seemed to have lowered her colours and it was assumed that she had struck. As *Algéciras* attempted to pass under her stern *Tonnant* had to manoeuvre to avoid being raked and the two ships then locked together, furiously exchanging broadsides. Firing at such close range, *Tonnant*'s crew had to direct their fire-fighting pump on to *Algéciras* to prevent the muzzle flashes setting fire to both ships. Musketry from *Algéciras*' rigging swept *Tonnant*'s upper decks until British gunnery smashed the masts of the French ship. During the fight with *Algéciras* Tyler had also targeted *Pluton* with the port batteries, actually firing over *Mars* at the French ship! After a failed attempt to board by *Algéciras*' crew, the superior discipline, heavier broadside and the more rapid rate of British fire pummelled *Algéciras*, until at about 2.30 p.m. she struck to *Tonnant*. In the desperate struggle *Tonnant* had lost 26 killed and 50 wounded, the latter including Captain Tyler. *Algéciras*' casualties totalled more than twice this number, and included Rear Admiral Magon who had remained at his post despite receiving a mortal wound and was later found dead at the foot of the poop ladder. In the meantime *Monarca*, freed from the *Tonnant*'s assault, had re-hoisted colours and dropped out of the battle line.

About fifteen minutes after *Tonnant* had cut the enemy line, the 74-gun 'Billy Ruffian', as *Bellerophon* was affectionately known, came upon the Combined Fleet. Determined, as the preceding ships had done, to follow Nelson's instructions, Captain John Cooke held his all-important first broadside. But with his ship receiving a steady stream of casualties, at about 12.20 p.m. a full ten minutes before *Bellerophon* got through the enemy line, he began firing, hoping the resultant sulphurous smoke would provide some cover for his ship. Aiming for the gap between *Montañes* and *Monarca*, in the increasingly poor visibility due to smoke and the confused nature of the enemy line, Cooke passed through and then almost immediately crashed into the French 74-gun *Aigle*. Sandwiched between *Aigle* on her starboard side and *Monarca* and *Montañes* to port, initial success went to the Combined Fleet as the soldiers stationed aloft in *Aigle* swept *Bellerophon* with musket fire while the Spaniards fired into her hull. Of the 58 men stationed on *Bellerophon*'s quarterdeck, all but four escaped unharmed. The Master received a fatal shot shattering his leg, the Captain of Marines was seriously wounded with eight musket balls lodged in his body and part of his right arm shot away, and, shortly after 1 p.m., Captain Cooke was killed. Command now devolved to Lieutenant Cumby, who removed everyone from the dangerously exposed poop deck. Soon the French *Swiftsure* and the Spanish *Bahama* had also joined in the fight, leaving *Bellerophon* the target of five enemy ships. Engaged on all sides, *Bellerophon* had to fend off at least two attempts at boarding from *Aigle*'s crew. Cumby himself tossed overboard a hand-grenade while another exploded in the gunner's storeroom, blowing open the magazine passage door and causing a dangerous fire, but luckily the blast forced the actual door to the magazine shut, preventing both vessels from being blown sky high. After a little over an hour of vicious combat, *Bellerophon* eventually gained the upper hand, superior British gunnery again turning the tide. At about 1.40 p.m. *Aigle* began to retire from the scene, and was raked by *Bellerophon* and the newly arrived *Revenge*. *Monarca* had by now hauled down her colours for the second time and was in the hands of a boarding-party from *Bellerophon*. It had been a hard-fought and desperate contest as reflected in the heavy casualties, 27 killed and 123 wounded in *Bellerophon* and a total of 250 dead and wounded in *Monarca*.

The Death of Captain Cooke

The men on the poop fell so fast, that Captain Cooke was obliged to call them down on his quarter-deck. The Master's leg was taken off, and another man wounded, as he was speaking to them; till at last only his first Lieutenant and a Midshipman were left on deck. It was now noticed by his Lieutenant to Captain Cooke, that he had his epaulets on, and that he was marked out by the men on the tops. His reply was, 'It is now too late to take them off, I see my situation. But I will die like a man.' His last orders to his first Lieutenant were, to go down and order the coins [sic] to be taken out of the guns to raise them, in order to force the decks of l'Aigle. This had the desired effect, for she disengaged herself immediately, and went off, receiving under her counter three broadsides from the Bellerophon. It was during the Lieutenants absence that Captain Cooke fell. He had discharged his pistols very frequently at the enemy, who as often attempted to board, and he killed a French officer on his own quarter-deck. He was in the act of re-loading his pistols when he received two musket balls in his breast. He immediately fell; and upon the Quarter-master's going up, and asking him if he should take him down below, his answer was, 'No, let me lie quietly one minute, tell Lieutenant Cumby never to strike.'

Source: Extract from Bellerophon's Battle, Naval Chronicle, III, pp. 226–8.

Captain James Morris' newly commissioned large 74-gun *Colossus* incurred the highest casualties among all the British ships at Trafalgar, losing 40 killed and 160 wounded, the latter including Morris. She received a heavy fire during the final minutes of her advance to the Franco-Spanish formation, cutting the line at about 1 p.m. As *Colossus* tried to pass in front of the French 74-gun *Swiftsure* (an ex-Royal Naval ship captured in 1801), the French ship had turned to leeward to prevent being raked. This caused the two ships to come alongside each other. In the smoke this manoeuvre caused confusion as *Colossus*' impetus brought her port side into contact with the French *Argonaute*. This was to the latter's great disadvantage as after about ten minutes of broadsides *Argonaute*'s guns had been almost silenced and she broke away.

Colossus was now attacked from port by the French *Swiftsure* and from the stern by the Spanish *Bahama*. The victim of well-directed and disciplined gunnery, *Swiftsure* was forced to break off the combat, leaving *Bahama* to tackle *Colossus* alone. Dismasted, *Bahama* soon surrendered, whereupon the French *Swiftsure* returned to the fray, attempting to rake *Colossus*' stern, which the British ship deftly manoeuvred to avoid. *Colossus* then managed to counter by raking *Swiftsure* and for a second time the two ships exchanged deadly broadsides, until eventually *Swiftsure*'s mizzen mast was brought down. At 3.30 p.m. Captain Codrington's *Orion*, originally from Nelson's division, weighed in, delivering a mortal broadside which brought *Swiftsure*'s mainmast crashing to the deck. After an epic fight *Swiftsure* struck to *Colossus*, herself in a shattered and unmanageable state. Later in the day *Colossus* was towed clear of the fight by *Agamemnon*. *Colossus* had been a victim of the Combined Fleet's inability to form an orthodox line of battle. At the rear the Franco-Spanish formation drew up two or even three ships deep in places, thereby absorbing the shock of Collingwood's attack and making it difficult for British ships to engage the enemy from leeward.

With the first six ships of Collingwood's division heavily engaged, the seventh, Captain Richard King's 74-gun *Achilles*, was fired upon the Spanish 74-gun *Montañes* before assisting the beleaguered *Belleisle* by pummelling the Spanish *Argonauta* for an hour, forcing her to drop to leeward. Built to French lines, *Achilles* then exchanged fire with two enemy 74s, the French *Achille* and *Berwick*. The former moved on, leaving the *Berwick* to be battered by Captain King's ship for nearly an hour before she struck, her decks littered with 250 dead and wounded including the body of Captain Jean Filhol-Camas.

Captain Moorsom's *Revenge* was next in action. Moorsom was one of the few officers who afterwards confided that he was unsure of how Nelson's plan was to be implemented. Like *Belleisle*, the excellent sailing qualities of *Revenge* had propelled her forward of her station during the advance and Collingwood had signalled for her to come abreast of the *Royal Sovereign* on a line of bearing. Although receiving hits from the enemy line, one thing that Moorsom did understand was the necessity of preserving his first broadside for close range where it could be devastatingly effective. According to seaman William Robinson, Moorsom declared: 'We shall want all of our shot when we get close in: never mind their firing: when I fire a carronade from the quarterdeck, that will be a signal for you to begin, and I know you will do your duty as Englishmen.'[114]

Aiming to cut off and isolate the rearmost five ships of the enemy line, Moorsom was frustrated as the line closed up and *Revenge* scraped across the bows of the 74-gun *Aigle*. Firing two broadsides into her opponent, *Revenge* worked free only to be engaged by Gravina's flagship, the 112-gun *Principe de Asturias*. At one point surrounded by four enemy ships, *Revenge* fought *Principe de Asturias* alone for an hour until joined by *Dreadnought* and then, at about 3 p.m., *Thunderer*, both ships beating off Gravina's ship. *Revenge*'s crew now undertook repairs to the hull and rigging, but she was unable to rejoin the battle proper. Several enemy ships raked her stern as she lay in the water and the *Revenge* returned fire as and when she could.

At about 2.20 p.m. the 74-gun *Defence* under Captain George Hope engaged *Berwick* for nearly an hour, sending her mizzen over the side and damaging the main

---

Extract from Captain Robert Moorsom to Richard Moorsom

4 December 1805

I have seen several plans of the action, but none to answer my ideas of it – indeed scarce any plan can be given; it was irregular and the ships just got down as fast as they could, and into any space where they found the enemy without attending to their place in the line. A regular plan was laid down by Lord Nelson some time before the action, but not acted upon; his great anxiety seemed to be to get to leeward of them, lest they should make off for Cadiz before he could get near.[115]

Source: Jackson II, p.244

Close action, William Robinson, HMS *Revenge*

[Following Captain Moorsom's speech] In a few minutes the gun was fired, and our ship bore in and broke the line, but we paid dear for our temerity, as those ships we had thrown into disorder turned round, and made an attempt to board. A Spanish three-decker ran her bowsprit over our poop, with a number of her crew on it, and, in her fore rigging, two or three hundred men were ready to follow; but they caught a Tartar, for their design was discovered, and our marines with their small arms, and the carronades on the poop, loaded with canister shot, swept them off so fast, some in the water and some on the decks, that they were glad to sheer off. While this was going on aft, we were engaged with a French two-deck ship on our starboard side, and on our larboard bow another, so that many of their shots must have struck their own ships and done severe execution. After being engaged about an hour, two other ships fortunately came up, received some of the fire intended for us, and we were now enabled to get at some of the shot-holes between wind and water and plug them up: this is a duty performed by the carpenter and his crew. We were now unable to work the ship, our yards, sails, and masts being disabled, and the braces completely shot away. In this condition we lay by the side of the enemy, firing away, and now and then we received a good raking from them, passing under our stern. This was a busy time for us, for we had not only to endeavour to repair our damage, but to keep to our duty. Often during the battle we could not see for the smoke whether we were firing at a foe or friend, and as to hearing, the noise of the guns had so completely made us deaf, that we were obliged to look only to the motions that were made. In this manner we continued the battle till nearly five o'clock, when it ceased.

Source: King, p. 162.

and foremasts, before the French ship dropped away, and was eventually taken by King's *Achilles*. The *Defence* now became the target for the Spanish 74-gun *San Idelfonso*, and although Hope's ship suffered several damaging hits, the Spaniard struck her colours just after 4 p.m. as *Polyphemus* was arriving to assist Hope. Again there was a large disparity in the total casualties, 160 in the Spaniard, including the wounded Commodore Vargas, compared to 36 in the *Defence*.

The 74-gun *Thunderer*, under Lieutenant John Stockham, entered the combat at about 3 p.m., by which time a number of enemy ships had already struck. Here again the nature of Collingwood's attack *en echelon* placed a great reliance on the initiative of individual ships' captains, and the acting commander Stockham was faced with the decision of where to best use his broadsides. He chose wisely, heading to support the outnumbered *Revenge* by raking *Principe de Asturias* from a position across her bows. After drawing the fire of the French *Neptune* for a short time, the two enemy vessels drew off, leaving *Thunderer* to answer Collingwood's signal to sail northwards to meet the threat posed by Admiral Dumanoir's squadron.

As we have already seen, Captain John Redmill's *Polyphemus* provided much needed assistance to the beleaguered *Belleisle*. During the advance Redmill had been

COMMODORE COSMÉ DAMIÁN CHURRUCA (1761–1805)

A fine seaman and professional naval officer, Churruca joined the Spanish navy at the age of 15 and was promoted to midshipman in 1778. As a sub-lieutenant he served in the epic Spanish blockade of Gibraltar 1779–82. Ashore in Cadiz after the War of American Independence, Churruca studied mathematics and navigation to improve his seamanship, then continued his education at Ferrol. In 1788 he embarked on a series of scientific expeditions to Spanish South America under the command of Antonio de Córdoba. In 1796, when Spain joined with France, Churruca served with the French Brest Squadron and ashore in Paris where he gained an immense distrust of his supposed allies. This was clearly exhibited during the Trafalgar campaign in his unwillingness to risk Spanish ships in a joint action with the French navy at the Cadiz conference of 8 October. Churruca strived to attain higher standards of training and discipline in his ship, the 74-gun *San Juan Nepomuceno*; his crew was one of the best in the Spanish fleet. He opposed the sailing from Cadiz, but before the battle his rousing speech to the crew promised eternal glory for those who fell and execution for those who withdrew from the fight! Churruca was killed at Trafalgar; his right leg being mangled by a roundshot, he bled to death on his quarterdeck.

instructed by Captain Conn to allow his notoriously slow *Dreadnought* to pass. *Dreadnought* was one of only three three-deckers in the Lee Division and with Collingwood's *Royal Sovereign* already engaged and Captain Richard Grindall's *Prince* bringing up the rear, it was imperative that Conn should get his powerful ship into action quickly. *Polyphemus* almost ran into Captain Rutherford's *Swiftsure* before both went on to engage the French *Achille*, forcing her out of the combat with *Belleisle*.

Rounding the rear of the Combined fleet at about 2 p.m., Conn headed for the Spanish *San Juan Nepomuceno*, unloading a devastating broadside into her as she attempted to manoeuvre into position to rake *Bellerophon*. Several British ships had already engaged *San Juan Nepomuceno*, causing heavy casualties and killing Commodore Churruca in the process. After ramming into the Spaniard, *Dreadnought* forced her to strike after about fifteen minutes of close-range fire. Leaving *San Juan Nepomuceno* to be later occupied by crew from *Defiance*, *Dreadnought* now moved on to attack the mighty *Principe de Asturias*. Although he gave the Spaniard a few good broadsides, Conn was unable to close because she fled from the battle carrying Admiral Gravina, mortally wounded by a shot from *Dreadnought*, towards Cadiz.

Captain Philip Durham of the 74-gun *Defiance* had resisted Sir Robert Calder's appeal for him to attend at his court-martial, instead wishing to stay with the fleet. Placed towards the rear of Collingwood's line, *Defiance* passed between the *San Ildefonso* and the French *Achille* before emptying a couple of broadsides into the *Principe de Asturias*. In return *Principe de Asturias* caused *Defiance* a great deal of damage aloft before Durham closed to within a few yards and engaged *Bellerophon*'s old foe the *Aigle*. With *Aigle* having already sustained a great deal of damage, the fight was apparently over quickly. The British boarding-party was in the process of raising a Union flag when they came under heavy small-arms fire from the forecastle and aloft, forcing them to flee back to the safety of the *Defiance*. Durham now subjected *Aigle* to a furious 25-minute cannonade before the French ship finally surrendered with about 270 casualties. This was much to the chagrin of *Bellerophon*'s officers who thought their ship had done all the hard work. Moreover, *Defiance* now proceeded to seize the drifting *San Juan Nepomuceno*, which had earlier been pounded by and surrendered to *Dreadnought*.

The rearmost ship of Collingwood's division was the 98-gun three-decked *Prince*. A powerful ship, she was late coming into action but used her heavy broadsides to spectacular effect. She engaged *Achille* at about 4.30 p.m., the French ship having already received heavy fire from at least four British ships, her captain being killed in the process. *Prince*'s second close-range broadside brought down *Achille*'s masts while a fire in the foretop began to spread and efforts to put out the blaze were

---

Extract from Don Antonio de Escaño to the Prince of the Peace

Cadiz, October 22 1805

… *It wanted eight minutes to noon when an English three-decker broke through the centre of our line, being seconded in this manoeuvre by the Vessels which followed in its wake. The other leading Ships of the Enemy's columns did the same; one of them passed down our Rear, a third laid herself between the* Achille *and the* St. Ildefonso, *and from this moment the Action was nothing but so many sanguinary single combats within pistol-shot: the greater part of them being between the whole of the Enemy's Fleet and the half of ours, several boardings necessarily took place. I do not possess the data necessary for giving your Highness a detailed and particular account of these single fights, nor can I speak with certainty of the movements of the Van, which, I am informed, tacked at the commencement of the Battle, in order to support those who were attacked. I can, however, confidently assure you that every Ship, French as well as Spanish, which fought in my sight, performed its duty to the utmost, and that this Ship, after a terrific contest of four hours with three or four of* the Enemy's Vessels, *its rigging destroyed, its sails shot through and through, its masts and topmasts riddled with balls, in every respect a most deplorable condition, was most reasonably relieved by the* San Justo, *a Spanish, and the* Neptune, *a French ship, which junction drove off the Enemy, and enabled the* Rayo, *the* Montañes, *the* Asís, *and the* San Leandro, *all of which had suffered severely, to unite with the other French ships, that were in just as bad a plight. As soon as this vessel found itself free of from the Enemy, it directed the Ships which had joined company to assist such Vessels as were in need of their aid; and at night-fall, the cannonade having ceased on both sides, the* Thémis *frigate was ordered to tow us towards Cadiz Bay, into which, however, we could not enter that night, in consequence of a severe gale from the S.S.E. accompanied by a heavy rain, which obliged us to ride at anchor, at half past one o'clock, in the Placer de Rota, with the other ships above mentioned; and the wind still continuing to freshen, we lost our main and mizzen masts, notwithstanding all our efforts to save them: a misfortune which likewise befell the* San Leandro, *also at anchor near us.*

Source: Nicolas, VII, p. 285

hampered by a roundshot having damaged the fire-fighting pump. Nevertheless, the French crew kept up a desultory fire until the progress of the fire became unstoppable. After drowning the powder stores, *Achille's* crew leapt overboard, abandoning the ship to her fate. *Prince* sheered away, fearing that a catastrophic explosion would engulf the two ships, but in company with the British *Swiftsure*, the cutter *Entreprenante* and the schooner *Pickle* lowered their boats to rescue what was left of the brave French crew from the water. With some of her remaining loaded guns firing off due to the heat, *Achille* burned until sometime between 5.30 p.m. and 5.45 p.m. when the flames detonated the magazines, sending her to the bottom with her tattered colours still clearly flying. One observer aboard the *Defence* recalled this macabre end to the battle:

> It was a sight the most awful and grand that can be conceived. In a moment the hull burst into a cloud of smoke and fire. A column of vivid flame shot up to an enormous height in the atmosphere and terminated by expanding into an immense globe, representing for a few seconds, a prodigious tree in flames, speckled with many dark spots, which the pieces of timber and bodies of men occasioned while they were suspended in the clouds.[116]

The explosion of *Achille* marked the end of the fighting for the Lee Division. Collingwood's assault had smashed the rear of the Combined Fleet. On the morning of 21 October 1805 Admiral Alava and Gravina had had nineteen ships under their command. By the time *Achille* blew up only five had escaped from furious onslaught, *Principe de Asturias*, *Argonaute*, *Montañes*, *Pluton* and *San Justo*, all of which fled to the safety of Cadiz.

It is interesting to note that one of *Achille's* survivors pulled from the water by the presumably startled British crew of the *Pickle* was a naked Frenchwoman. Jeanette, as she was called, had gone to sea in the *Achille* disguised as a man to follow her husband. She saw him killed in action and when the disastrous conflagration began to consume the ship, she had to throw off her clothes before plunging into the water. Here she was assisted by one of *Achille's* crew, who kept her afloat before the *Pickle* came to their rescue. Brought on board the *Victory*, she was dressed in theatre clothing used for entertaining the crew. She was then moved to the *Revenge* where she was provided with a couple of shirts to make a petticoat. (CPL)

NELSON'S WEATHER COLUMN

While Collingwood was leading his element of the British fleet into battle, Nelson had been directing his own attack. The Weather column, in an uncomplicated line ahead formation, had maintained a more compact cohesion than Collingwood's more diffuse rough line abreast. With his heavy ships to the fore, Nelson's attack would pack an almighty punch; the key question was where should he deliver it?

It was not until the final part of his advance that Nelson could be sure where to direct his blow. He was specifically searching out the flagship of the enemy fleet, Villeneuve's *Bucentaure*. Thinking that perhaps the enemy commander would have flown his flag in the mighty *Santíssima Trinidad*, his initial aim was a little to the north of *Bucentaure*'s actual position in the centre of the line. By heading towards the van it has been argued that Nelson was making an intentional feint before delivering his blow farther towards the centre, though the evidence remains inconclusive.[117] Perhaps the reversal of the Combined Fleet and the disorganised nature of their line confused matters. What is certain is that the Weather column headed towards the van before making a slight turn to starboard before, once the enemy colours were unfurled, dropping down the enemy line and heading for *Bucentaure*.

The difficulty of providing exact timings for events is highlighted by the fact that *Victory* and the ship astern of her, *Téméraire*, both give different times for the start of the engagement. For instance *Victory*'s log reads 'At 11.50 the enemy began firing upon us. At 4 minutes past 12, opened our larboard guns at the enemy's van.' Whereas according to *Téméraire*'s log 'At 18 minutes past noon the enemy began to fire. At 25 minutes past noon *Victory* opened fire.'[118]

Recollection of Midshipman William Stanhope Babcock, HMS Neptune

Some of [the Combined Fleet] were painted like ourselves – with double or yellow sides, some with a broad single red or yellow streak, others all black, and the noble Santíssima Trinidad *with four distinct lines of red, with a white ribbon between them, made her seem to be a superb man-of-war, which, indeed she was. Her appearance was imposing, her head splendidly ornamented with a colossal group of figures, painted white, representing the Holy Trinity, from which she took her name. This magnificent ship was destined to be our opponent. She was lying-to under topsails, top-gallant-sails, royals, jib, and spanker; her courses were hauled up, and her lofty towering sails looked beautiful, peering through the smoke as she awaited the onset. The flags of France and Spain, both handsome, chequered the line, waving defiance to that of Britain.*

Then in our own fleet, union jacks and ensigns were made fast to the fore and fore-topmast-stays, as well as to the mizzen rigging, besides one at the peak, in order that we might not mistake each other in the smoke, and to show the enemy our determination to conquer. Towards eleven, our two lines were better formed, but still there existed long gaps in Vice Admiral Collingwood's division. Lord Nelson's van was strong: three three-deckers and four seventy fours, their jibbooms nearly over the other's taffrails, the bands playing 'God save the King', 'Rule Britannia', and 'Britons Strike Home'; the crews stationed on the forecastles of the different ships, cheering the ship ahead of them when the enemy began to fire, sent those feelings to our hearts that insured victory.

Source: Fraser (1913), p. 218.

What is clear is that, as with Collingwood's attack to the south, the light winds slowed the pace of Nelson's advance and as a result the lead ship suffered an incredible amount of fire before she cut the line. At first the enemy fire was limited to ranging shots, but as *Victory* closed with the van of the line she was exposed to the combined fire of seven or eight enemy ships. Unable to return fire, Nelson instead offered a rousing verbal broadside, 'I'll given them such a dressing as they never had before!' The enemy ships' flags and ensigns were now unfurled, confirming the position of Villeneuve's *Bucentaure* as the eleventh ship in the line. Nelson directed *Victory* to make for the enemy flagship, a move that entailed passing in front of part of the enemy line at fairly close range. As she closed to about 500 yards of the enemy line, *Victory*'s mizzen topmast was shot away and her wheel was destroyed; from now on steering was conducted by a tiller in the gunroom with orders possibly being conducted by copper speaking-tubes.[119]

John Scott, Nelson's private secretary, was one of the first casualties. Talking with Captain Hardy, Scott was almost sliced in two by a round shot, splattering the decks with blood. Nelson glimpsed the remains of his carcass being thrown overboard. 'Was that Scott?' he inquired; when the answer came in the affirmative he remarked 'Poor fellow'. Just after Scott's death, Nelson and Hardy had a remarkable escape while calmly pacing the quarterdeck. As later recalled by *Victory*'s Surgeon William Beatty:

In a few minutes afterwards a shot struck the fore-brace-bits on the quarterdeck, and passed between Lord Nelson and Captain Hardy; a splinter from the bits bruising Captain Hardy's foot and tearing the buckle from his shoe. They both stopped; and were observed by the Officers on deck to survey each other with inquiring looks, each supposing the other to be wounded. His Lordship then smiled, and said: 'This is too warm work, Hardy, to last long' and declared that through all the battles he had been in, he had never witnessed more cool courage than was displayed by the *Victory*'s crew on this occasion.[120]

Unlike *Royal Sovereign*, which had outpaced the rest of her division, leaving Collingwood isolated in the enemy line, *Victory* was slowed down even more by the amount of damage to her sails and rigging. However, this would prove to be of some benefit for immediately astern of *Victory* was Captain Harvey's *Téméraire* which would provide much needed assistance over the next few hours. Furthermore, unlike Collingwood's attack, four out of the first five ships in Nelson's division were powerful three-deckers. In other parts of the line ships were also closing up, creating a very powerful compact punch that would land right on Villeneuve's chin. This would cut the line ahead of Collingwood's attack and enable him to isolate and destroy the rear while the remainder of Nelson's line would prevent the van of the Combined Fleet turning to provide assistance to their comrades.

With French and Spanish ships bunching up to prevent the British penetrating the line near Villeneuve's flagship, a dangerously large gap had opened between the stern of *Redoutable* and the bows of *Santa Ana*. But it also had the effect of presenting Captain Hardy with a compact target. Unlike the situation at the rear of the Combined Fleet, where several gaps had opened up in the line, *Bucentaure* was closely supported by Captain Lucas' *Redoutable*, to her rear, and by *Neptune*, a little

French engraving of the combat between the *Redoutable* and *Victory*. Captain Lucas' ship was perhaps the best trained and led in the Combined Fleet. In running *Victory* alongside her, Hardy could not have chosen a worse opponent. (CPL)

to leeward off her starboard quarter. Realising that to cut the line and engage the flagship from leeward would probably entail colliding with at least one ship, Hardy raised the point with Nelson, who replied that the choice of where to impact rested with Hardy. He made the fateful decision to head for *Redoutable*, a small 74-gun two-decker under the command of Captain Jean-Jacques Lucas, whose forward guns were at that moment firing on the *Victory*.

Setting the required course, Hardy sailed *Victory* through the line, astern of *Bucentaure* and ahead of *Redoutable* at about 1p.m. On *Victory*'s forecastle her port 68pdr carronade was fired by the boatswain William Wilmet, unleashing a hail of 500 musket balls followed by a roundshot through *Bucentaure*'s stern gallery, which showered the deck with broken timbers. As *Victory* continued to pass under *Bucentaure*'s stern, a devastating rolling broadside from double and triple-shotted port guns ripped through Villeneuve's ship, destroyed her stern, caused horrific casualties and in one move virtually removed the flagship from the fight. After firing the starboard guns into *Redoutable* at 1.10 p.m. Hardy, unable to engage *Bucentaure* from the leeward side, ran *Victory*'s starboard side on to Lucas' ship, in the process receiving a raking broadside from *Neptune*.

Redoutable, a 74-gun two-decker of the smallest type in the French Navy, was perhaps the best officered and manned ship in Villeneuve's fleet. *Redoutable* could not match *Victory* in terms of big gun firepower, but where she could gain an advantage was in small-arms fire. Like many in the Combined Fleet, *Redoutable* had embarked soldiers at Cadiz; they were now stationed aloft to sweep the enemy decks with musket fire as a precursor to boarding. Lucas had paid particular attention to boarding techniques, increased the effectiveness of his crew by training them in hand-to-hand combat, gave a great deal of practice to marksmen and distributed a large number of hand-grenades to be thrown on to an enemy's deck. Now locked in

Captain Lucas survived the devastation inflicted on his ship *Redoutable* to leave a valuable account of the action with Nelson's *Victory*. (CPL)

Captain Jean Jacques Étienne Lucas (?–1819)

Captain Lucas commanded *Redoutable* at Trafalgar, the ship that became locked in a deadly combat with Nelson's *Victory*. Standing at a little under five feet tall, Lucas may not have seemed the most ferocious of opponents but he was a highly competent and tenacious captain. He was a protégé of the French Admiral Latouche Tréville, having served under the great man in the War of American Independence. One of the many officers from a non-aristocratic background who benefited from the Revolution, he soon made Captain. Held prisoner in England for a short time after his capture at Trafalgar, he was allowed to attend Nelson's funeral and in April 1806 was exchanged and returned to France. Unlike Villeneuve, Lucas received a warm reception. Summoned by Napoleon, he was awarded the *Légion d'honneur* and raised to flag rank as Rear Admiral. Forever known to his countrymen as *le Redoutable Lucas*, he died in 1819 and was buried at Brest.

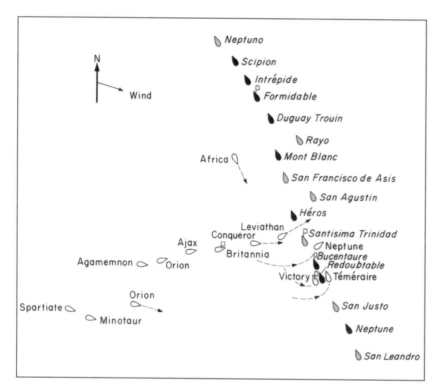

The action between Nelson's division and Villeneuve's centre at about 12.45 pm.

deadly combat with the British flagship, Lucas' men on the upper decks and in all three tops unleashed a hail of lead against *Victory*'s upper decks. Musket balls peppered *Victory*'s woodwork and her crew, while the grenades exploded in sulphurous flashes, causing death and destruction and spreading smoke and confusion. In a short space of time *Victory*'s upper deck was a scene of carnage and cleared of the majority of her crew including Nelson. At about 1.15 p.m. he was struck by a musket ball, fell to the deck and was taken below to the cockpit.

But the men stationed on *Victory*'s infernal lower decks, stripped to the waist, bodies blackened by the smoke, kept up their demonic activity, pounding double and even triple shot into *Redoutable*. With such intensive fire in a concentrated area, there was a very real danger that the ships might be engulfed in a conflagration. The 'fireman' stationed at each of *Victory*'s guns sent a bucketful of water out her gunports after each shot to dampen down *Redoutable*'s sides.

It seems that *Redoutable*'s larboard lower deck gunports may have been intentionally closed to stop boarding-parties entering through them, though Lucas afterwards maintained that they were held firmly shut by *Victory*'s hull. Whatever

---

Marine Second Lieutenant Lewis Rotely, HMS Victory

We were engaging on both sides; every gun was going off. A man should witness a battle in a three-decker from the middle deck, for it beggars all description: it bewilders the senses of sight and hearing. There was the fire from above, the fire from below, besides the fire from the deck I was

upon, the guns recoiling with violence, reports louder than thunder, the decks heaving and the sides straining. I fancied myself in the infernal regions, where every man appeared a devil. Lips might move, but orders and hearing were out of the question; everything was done by signs.
Source: Fenwick, p. 274.

> *Recounting the previous day's action, the Log of HMS* Victory *for Tuesday*
> 22 October 1805
> *Modt Wd at 11.40 the action commenced between the* Ry Sovereign *and the rear of the enemy's line, at 11.50 the van of the enemy's line opened their fire on us, all sail set, at 12.12 opened our fire, at 12.20 in attempting to break through the enemy's line fell on board the 10th and 11th ships, the action became general with the van ships of both columns, at 1.15 the Right Honble Lord Viscount Nelson was wounded, at 1.30 the* Redoutable *having struck ceased firing our starboard guns, the action continued larboard side with the* San Tissima Trinidada *and some other ships, at 3.0 all the enemy's ships near us having struck ceased firing, observed the* Royal Sovereign *had lost her main and mizen mast, and several dismasted prizes around her, at 3.10 4 of the enemy's van tack'd and stood along our line and engaged us in*
>
> *passing, at 3.40 made the signl for our own ships to keep their wind, for the purpose of attacking the enemy's van, at 4.45 the Spanish Rear Adm struck and one of the enemy's ships blew up, the Right Honble Lord Viscount Nelson departed this life, at 5 the mizzen mast fell, our ships employd in taking possession of the prizes, Vice Admiral Collingwood hoisted his flag on board the* Euryalus, *employd securing the masts and bowsprit, sounded occasionally from 19 to 13 fathoms, observed 14 sail of the enemy standing to the northward and three to the southward AM struck the fore top mast to fish the fore masts at noon the fleet and prizes in company but not having communication of any of our ships remain ignorant of the no. taken our loss on board the* Victory *is as follows*
> *6 Officers and 48 Seamen and Marines killed*
> *7 Officers and 74 Seamen and Marines wounded*
> *Source: TNA ADM 51/4514*

the reason, with most of *Victory*'s upper deck 12pdrs silent and the deck itself almost deserted, Lucas gathered his crew for a mass boarding of the British flagship. It was a critical time for Nelson's attack; if Lucas could capture the *Victory* it would inspire his fellow French and Spanish crews to greater efforts. But the intricacies of naval architecture provided an initial frustration because, although the sides of each ship were touching at the waterline, the hull shape, or tumblehome, left a gap between them at the level of the upper deck. To bridge it Lucas ordered *Redoutable*'s main yard to be placed across the gap, but at that very moment the two ships drifted towards *Téméraire*. At about 1.40 p.m. *Redoutable* crashed into Captain Harvey's ship, placing Lucas in the unenviable and uncomfortable position of being sandwiched between two British three-deckers. A 68pdr carronade on *Victory*'s quarterdeck was now fired with devastating effect into the mass of boarders while a broadside from *Téméraire* smashed into her hull. Lucas, sustaining his own wound from this broadside, later stated that it alone killed or wounded more than 200 of his crew.

As *Redoutable* received numerous fearsome broadsides and a withering fire from her opponents carronades, Lucas' rapidly diminishing crew continued to use their muskets and grenades' with great effect. Many of their heavy guns had been shot to pieces. But the fate of his ship had already been determined by *Téméraire*'s first broadside, which had caused several leaks that could not be sealed. Four of *Redoutable*'s six pumps were destroyed and the influx of water could not be halted.

Following immediately in *Victory*'s wake and receiving a heavy fire in the advance, the second ship in Nelson's attack, the 98-gun *Téméraire* had passed to the stern of *Bucentaure* but in the process of cutting the line had received a devastating raking broadside from *Neptune*. Harvey's ship suffered a great deal of damage and was left virtually unmanageable as *Redoutable* to port and *Neptune* off her starboard bow poured in a constant stream of shot. At 1.40 p.m. as *Redoutable* crashed into *Téméraire*, her bowsprit went through the main entry port. This was quickly secured leaving the French ship trapped while *Téméraire* poured shot after shot into her hull and used her 32pdr carronades to sweep the upper deck of the French ship.

So far *Téméraire*'s starboard guns had been unemployed, but now she fired them at the passing *Fougueux*. Already engaged by *Belleisle* and *Mars* from Collingwood's division, *Fougueux* had come up to assist the flagship. Unleashing a terrifying broadside into the stationary *Téméraire*, whose Union flags had been shot away and her upper deck apparently deserted, Captain Louis Beaudouin prepared to board and seize the British three-decker. But the crews manning *Téméraire*'s starboard lower deck guns held their fire until *Fougueux* was within 100 yards before taking the French ship by surprise, delivering a frightening broadside, shortly followed by a second volley. The result was devastating. Beaudouin was lying mortally wounded; his ship, wrecked and unmanageable, careered into *Téméraire*. Like *Redoutable*, *Fougueux* was lashed to the British ship and after about ten minutes was boarded and struck to the 'Fighting *Téméraire*'.

Victory to leeward of the mighty four-decker *Santíssima Trinidad*. With four distinct lines of red, with a white ribbon between them, the *Santíssima Trinidad* was the largest warship in the world but by the end of the fight had been reduced to a floating wreck by British gunnery. (CPL)

At about 2 p.m. *Victory* worked free of the tenacious *Redoutable*, moving off a little to the north. *Téméraire*, *Redoutable* and the captured *Fougueux* were now drifting as unmanageable hulks. At about 2.20 p.m. *Redoutable's* mizzen mast was brought down, providing a bridge for *Téméraire's* crew to board and seize the ship. With more than 300 dead, and his ship smashed, dismasted, her rudder gone and several fires breaking out Lucas, realising that continued resistance was pointless, struck his flag. But so fierce had been the fight from the small 74-gun ship, her crew and the resolute Captain Lucas, that *Victory*, the British flagship, could play little further part in the battle. Taken in tow by the British *Swiftsure* later in the day, *Redoutable* was a wreck and only with great efforts could she be kept afloat.

The action between Nelson's division and Villeneuve's centre at about 2.00 pm. (Note: French *Neptune* not *Neptuno*)

With Nelson's division attacking in line ahead, *Bucentaure* and the enemy ships around her took a terrible pounding from successive British ships. The third ship in the Weather Column, Captain Thomas Fremantle's 98-gun *Neptune*, also emptied a broadside into the stern of *Bucentaure*. Rounding the stern of the massive four-decked 136-gun *Santíssima Trinidad*, he luffed up alongside and pounded his heavier opponent. At about 1.50 p.m. her main and mizzenmasts were brought down, to the sound of three cheers from the British crew, and at 2.30 p.m. her foremast went over. With *Conqueror* and *Africa* also weighing into the fight, *Santíssima Trinidad* was left a floating wreck and an officer draped a Union flag over her side to show that she had surrendered. Fremantle was, however, unable to claim his prize as his ship was needed to stave off the threat posed by the movement of the Combined Fleet's van. *Santíssima Trinidad* was left to drift until seized by Captain Grindall's *Prince*.

Hot on the heels of Fremantle came Captain Henry Bayntun's 74-gun *Leviathan*, which also fired into *Bucentaure* before heading towards *Santíssima Trinidad*. After emptying a few broadsides into the four-decker, Bayntun could see that *Neptune's* gunnery was so accurate that she needed little help. Using the initiative that Nelson so valued, he looked for another opponent, settling on the French *Neptune*, an 80-gun ship under Captain Esprit Tranquille Maistral. Aware that the *Leviathan* was bearing down on his ship, Maistral promptly made off to leeward. By now several ships from the van of the Combined Fleet were coming round and threatening to attack the ships from the head of Nelson's Weather Column. Bayntun headed to intercept one of the ships that had abandoned Dumanoir's formation to sail down

Extracts from Captain Lucas' report to the Minister of Marine

… At a quarter to twelve the Redoutable opened fire with a shot from the first gun division. It cut through the foretopsail yard of the Victory, whereupon cheers and shouts resounded all over the ship. Our firing was well kept up, and in less than ten minutes the British flagship had lost her mizen-mast, foretopsail, and main topgallant mast….

The damage done to the Victory did not affect the daring manoeuvre of Admiral Nelson. He repeatedly persisted in trying to break the line in front of the Redoutable, and threatening to run us down if we opposed. But the proximity of the British flagship, though closely followed by the Téméraire, instead of intimidating my intrepid crew, only increased their ardour; and to show the English admiral that we did not fear his fouling us, I had grappling irons made fast at all the yardarms.

The Victory having now succeeded in passing astern of the French admiral, ran foul of us, dropping alongside and sheering off aft in such a way that our poop lay alongside her quarter-deck. From this position the grappling irons were thrown on board her. Those at the stern parted, but those forward held on; and at the same time our broadside was discharged, resulting in a terrible slaughter. We continued to fire for some time, although there was some delay at the guns. We had to use rope rammers in several cases, and fire with the guns run in, being unable to use them, as the ports were masked by the sides of the Victory. At the same time, elsewhere, by means of muskets fired through the ports into those of the Victory, we prevented the enemy from loading their guns, and before long they stopped firing on us altogether. What a day of glory for the Redoutable if she had had to fight only with the Victory! The English batteries, not being able to resist us longer, ceased firing. Then I became aware that the crew of the enemy were about to attempt to board us. At once I had the trumpets sounded, giving the divisional call for boarding. All hastened up from below instantly, in fine style; the officers and midshipmen sprang to the head of their men, as though at a parade. In less than a minute our decks swarmed with armed men, who spread themselves with rapidity on the poop and in the nettings and the shrouds…

Our firing, though, became so rapid, and was so much superior to his, that in less than a quarter of an hour we had silenced that of the Victory altogether. More than two hundred grenades were flung on board her, with the utmost success; her decks were strewn with the dead and wounded. Admiral Nelson was killed by the firing of our musketry. Immediately after this, the upper deck of the Victory became deserted, and she again ceased firing, but it proved difficult to board her because of the motion of the two vessels, and the height of the Victory's upper tier and battery. On that I gave the order to cut the supports of the main-yard so that it might serve as a bridge. At the same time Midshipman Yon and four seamen sprang on board the Victory by means of her anchor, and we then knew that there was nobody left in the batteries. At that moment, when my brave fellows were hastening to follow, the three-decker Téméraire, which had seen that the Victory fought no longer and must without fail be taken, came down, full sail, on our starboard side. We were immediately under the full fire of her artillery, discharged almost with muzzles touching.

It is impossible to describe the carnage produced by the murderous broadside of this ship. More than two hundred of our brave men were killed or wounded by it. I was wounded also at the same time, but not so seriously as to make me abandon my post. Not being able to undertake anything on the side of the Victory, I now ordered the rest of the crew to man the batteries on the other side and fire at the Téméraire with what guns the collision when she came alongside had not dismounted.

The order was carried out; but by this time we had been so weakened, and had so few guns left available, that the Téméraire replied to us with great advantage. A short time afterwards another ship, a two-decker, whose name I cannot recall, placed herself across the stern of the Redoutable and fired on us within pistol-shot. In less than half an hour our ship had been so fearfully mauled that she looked like little more than a heap of debris. Judging by appearances, no doubt, the Téméraire now hailed us to surrender and not prolong a useless resistance. My reply was instantly to order some soldiers who were near me to fire back; which they did with great alacrity. At the same moment almost, the mainmast of the Redoutable fell on board the English ship. The two topmasts of the Téméraire then came down, falling on board of us. Our whole poop was stove in, helm, rudder, and stem post all shattered to splinters, all the stern frame, and the decks shot through. All our own guns were either smashed or dismounted by the broadsides of the Victory and Téméraire. In addition, an 18-pounder gun on the lower deck, and a 32-pounder carronade on the forecastle had burst, killing and wounding a great many men. The hull itself was riddled, shot through from side to side; deck beams were shattered;

port-lids torn away or knocked to pieces. Four of our six pumps were so damaged as to be useless. The quarter-deck ladders were broken, which rendered communication with the rest of the ship very difficult. Everywhere the decks were strewn with dead men, lying beneath the debris. Out of a crew of 634 men we had 522 hors de combat; of whom 300 were killed and 222 wounded – nearly all the officers among them… The batteries and upper decks were practically abandoned-bare of men, and we were unable longer to offer any resistance. No one who had not seen the state of the Redoutable could ever form an idea of her awful condition. Really I know of nothing on board that had not been hit by shot. In the midst of this horrible carnage and devastation my splendid fellows who had not been killed, and even, too, the wounded below on the orlop, kept cheering ' Long live the Emperor! We are not taken yet! Is the Captain still alive?' Some tarred canvas at the stern took fire about this time, but happily the flames were held in check, and we succeeded before long in extinguishing them.

The Victory by this time fought no longer. She busied herself only with getting clear of the Redoutable. We, however, meanwhile, were being cut to pieces by the cross fire from the Téméraire, with whom we still fought, and from the other ship, which was still firing into us at the stern. Unable to meet that fire, and not seeing any chance of rescue, the rest of our ships being all too far to leeward to be able to come to our assistance, I hesitated no longer about surrendering. The leaks were sufficiently serious to ensure the ship going to the bottom, so that the enemy would not keep her. When I satisfied myself finally about this, I gave orders to lower the colours.
Source: Fraser, (1906), pp. 158–73.

An engraving of HMS *Victory* at Portsmouth in 1828. (Warwick Leadlay Gallery)

A typical Victorian image portraying Nelson as the calm, confident leader on deck amongst the chaos of battle. In fact *Victory's* upper deck had been largely cleared by small-arms fire from *Redoutable*. (Warwick Leadlay Gallery)

and assist her comrades, the Spanish 74-gun *San Augstin*. Waiting until the British ship was about 100 yards away, the Spaniard turned hard to starboard to try and rake *Leviathan*, Bayntun responded with a swift turn to port, catching the *San Augstin* with a treble-shotted raking broadside, sending her mizzenmast crashing to the deck. *Leviathan* had already sustained damage aloft in her previous combat with *Santíssima Trinidad*. Bayntun, fearing that the Spaniard would escape like the *Neptune*, sent his ship crashing into *San Augstin*. With her 32pdr carronades sweeping *San Augstin*'s decks, Bayntun sent over a boarding-party, which seized the Spaniard without too much fuss. Although *Leviathan* had sustained a great deal of material damage, particularly aloft, casualties to her crew were minimal, 26 in total. There is no

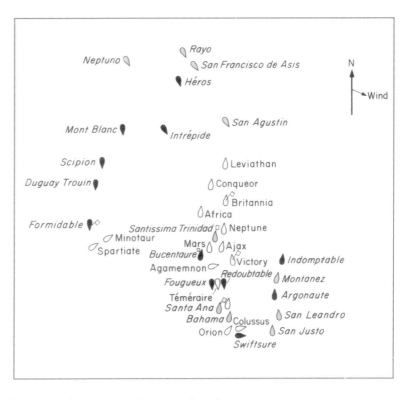

Dumanoir's division trying to support Villeneuve's centre at about 3.30 pm.

greater testament to the superiority of the British gunnery than the fact that *San Augstin*'s casualties numbered 380, more than *half* of her crew.

There would be no respite for Bayntun and his men as she almost immediately came under attack from another of Dumanoir's ships, *Intrépide*, commanded by the splendidly named Captain Infernet. Breaking ranks from Dumanoir's formation, in the process colliding with *Mont-Blanc*, he sailed directly to assist *Bucentaure*. Reaching the action he placed *Intrépide* across *Leviathan*'s bows, unleashing a deadly raking broadside before taking up a position to starboard where the two ships engaged in a furious fight.

Assistance for *Leviathan* came in the form of one of the smallest battleships in the British fleet. Having become separated from the main part of Nelson's fleet during the night, Captain Henry Digby's 64-gun *Africa* initially operated independently of either attack. Throwing a large number of provisions overboard to increase her speed before opening fire soon after *Royal Sovereign* cut the Combined Fleet, *Africa* targeted the leading ship of the enemy van, before exchanging fire with several more ships as she passed down the line. Once the signal to 'engage the enemy more closely' had been hoisted, she made for the enemy's centre to tackle *Santíssima Trinidad*. Arriving after the four-decker had been pulverised by Fremantle's *Neptune*, Digby, thinking the Spaniard had given up the fight, organised a boarding-party to seize her. Finding a Spanish officer,

Extract from Admiral Villeneuve's official report on board the English frigate **Euryalus,**

15th November 1805.

At midday I signalled to the fleet to begin firing as soon as the enemy was within range and at a quarter past twelve the opening shots were fired by the Fougueux *and the* Santa Ana – *at the* Royal Sovereign, *which led the enemy's starboard column, with the flag of Admiral Collingwood. The firing broke off for a brief interval, after which it re-opened fiercely from all the ships within range. It could not, however, prevent the enemy from breaking the line astern of the* Santa Ana.

The port column, led by the Victory, *with the flag of Admiral Nelson, came on in much the same way. She appeared as if she was aiming to break the line between the* Santíssima Trinidad *and the bows of the* Bucentaure. *Whether, however, they found our line too well closed up at that point, or from some other reason, when they were almost within half pistol-shot – while we, for our part, prepared to board and had our grappling-irons ready for throwing – they swung off to starboard and passed astern of the* Bucentaure. *The* Redoutable *had the station of the* Neptune, *which had fallen to leeward, and she heroically fulfilled the duties of the second astern to the flagship. She ran*

on board the Victory, *but the lightness of the wind had not prevented the* Victory *passing close under the stern of the* Bucentaure *and firing into us as she passed several treble-shotted broadsides, with effects that were murderous and destructive. At that moment I made the signal, 'All ships not engaged owing to their stations, are to get into action as soon as possible!' It was impossible for me to see how things were going in the centre and rear of the fleet because of the dense smoke which enveloped us.*

To the Victory *succeeded two others of the enemy, three-deckers, and several seventy-fours. These one after the other came up and filed by, slowly past the stern of the* Bucentaure. *I had just made the signal to the van to put about when the main and mizen masts both came down. The English ships which had passed through astern of us were attacking us from leeward, but, unfortunately, without suffering any serious loss in return from our batteries. The greater part of our guns were already dismounted and others were disabled or masked by the fall of the masts and rigging. Now, for one moment, the smoke-fog cleared and I saw that all the centre and rear had given way. I found, also, that my flagship was the most to windward of all. Our foremast was still standing, however. It offered a means for our making sail to get to leeward to join a group of ships at a little distance which did*

they were surprised when he declared that the ship had not surrendered, and they were allowed to withdraw back to the *Africa*. With *Santíssima Trinidad* still active, though playing little part in the fight, Digby looked for a target on which to use his broadsides to greater effect. With *Leviathan* now targeted by *Intrépide*, Digby rounded her stern before taking up a position off her port side, distracting the French ship from engaging the *Leviathan*. It was an unequal contest, as *Africa* took a hard pounding for 45 minutes leaving her almost silent and causing much damage aloft though her casualties were the surprisingly low total of sixty-two, not seem much damaged: but immediately afterwards the foremast came down like the others. I had had my barge kept ready, so that in the event of the Bucentaure being dismasted, I might be able to go on board some other ship, and rehoist my flag there. When the mainmast came down I gave orders for it to be cleared for launching, but it was found to be unserviceable, damaged irreparably, either from shot or crushed in the fall of the masts. Then I had the Santíssima Trinidad hailed – she was just ahead of us – and asked them either to send a boat or take us in tow. But there was no answer to the hail. The Trinidad at that moment was hotly engaged. A three-decker was attacking her on the quarter astern, and another enemy was on the beam to leeward. Being now without any means of repelling my antagonists, the whole of the upper deck and the twenty-four-pounder batteries on the main deck having had to be abandoned, heaped up with dead and wounded, with the ship isolated in the midst of the enemy and unable to move, I had to yield to my destiny. It remained only to stop further bloodshed. That, already immense, could only have been in vain.

All the fleet astern of the Bucentaure was, as I have said, broken up. Many ships were dismasted; others were still fighting, in retreat towards a body of ships to the east. Some of Rear-Admiral Dumanoir's squadron attempted to rally on the vessels to leeward, while five others kept to windward and exchanged shots with their enemy in passing, but only at long range. The rearmost of the five, I believe the Neptuno, a Spanish ship, which was a little to leeward of the others, had to surrender.

From the nature of the attack that the enemy delivered there could not help resulting a pêle-mêle battle, and the series of ship-to-ship actions that ensued were fought out with the most noble devotion. The enemy had the advantage of us, owing to his powerful ships, seven of which were three-deckers, the smallest mounting 114 guns [98 guns] in weight of metal of his heavy guns and carronades; and in the smartness with which his ships were handled, due to three years' experience at sea – a form of training which, of course, had been impossible for the Combined Fleet. The courage and the devotion to France and the Emperor, shown by the officers and men, could not be surpassed. It had evinced itself on our first putting to sea, and also in preparing for battle, by the cheers and shouts of 'Vive l'Empereur!' with which the flagship's signals were received. I did not see a single man blench at the sight of the enemy's formidable column of attack, headed by four three-deckers, which came down on the Bucentaure.

Source: Fraser (1906), pp. 128–33.

until she was rescued by Codrington's Orion. Digby's brave conduct had saved Bayntun's ship from suffering great damage.

Bucentaure had been effectively taken out of the battle by Victory's first deadly raking broadside, and Villeneuve's situation had been exacerbated by successive British ships engaging his unmanageable ship. He now decided to move his flag to another ship in an endeavour to gain control of his fleet. With all of Bucentaure's boats smashed to bits, he made several attempts to signal his frigates to provide assistance and for Santíssima Trinidad to send over a boat – but no help came. At

The Spanish
Santíssima Trinidad,
the largest ship in
the world when she
was built at Havana
in 1769. (CPL)

about 1.35 p.m. *Conqueror* became the latest British ship to fire into the *Bucentaure's* stern from a distance of 30 yards. Despite the French flagship's being a virtual hulk, her crew maintained a withering small-arms fire against *Conqueror*, forcing the men manning the quarterdeck and forecastle guns to be withdrawn and causing much damage aloft, particularly to the rigging.

With a huge amount of fire poured into *Bucentaure* that afternoon, in particular the raking broadsides from *Victory*, *Leviathan* and *Conqueror*, it is remarkable that among the broken bodies and severed limbs, Villeneuve escaped unharmed. Captain Magendie had received a shot in the face and Captain Prigny received a wound to the leg; *Bucentaure's* total casualties were 209. At 2 p.m. Villeneuve took the inevitable decision to strike his flag to *Conqueror*, saving his crew from further suffering. Sent across with five Royal Marines to collect Villeneuve, *Conqueror's* Captain of Marines James Atcherley found a scene of utter horror:

> The dead, thrown back as they fell, lay along the middle of the decks in heaps,
> and the shot passing through had frightfully mangled the bodies... An

extraordinary proportion had lost their heads. A raking shot, which entered the lower deck, had glanced along the beams and through the thickest of the people, and a French officer declared that this shot alone had killed or disabled nearly forty men.[121]

On hearing that it was Captain Pellew of the *Conqueror* to whom he had surrendered, Villeneuve is reported to have remarked 'It is a satisfaction to me that it is to one so fortunate as Sir Edward Pellew I have lowered my flag.' When corrected that *Conqueror* was commanded by Pellew's brother Israel, Villeneuve was taken aback: 'His Brother. What, are there two of them? *Hélas!*'. With *Conqueror* by now engaged elsewhere, Villeneuve was taken to the *Mars* where he remain until the end of the battle.

The oldest ship in the British fleet, launched in 1762, was the three-decked 100-gun *Britannia*, flagship to Rear Admiral the Earl of Northesk. Naturally hesitant, Northesk was the third in the chain of command and once Nelson and Collingwood were engaged was the only man capable of issuing instructions to the unengaged part of the fleet. In this respect he missed the opportunity to react to the battle developing in front by organising the rear of the Weather Line and bearing down to the combat, possibly increasing the magnitude of victory. Captain Rotherham later recalled that he thought that Northesk 'behaved notoriously ill in the Trafalgar action'. There were later reports of a disagreement between Northesk and Charles Bullen his Flag Captain, with the former apparently wanting to slow his advance and the latter flatly refusing.[122] Northesk was certainly cautious, evidenced by the fact that although fired on at 1p.m., *Britannia* took a further two hours to pass through the degenerating enemy line behind several ships originally stationed to his rear, then firing on the departing *Rayo* and *San Francisco de Asís*.

As tenth in the Weather Line, Codrington had ample time to watch carefully and then choose where to deploy his ship the *Orion* with the greatest effect. Holding his own fire despite attracting a steady stream of shot, he looked for a suitable enemy on whom to unleash his own first broadside. Settling on the French *Swiftsure*, he raked her from astern, bringing down all three masts in one dreadful broadside. 'Having repeatedly pointed out to my men the waste of shot from other ships,' Codrington later wrote, 'I now had a fine opportunity of convincing them of the benefit of cool reserve.'

Demonstrating his superb leadership and the expert seamanship of his crew, Codrington headed to assist *Leviathan*, sandwiched between the Spanish *San Augstin* and the *Intrépide*. With a gallantry that shamed Dumanoir's caution, Infernet had brought his ship down into action, firing into *Leviathan* and almost silencing *Africa*. Codrington now managed to bring *Orion* into action against *Intrépide*. However, a number of British ships were firing on *Intrépide* from long range, thereby blocking his path. Codrington later recalled how he solved this problem:

I managed, first to back all sail so as to get under *Ajax*'s stern, and then to make all sail so as to pass across *Leviathan*'s head, who hailed me and said he hoped

I should make a better fist of it... and then on to bear down sufficiently to get our starboard guns to bear on *L'Intrépide*'s starboard quarter, and then to turn gradually round from thence under his stern, pass his broadside, and bring to on his larboard bow.

Captain Inferent had previously made it known that he would keep fighting until his masts and rudder were shot away. Codrington laconically noted to his wife, 'this we did for him in so handsome a way that he had no time to do us much injury', a point reflected in his casualty figures of 1 dead and 23 wounded.[123]

With the majority of the British fleet now in action, Nelson's wish for a 'pell-mell' battle was certainly granted. His plan to impact upon the enemy centre leaving Collingwood to smash the rear depended to a large degree on the weather division preventing the van of the Combined Fleet turning to intervene. The tenacious fighting of many Spanish and French ships drew comments of admiration and surprise from many in the British fleet. They were also buying time for the van of the Combined Fleet to turn and sail to their assistance.

Perhaps the most confusing aspect of Trafalgar is why the van of the Combined Fleet under Rear Admiral Dumanoir de Pelley remained a passive spectator for so long. While the rear and centre of Villeneuve's fleet were being smashed by the British attacks, the van, apart from some sporadic fire from the *Africa*, was entirely fresh. With many British ships lying dismasted and vulnerable to fresh enemy ships, the intervention of Dumanoir's squadron could have had a massive influence on the final outcome of the battle. Nelson himself had surmised that in the light airs it would not be easy for the head of the Combined Fleet to turn into the wind and assist the centre and tail of the line. Moreover, one of the tasks for the rear of his line was to prevent any such movement.

Dumanoir's failure to support the centre of his fleet had already drawn stinging criticism from Villeneuve. At about 1.50 p.m. one of the last orders given by Villeneuve before he surrendered the *Bucentaure* was to signal for Dumanoir to bear down and assist the centre and rear of the line as soon as possible. But as Nelson had foreseen, given the light winds Dumanoir had to use ships' boats to manoeuvre his ships around into the wind. After an intolerable delay, at about 3 p.m. Dumanoir in his flagship the 80-gun *Formidable* managed to lead three 74-gun two deckers, *Duguay-Trouin*, *Scipion* and *Mont-Blanc*, to windward of the, by now disorganised, British fleet. Three other ships, the Spanish 100-gun *Rayo*, 74-gun *San Francisco de Asís* and the French 74 *Héros*, ignoring signals from both Villeneuve and Dumanoir, headed north away from the action.

As Dumanoir was turning, two British ships that had failed to lay themselves alongside an opponent now made an important contribution to the fight. The 74-gun *Ajax* is reported to have joined the general action early, firing off her first shots at about 1p.m., shortly after coming upon the enemy line. With Captain Berry's 64-gun *Agamemnon* opening fire at 1.30 p.m., both ships took up a position between *Intrépide* and Dumanoir's squadron to windward, firing on the latter's ships as they passed.

It was now that the light winds finally favoured the British, for to windward of the fighting and yet to get into action were the last two ships of Nelson's Weather Line, the 74-gun *Spartiate*, Captain Francis Laforey, and *Minotaur*, Captain John Mansfield. Acting on the individual initiative that Nelson so favoured, they reacted instinctively. With the faster *Spartiate* leading, both ships placed themselves across Dumanoir's T. Opening fire at about 25 paces, both ships raked *Formidable*, then took up a position to protect *Victory*. Exchanging broadsides with Dumanoir, who could see that *Bucentaure* had struck and was therefore unwilling to press the matter, *Spartiate* and *Minotaur* closed with the isolated Spanish 80-gun *Neptuno*, which had fallen behind and was a little to leeward of the other four ships. Cutting off her escape route after an hour's pounding that brought down her mizzenmast, *Neptuno* struck at about 5.10 p.m. then drifted on the swell before becoming the third enemy ship to crash into *Téméraire*.

Although fired on by *Agamemnon* and *Ajax*, Dumanoir continued his movement behind the British fleet, firing at long range into the mass of ships concentrated around the two flagships, sending round shot into friend and foe alike. *Victory*, *Royal Sovereign*, *Belleisle* and *Téméraire* lay in a wretched state, and were vulnerable to this new threat, as were the enemy ships now taken as prizes. While *Spartiate* and *Minotaur* had prevented Dumanoir from attacking the British centre, he now abandoned *Neptuno* and *Intrépide* to their fate and made to support the remaining ships of Gravina's squadron to the south.

The Combined Fleet's line was cut in two places by Nelson's attack. (From Jenkins' *Naval Achievements* reprinted by Sim Comfort Associates)

Once he had been informed of Nelson's mortal wound, Collingwood had moved his flag from the shattered *Royal Sovereign* into the *Euryalus* to provide him with mobility and the capacity to transmit orders to the fleet. Now aware of the danger posed by Dumanoir, he signalled the Weather division to form a line to windward of the main enemy fleet. Although many ships did not see the signal or were otherwise engaged with enemy ships, or were in no position to comply, six ships did now manage to block Dumanoir's way. Unwilling to engage these ships, Dumanoir could see the *Principe de Asturias* fleeing to leeward, flying the signal for the remaining French and Spanish ships to rally on her. Dumanoir headed in the direction of Gibraltar, before deciding that his ultimate destination would be Rochefort. With Dumanoir leading his ships to the south and several ships following *Principe de Asturias* towards the safety of Cadiz, any chance of a counter-attack by the Combined Fleet had now gone.

As the firing stopped, some time between 5.15 and 5.30, when the French *Achille* exploded, shattered ships littered the scene. *Spartiate*'s log states: 'observed fourteen ships of the Enemy in our possession, including *Santíssima Trinidad*, and *Santa Ana*, three-deckers, two Admiral's ships, and *Bucentaure*, Admiral Villeneuve'. But many of the French and Spanish prizes were in a dreadful state, eight were completely dismasted, and a number of British ships were in a comparably bad way. With dark clouds gathering, Nelson's prediction that a storm would follow the battle would be devastatingly correct, but it was a prophecy he would not live to see.[124]

The French *Achille* engulfed in flames. Her explosion between 5:15 and 5:30 p.m. marked the end of a hard day's fighting. (From Jenkins' *Naval Achievements* reprinted by Sim Comfort Associates)

THE DEATH OF NELSON

If there is one single event that Trafalgar is remembered for it is the death of Nelson. His naval career had marked him out as the greatest exponent of naval warfare. Already the first real popular celebrity with a controversial private life, Nelson was recognised wherever he went ashore. With typical Nelsonic drama the nature of his suffering came to overshadow the great victory achieved by the Royal Navy. It was not an instantaneous death, being truncated or decapitated by a roundshot, or suffering an immediately fatal musket shot, but a mortal wounding and lingering death. He did not die on deck among his crew but below decks in the dark and cramped confines of the cockpit, recorded by eye-witnesses and almost immediately portrayed in quasi-religious imagery. It raised him from the ranks of normal humanity into an immortal figure revered as a demigod. For a society which was being transformed by the wars against France, moving away from the age of Enlightenment through to the romantic movement of post-war peace, Nelson's demise was legendary: 'it was the ideal romantic death'.[125]

Nelson was a victim of circumstance. Captain Hardy, in choosing to lay alongside the small 74-gun *Redoutable* could not have made a more fateful decision. *Redoutable*'s crew was the best trained and officered in Villeneuve's fleet. Her captain Jean Jacques Lucas had spent a great deal of time training his men in small-arms fire and boarding tactics to combat the superior gunnery skills of the Royal Navy. With marksmen stationed in her tops and upper deck, *Redoutable* swept *Victory*'s deck with musket fire to clear it of defenders before a boarding attempt could be launched.

At 1.15 p.m. Nelson was pacing the quarterdeck with Hardy. As they turned by the hatchway to retrace their steps Nelson was struck by a musket ball fired from

Redoutable's mizzen top. The force of the ball threw Nelson to his knees, he then briefly supported his frame using his left arm, before collapsing into the pool of blood left by Scott, his deceased secretary. Nelson immediately knew it was a fatal wound: 'They have done for me at last Hardy, my backbone is shot through.' The musket ball had struck Nelson's left shoulder, smashing two ribs, passed through his left lung, cut through a major artery, broke his spine and lodged under his right shoulder blade.

Whether the shot was deliberately aimed has been a matter of conjecture. In his blue undress uniform frockcoat with his four orders of chivalry embroidered on the left breast, Nelson was not an overly conspicuous target in the confusion of battle. But Hardy for one had expressed concern during the advance that they did make him stand out, and Nelson replied that it was too late to change. For a marksman to have picked him out amidst the smoke and then to have fired an inaccurate smoothbore musket from a moving platform at a moving target 40 feet away, deliberately avoiding the large frame of Captain Hardy, is a little far fetched. Most likely it was either a lucky snapshot or a deflected musket ball, the latter highly probable given the amount of small-arms fire directed at *Victory*'s poop and quarterdeck. After the battle various stories circulated in France as to the identity of the gunman; in 1826 an account appeared stating that Sergeant Robert Guillemard had claimed he was the man who fired the fatal shot. This claim was disproved by members of *Victory*'s crew, in particular midshipman John Pollard, who asserted that

Nelson falls to the quarter deck of Victory *after receiving his mortal wound. Shot in the left shoulder, Nelson fell to his knees in the very spot where his Private Secretary John Scott had been cut in two by a round shot. (National Maritime Museum)*

all the marksmen in *Redoutable*'s mizzen top were slain in revenge for the shooting. In fact the 1826 publication was a work of pure fiction.

Sergeant Secker of the Marines and two seamen carried Nelson below deck. Knowing the effect his wounding would have had on the crew, he attempted to cover his face and decorations with his handkerchief. He was taken to the gruesome dark confines of the cockpit, located below the waterline on the orlop deck. This was where the surgeons went about their grisly business; wounded men lay in every inch of deck space. The orlop was immediately below the lowest gun deck; the deafening sound of 32pdrs and the shuddering recoil of their carriages were immediately overhead. It was a nauseous hellish place. *Victory*'s chaplain, Alexander Scott, one of the key witnesses who recorded the last few hours of Nelson, had nightmares about this place for the rest of his life. In all his remaining years Scott could only bring himself to talk about it once, when he referred to the scene: 'it was like a butcher's shambles!' It all proved too much for Scott at one point; in utter shock he rushed up the ladders 'slippery with gore' to the deck, where he regained a modicum of composure.

Surgeon Beatty was immediately called over to examine the wounded Admiral who was on a bed in the midshipmen's quarters against the port side of the hull and covered with a sheet. 'Ah Mr Beatty!' Nelson wheezed, 'You can do nothing for me. I have but a short time to live: my back is shot through'. Beatty had the Admiral's clothes removed, examined the wound and confirmed Nelson's self-diagnosis. He left the Admiral to attend to other cases, leaving Nelson to be cared for by Scott and Walter Burke the purser. Despite his belief that death would come soon, Nelson lingered for two and three-quarter hours, his pain and suffering increasing. It seemed as if he was waiting for the important news of the outcome of the battle. He felt a 'Gush of blood every minute' in his chest, he told Scott, and referring to the musket ball stated, 'I felt it break my back'. Paralysed below the waist and with his lungs filling with blood, he became increasingly short of breath. He was given lemonade and watered wine to assuage his raging thirst, while Scott fanned him with papers.

SIR WILLIAM BEATTY (?–1842)

Synonymous with the story of Nelson and Trafalgar, Beatty's *An Authentic Narrative of the Death of Lord Nelson* remains a key text in any examination of Trafalgar. Beatty entered the navy at the start of the war with Revolutionary France in 1793. He joined the *Victory* in December 1804 as her surgeon, a position he held throughout the momentous year of 1805. More than just an account of the Admiral's demise, Beatty's *Narrative* describes the events of the day leading up to the battle, including his concerns for Nelson's safety, and the conclusions of the autopsy. He was also responsible for preserving Nelson's remains, which he placed in a large cask filled with brandy. The bullet fired from the tops of the *Redoutable* was recovered by Beatty during the autopsy and was presented by him to William IV (who knighted Beatty in 1831). After the wars Beatty served as Physician of Greenwich Hospital.

While Nelson was carried below Hardy had remained on deck. Nelson expressed great concern that his friend had been killed, but Hardy managed to visit the cockpit about an hour after Nelson had been hit. He brought the news that between twelve and fourteen enemy ships had struck to the British fleet. 'I hope none of our ships have struck,' Nelson naturally retorted, to which Hardy reassured the Admiral, 'No my Lord, there is no fear of that.' Nelson told Hardy, 'it will be all over with me soon', then motioning his flag captain over, said weakly, 'Pray let my dear Lady Hamilton have my hair, and all other things belonging to me.' Hardy then returned to the quarterdeck to attend to his duties, one of which was to inform Collingwood of Nelson's wound.

Alexander Scott's account of Nelson's death
Scott to Mr Rose,
22 December 1805

It is my intention to relate everything Lord Nelson said, in which your name was in any way connected. He lived about three hours after receiving his wound, was perfectly sensible the whole time, but compelled to speak in broken sentences, which pain and suffering prevented him from always connecting. When I first saw him, he was apprehensive he should not live many minutes, and told me so; adding, in a hurried, agitated manner, though with pauses, 'Remember me to Lady Hamilton! remember me to Horatia! remember me to all my friends. Doctor remember me to Mr Rose: tell him I have made a will, and left Lady Hamilton and Horatia to my Country.' He repeated his remembrances to Lady Hamilton and Horatia, and told me to mind what he said, several times. Gradually he became less agitated, and at last calm enough to ask questions about what was going on; this led his mind to Captain Hardy, for whom he sent and inquired with great anxiety, exclaiming aloud, he would not believe he was alive, unless he saw him. He grew agitated at the Captain's not coming, lamented his being unable to go on deck, and do what was to be done, and doubted every assurance given him of the Captain's being safe on the quarter-deck. At last the Captain came, and he instantly grew more composed, listened to his report about the state of the Fleet, directed him to anchor, and told him he should die, but observed, he should live half an hour longer. 'I shall die, Hardy,' said the Admiral. 'Is your pain great, Sir?' 'Yes, but I shall live half an hour yet. – Hardy, kiss me!' The Captain knelt down by his side, and kissed him. Upon the Captain leaving him to return to the deck, Lord Nelson exclaimed very earnestly more than once, 'Hardy, if I live I'll bring the Fleet to an anchor; if I live I'll anchor;' and this was earnestly repeated even when the Captain was out of hearing. I do not mean to tell you everything he said. After this interview, the Admiral was perfectly tranquil, looking at me in his accustomed manner when alluding to any prior discourse. 'I have not been a great sinner, Doctor,' said he. 'Doctor, I was right – I told you so – George Rose has not yet got my letter: tell him –' he was interrupted here by pain. After an interval, he said, 'Mr. Rose will remember – don't forget, Doctor: mind what I say.' There were frequent pauses in his conversation.
Source Nicolas, VII, p. 246.

Surgeon Beatty
His Majesty's Ship **Victory**,
15th December 1805

About the middle of the action with the combined fleets, on the 21st of October last, the late illustrious Commander in Chief, Lord Nelson, was mortally wounded in the left breast by a musket ball, supposed to be fired from the mizzen-top of the Redoutable, *French ship of the line, which the* Victory *fell on board of early in the battle. His Lordship was on the act of turning on the quarter-deck, with his face towards the enemy, when he received his wound; he instantly fell, and was carried to the cockpit, where he lay about two hours. On his being brought below, he complained of acute pain about the sixth or seventh dorsal vertebra; of privation of sense, and motion of the body, and inferior extremities; his respiration short and difficult; pulse weak, small and irregular. He frequently declared his back was shot through; that he felt every instant a gush of blood within his breast; and that he had sensations which indicated to him the approach of death. In the course of an hour, his pulse became indistinct, and was gradually lost in the arm; his extremities and forehead became soon afterwards cold: he retained his wonted energy of mind, and exercise of his facilities, until the latest moment of his existence; and when victory, as signal as decisive, was announced to him, he expressed his pious acknowledgements thereof, and heartfelt satisfaction at the glorious event, in the most emphatic language. He then delivered his last orders with his usual precision; and in a few minutes afterwards expired without a struggle.*

Source: Naval Chronicle, III, p. 207.

Below in the cockpit, Nelson used his last hours to impress upon Scott that Emma and his daughter Horatia must be looked after, as he had declared in the codicil to his will. When Hardy next visited it was clear that Nelson was in severe pain. Hardy confirmed that fourteen or fifteen enemy ships had been taken, in typical fashion Nelson replied that he had counted on capturing twenty. Ever the consummate seaman, Nelson still had enough presence of mind to urge Hardy to anchor the fleet after the battle. He then voiced concern that his body might be thrown overboard, to which Hardy reassured him, 'Oh no, certainly not.' He asked Hardy to take care of Emma, then asked him for the famous kiss. The concept of Nelson the hero asking to share a touching and emotional moment with his friend embarrassed the Victorians, giving rise to the belief that he had said '*Kismet* Hardy', kismet being the Turkish word for fate. All the eye-witnesses agree that Nelson said 'Hardy, kiss me', to which Hardy knelt beside his great friend and kissed him on the cheek. Rising, Hardy stood for a moment's contemplation before leaning forward to kiss Nelson on the forehead. 'Who is that?' Nelson inquired. 'It is Hardy'. 'God bless you Hardy,' the Admiral replied.

After Hardy had returned above deck, Nelson was turned on to his right side. His breathing became increasingly difficult as blood flooded into his right lung, his left already being saturated. Scott massaged his chest in a vain effort to help his breathing. Nelson said to him 'Doctor, I have not been a great sinner.

'The Death of Nelson' portrays the dying admiral lying in *Victory*'s cockpit. While capturing the emotion of the scene, many details in the composition are incorrect, most notably the grossly exaggerated height between decks. In reality the cockpit was a cramped and gruesome place. (CPL)

Remember I leave Lady Hamilton and my daughter Horatia as a legacy to my country.' As his speech became more intermittent and confused, he asked for 'Drink, drink' and 'fan, fan'. He then repeated the words 'Thank God I have done my duty', and died so quietly that no one could determine the precise time of death. Beatty was called over and finding no pulse in the wrist, declared him dead at 4.30 p.m.

Next day Nelson's body was briefly examined by Beatty, who confirmed the course of the musket ball but could not find its ultimate resting place. The corpse was then stripped of all but a shirt, placed in a large cask and covered with brandy. The cask was lashed to the deck during the storms which rocked the fleet over the next few days, as new brandy was fed into the top while some was drawn off at the bottom. On the 24th, Beatty informs us 'there was a disengagement of air from the body to such a degree, that the sentinel became alarmed on seeing the head of the cask raised: he therefore applied to the Officers, who were under the necessity of having the cask spiled to give the air a discharge'.[126]

THE STORM

With Nelson dead, command of the British fleet now rested with Collingwood. For him, like many of others who survived the battle of Trafalgar, the worst was yet to come. Statistically, during the age of sail sailors were more at risk from disease, accidents and the general dangers of the sea than from dying in action. The main cause of death was disease, killing 70–80,000 men during the French Revolutionary and Napoleonic Wars, followed by shipwreck and fire, 13,000 men, with combat claiming 6,500 lives. Accidental loss accounted for 101 Royal Naval warships during the wars. It is not surprising that Nelson had been extremely anxious that the British fleet and their prizes should anchor. He could clearly see a storm approaching from the west, a dangerous prospect with the fleet about seven miles off a lee shore at the conclusion of a hard day's fighting.[127]

There was no time for elation, reflection or mourning as the British crews tried desperately to get their own ships and the prizes into a seaworthy condition and into the safety of Gibraltar. With *Belleisle* completely dismasted and the majority of British ships suffering from damage aloft, all those without the ability to anchor were drifting on the heavy swell. The fleet was now in grave danger of being wrecked, undoing all the good work achieved during the afternoon. After hauling up on deck and heaving overboard the bodies of those who had died of their wounds, the crews were set to repairing the material damage. Priority was given to pumping out water, plugging holes between wind and water and setting up 'jury' rigging aloft. The French and Spanish prisoners were held in their captured ships, guarded by British prize crews who also had the responsibility for sailing the heavily damaged ships.

*Clearing after a battle,
William Robinson, HMS
Revenge*

*We were now called to clear the decks, and
here might be witnessed an awful and
interesting scene, for as each officer and
seaman would meet, they were inquiring for
their mess-mates. Orders were now given to
fetch the dead bodies from the after cock-pit,
and throw them over-board; these were the
bodies of men who were taken down to the
doctor during the battle, badly wounded,
and who by the time the engagement was
ended were dead. Some of these, perhaps,
could not have recovered, while others
might, had timely assistance been rendered,
which was impossible; for the rule is, as
order is requisite, that every person shall be
dressed in rotation as they are brought down
wounded, and in many instances some have
bled to death.*

*… we had now a good night's work before
us; all our yards, masts, and sails were sadly
cut, indeed the whole of the sails were
obliged to be unbent, being rendered*

*completely useless, and by the next morning
we were partly jury-rigged: we now began to
look for our prizes, as it was coming on to
blow hard on the land, and Admiral
Collingwood made signals for each ship that
was able to take a prize in tow, to prevent
them drifting into their own harbour, as
they were complete wrecks and
unmanageable.*

*We took an eighty gun Spanish ship in
tow for a day and a night, but were obliged
to cast her off, it blew so hard, and our ship
being so very much disabled, indeed we
were obliged to scuttle a few of them; some
we contrived to take into Gibraltar; some
were wrecked near Cadiz harbour; and
others drifted into the harbour from whence
they had only come out two days before. It
was a mortifying sight to witness the ships
we had fought so hard for, and had taken as
prizes, driven by the elements from our
possession, with some of our own men on
board as prize masters, and it was a great
blight to our victorious success…*
Source: King, pp. 163–4.

Collingwood's controversial decision after the battle to ignore Nelson's instruction to order the fleet to anchor immediately has drawn criticism from contemporaries and historians alike. Codrington was scathing of the decision while the historian Alan Schom notes 'Collingwood arrogantly rescinded that order'.[128] Anchoring immediately might seem to have been the obvious thing to do, giving the crews time to make good sails, masts and rigging. Perhaps Collingwood took a little time to adjust to his new position as commander. Emotionally and mentally exhausted and without his staff, he was extremely concerned at his fleet's close proximity to a dangerous lee shore. Initially he may have wanted to put as much distance between shore and fleet by heading out to sea. Moreover, though many ships were much damaged aloft and would be difficult to move, many had also anchors and cables shot away preventing them from anchoring. Collingwood may have thought that with Gibraltar close by, the fleet could make that safe harbour before the full storm hit. Finally, with repairs well under way at about 9 p.m., Collingwood made the signal for the fleet to anchor.[129] Collingwood himself clearly stated in his dispatch:

…after the action, I shifted my flag to her [*Euryalus*] that I might more easily communicate my orders to, and collect the ships, and towed the *Royal Sovereign* out to seaward. The whole fleet were now in a very perilous situation, many dismasted, all shattered, in thirteen fathom water, off the Shoals of Trafalgar, and when I made the signal to prepare to anchor, few of the ships had an anchor to let go, their cables being shot; but the same good Providence which aided us through such a day, preserved us in the night, by the wind shifting a few points, and drifting the ships off the land.[130]

As Andrew Lambert has concluded, it was 'the right decision in the circumstances'.[131] Most of the ships passed an uncomfortable, but not dangerous first night.

Collingwood was anxious to get the rest of the fleet to the west and away from the shore. Still flying his flag in *Euryalus*, on 22 October he ordered the prizes to rendezvous around the *Royal Sovereign*, currently under tow herself by *Neptune*. But problems started to arise at about 11.30 a.m. when the weather began to degenerate. All the activities of the previous day were put aside as on board the prize ships the French and Spanish were freed to help prevent the ships being destroyed. By evening a full-blown gale had struck the fleet and despite their best efforts three prize ships would not even survive the night of Tuesday 22 October. *Téméraire*'s broadsides had left Lucas' *Redoutable* an absolute wreck. With her pumps out of action and taking in water, at about midday the inevitable conclusion was reached when boats arrived to remove as many of the crew as could be saved. Unfortunately, when she finally slipped beneath the waves at 10 p.m., the majority of her wounded had not been evacuated. British ships

The severely damaged HMS *Victory* limps into the relative safety of Gibraltar under tow from Captain Fremante's *Neptune*. Nelson's body was lying in a cask of brandy lashed to the deck. (National Maritime Museum)

continued to pick up a few more survivors from the water, but the figures alone tell the ordeal that *Redoutable* had endured from British gunnery; of her entire crew of 643 only 169 survived. *Téméraire*'s other prize, the *Fougueux*, the French ship that had fired the first shots of the battle, was taken in tow by the frigate *Phoebe*. During the night the cable separated and *Fougueux* was sent crashing against the shore, the majority of those on board being killed including the thirty-strong prize crew from *Téméraire*. The fifty-man prize crew sent from *Tonnant* to seize the *Algéciras* were rather more fortunate. The French ship was little more than a shattered hulk, dismasted and drifting on the swell towards the shore a mile and a half away. With no ship answering his distress signals, the commander

Vice Admiral Cuthbert Collingwood's Dispatch To William Marsden Esq., Admiralty, London

Euryalus, off Cape Trafalgar, Oct. 22.

Sir, The ever to be lamented death of Vice Admiral Lord Viscount Nelson, who, in the late conflict with the enemy, fell in the hour of victory, leaves to me the duty of informing my Lord Commissioners of the Admiralty, that on the 19th inst. it was communicated to the Commander in Chief from the ships watching the motions of the enemy in Cadiz, that the combined fleet had put to sea; as they sailed with light winds westerly, his Lordship concluded their destination was the Mediterranean, and immediately made all sail for the Streights' entrance, with the British squadron, consisting of twenty-seven ships, three of them sixty-fours, where his Lordship was informed by Captain Blackwood (whose vigilance in watching, and giving notice of the enemy's movements, has been highly meritorious) that they had not yet passed the Streights.

On Monday, the 21st instant, at day light, when Cape Trafalgar bore E. by S. about seven leagues, the enemy was discovered six or seven miles to the eastward, the wind about west, and very light, the Commander in Chief immediately made the signal for the fleet to bear up in two columns, as they are formed in order of sailing; a mode of attack his Lordship had previously directed, to avoid the inconvenience and delay in forming a line of battle in the usual manner. The enemy's line consisted of thirty-three ships (of which 18 were French and 15 Spanish) commanded in chief by Admiral Villeneuve; the Spaniards under the direction of Gravina, wore, with their heads to the northward, and formed the line of battle with great closeness and correctness;– but as the mode of attack was unusual, so the structure of their line was new; it formed a crescent convexing to leeward – so that, in leading down to their centre, I had both their van and rear, abaft the beam; before the fire opened, every alternate ship was about a cable's length to windward of her second a-head, and a-stern, forming a kind of double line, and appeared, when on their beam, to leave a very little interval between them; and this without crowding their ships. Admiral Villeneuve was in the Bucentaure in the centre, and the Prince of Asturias bore Gravina's flag in the rear; but the French and Spanish ships were mixed without any apparent regard to order of national squadron.

As the mode of our attack had been previously determined on, and

of the prize crew, Lieutenant Charles Bennett, was faced with no alternative but to agree to release the prisoners and all on board now set about saving the ship. *Algéciras* was successfully brought into Cadiz harbour, where the prize crew were promptly seized as prisoners of war.

Villeneuve's former flagship *Bucentaure* was not so fortunate. On the evening of the 22nd *Conqueror* made several attempts to take the prize in tow and it is still debated as to whether or not she was successful. What is certain is that *Conqueror* virtually abandoned the prize at about 4.30 p.m. on 23 October, leaving her drifting. With little option the prize crew handed over control of the ship to the French crew, but she ran aground off Cadiz harbour where many of those on board,

communicated to the Flag Officers and Captains, few signals were necessary, and none were made, except to direct close order as the lines bore down. The Commander in Chief in the Victory *led the weather column, and the* Royal Sovereign, *which bore my flag, the lee.*

The action began at twelve o'clock, by the leading ships of the columns breaking through the enemy's line, the Commander in Chief about the tenth ship from the van, the Second in Command about the twelfth from the rear, leaving the van of the enemy unoccupied; the succeeding ships breaking through, in all parts, astern of their leaders, and engaging the enemy at the muzzles of their guns: the conflict was severe; the enemy's ships were fought with a gallantry highly honourable to their officers, but the attack on them was irresistible, and it pleased the Almighty Disposer of all Events, to grant his Majesty's arms a complete and glorious victory.

About three P.M. many of the enemy's ships having struck their colours, their line gave way: Admiral Gravina, with ten ships, joining their frigates to leeward, stood towards Cadiz. The five headmost ships in their van tacked, and standing to the southward, to windward, of the British line, were engaged, and the sternmost of them

taken:-the others went off, leaving to his Majesty's squadron, nineteen ships of the line, (of which two are first-rates, the Santísima Trinidad *and the* Santa Anna) *with three Flag Officers, viz. Admiral Villeneuve, the Commander in Chief, Don Ignatio Maria D'Aliva, Vice Admiral, and the Spanish Rear Admiral Don Baltazar Hidalgo Cisneros.*

After such a victory it may appear unnecessary to enter into encomiums on the particular parts taken by the several Commanders; the conclusion says more on the subject than I have language to express; the spirit which animated all was the same; when all exerted themselves zealously in their country's service, all deserve that their high merits should stand recorded; and never was high merit more conspicuous than in the battle I have described.

The Achille (a French 74), after having surrendered, by some mismanagement of the Frenchmen took fire and blew up; two hundred of her men were saved by the tenders. A circumstance occurred during the action, which so strongly marks the invincible spirit of British seamen, when engaging the enemies of their country, that I cannot resist the pleasure I have in making it known to their Lordships; the Temeraire was boarded by accident, or design, by a

including the British prize crew, were rescued by two of Cosmao-Kerjulien's ships.

A member of the prize crew aboard *Monarca*, Midshipman Henry Walker of *Bellerophon* was more lucky. He later recalled how he had 'felt not the least fear of death during the action'. But once aboard the prize he reflected:

> …upon the approach of death either from the rising of the Spaniards upon so small a number as we were composed of, or what latterly appeared inevitable from the violence of the storm, I was most certainly afraid, and at one time, when the ship had made over three feet of water in ten minutes, when our people were lying almost drunk on deck, when the Spaniards, completely worn out with fatigue, would no longer work at the only chain pump left serviceable;

French ship on one side, and a Spaniard on the other; the contest was vigorous, but, in the end, the combined ensigns were torn from the poop, and the British hoisted in their places. [Later proved to be false.]

Such a battle could not be fought without sustaining a great loss of men. I have not only to lament in common with the British Navy, and the British Nation, in the fall of the Commander in Chief, the loss of a Hero, whose name will be immortal, and his memory ever dear to his country; but my heart is rent with the most poignant grief for the death of a friend, to whom, by many years intimacy, and a perfect knowledge of the virtues of his mind, which inspired ideas superior to the common race of men, I was bound by the strongest ties of affection; a grief to which even the glorious occasion in which he fell, does not bring the consolation which perhaps it ought; his Lordship received a musket ball in his left breast, about the middle of the action, and sent an officer to me immediately with his last farewell; and soon after expired. I have also to lament the loss of those excellent officers, Captains Duff, of the Mars, *and Cooke, of the* Bellerophon; *I have yet heard of no others.*

I fear the numbers that have fallen will be found very great, when the returns come to

me; but it having blown a gale of wind ever since the action, I have not yet had it in my power to collect any reports from the ships. The Royal Sovereign *having lost her masts, except the tottering foremast, I called the* Euryalus *to me, while the action continued, which ship lying within hail, made my signals, a service Captain Blackwood performed with great attention; after the action, I shifted my flag to her, that I might more easily communicate my orders to, and collect the ships, and towed the* Royal Sovereign *out to seaward. The whole fleet were now in a very perilous situation, many dismasted, all shattered, in thirteen fathom water, off the Shoals of Trafalgar, and when I made the signal to prepare to anchor, few of the ships had an anchor to let go, their cables being shot; but the same good Providence which aided us through such a day, preserved us in the night, by the wind shifting a few points, and drifting the ships off the land.*

Having thus detailed the proceedings of the fleet on this occasion, I beg to congratulate their Lordships on a victory, which, I hope will add a ray to the glory of his Majesty's Crown, and be attended with public benefit to our country.
Source: Collingwood, pp. 119-23.

when I saw the fear of death so strongly depicted on the countenances of all around me, I wrapped myself up in a Union Jack and lay down upon the deck.[132]

The *Orion* came to the timely rescue of *Monarca* and, but relief was short lived as the Spanish ship was wrecked on 25 October..

On 23 October the wind blew even harder than the previous day and the situation in some of the shattered British ships was just as bad as in the prizes. Most importantly, *Victory* was in great danger. Having led the attack of the Weather Line, the flagship had been subjected to a fearsome fire from the French and Spanish ships. She had many holes between wind and water, a great deal of damage to the hull superstructure and her pumps were working furiously to combat the twelve inches of water per hour she was taking in. With a storm in the offing she had much damage aloft to repair:

The mizzen mast shot away about nine feet from the deck; the main mast shot through and sprung; the main yard gone; main topmast and cap shot in different places and reefed, the main topsail yard shot away; the foremast shot through in a number of different places and is at present supported by a topmast and part of the topsail and crossjack yards; the fore yard shot away; the bowsprit jibboom and cap shot, and the spritsail, spritsail yards, and flying boom are gone; the fore and main tops damaged…

While the carpenter plugged the shot holes the men worked aloft to hoist a jury rig. On the 24th the weather degenerated and *Polyphemus* took *Victory* in tow. Next day the crew managed to hoist more temporary masts and sails, but on the 26th the storm damaged some of the jury rigging and masts, and the tow cable was cut because *Victory* was becoming increasingly unmanageable. Taken in tow again, this time by *Neptune*, on the 27th Fremantle set course for Gibraltar.[133]

Aboard *Belleisle*, the only completely dismasted British ship, the crew worked tirelessly to hoist temporary masts on which to set at least some canvas. Taken in tow by the frigate *Naiad*, they set sail for Gibraltar after the battle. But as the storm intensified during the night of the 23rd, *Belleisle* was battered by the wind, water rushed in through her ports and over her sides, a 24pdr gun broke loose and careered across the deck. The shattered hulk parted her tow cable on more than one occasion while those on board listened for the terrifying sound of surf crashing onto the rocks. At 3.30 a.m. next day, with the hawser having again parted, breakers could be seen about a mile to leeward. Fortunately the jury rig held and she wore away from certain destruction before *Naiad* could take her back in tow. At 1.20 p.m., much to the relief of all on board, *Belleisle* was the first battleship from Trafalgar to anchor at Gibraltar.

Cosmao-Kerjulien's Sortie

The British efforts to save their own ships as well as the prizes were hampered by a sortie from Cadiz by a number of French and Spanish ships. Occurring right in the middle of the worst of the storm, the squadron under the remaining senior officer, the gallant and aggressive Commodore Jean Marie Cosmao-Kerjulien forced the British ships to prepare for action once more. Cosmao-Kerjulien's ship was the *Pluton* and his actions on 22 July in supporting his Spanish comrades meant that he was probably the only French officer the Spaniards truly respected. On the morning of 23 October, with the wind shifting round to the north-west, he decided to take advantage of the conditions and attempt to retake some of the prizes now in the hands of the British.

Collecting a small squadron of *Pluton*, *Indomptable*, *Neptune*, *Rayo* and *San Francisco de Asís*, with the five frigates and a couple of brigs, he cleared Cadiz harbour on the morning of 23 October. Approaching the British fleet at about midday, he saw the British respond by abandoning the prizes and, with ten of the least damaged vessels, form a line of battle between himself and the drifting prize ships. By now the wind had increased and moved round to west-south-west, and an attack against such numbers in the rapidly degenerating conditions was out of the question. However, two of the prizes, *Neptuno* and *Santa Ana*, were lying close enough to allow Cosmao-Kerjulien's frigates to isolate them from the main British fleet. They were retaken and eventually limped back into Cadiz.

As well as losing *Neptuno* and *Santa Ana*, the sortie had prevented the British from reaping the full benefits of the battle. With Cosmao-Kerjulien approaching his fleet, Collingwood, in the middle of the storm, was faced with little option but to abandon, scuttle or burn the prize ships rather than see them recaptured. With the signal to destroy the prizes made at 9 a.m., the British crews were faced with the horrible task of trying to rescue the many wounded aboard the prize ships.

The *Santísma Trinidad*, under tow by *Prince*, had already parted her hawser more than once and was being kept afloat with great difficulty when the signal came. Setting her loose, *Prince*, assisted by *Ajax* and *Neptune*, managed to rescue 500 men and the ship's cat before cutting her anchor cables and scuttling the once mighty ship. *Conqueror* had spotted the *Bahama* drifting helplessly to the south on the morning after the battle. She was taken in tow by *Orion*, and Codrington set a course for Gibraltar. Next morning the swell was driving the two ships towards land and Codrington, pushing his anchor cables to the maximum depth, took the decision to anchor. Witnessing Cosmao-Kerjulien's sortie, he cut the hawser, hoping the prize could make it to safety without falling into enemy hands. When Cosmao-Kerjulien returned to Cadiz, *Orion* took *Bahama* back under tow, but when the worst of the storm hit he had to cut the cable again, setting the prize adrift. Luckily, *Bahama* fell in with the *Donegal*, part of Louis' squadron, and was taken safely into Gibraltar.

Several of *Revenge*'s crew had been sent to help with the pumps to keep the prize *Argonauta* afloat. Once on board they found a 'scene of carnage horrid to behold: there were a number of their dead bodies piled up in the hold; many, in a wounded or mutilated state, were found lying amongst them'. Unable to stem the flooding in the rising gale, at about 10 a.m. *Revenge* had to let the prize go. Even when boats from *Defiance* and *Melpomene* provided assistance, not all of the Spanish crew could be taken off; those remaining were left in a grim situation. *Defiance* was still in company with *Aigle*, but a tow rope could not be attached and the prize was left to drift towards shore, eventually reaching the safety of Cadiz.

Of the total captures made on the afternoon of 21 October, only one French and three Spanish ships made it back to England as prizes. Once the prize ships had been released there was no way to get them back under-tow. Many French and Spanish men could not be saved and vanished beneath the waves with their ships. The cost to Cosmao-Kerjulien was also high. On the 24th *Indomptable* grounded off Rota and was smashed to bits in the surf; of 1,000 men on board only 100 made it ashore. The *San Francisco de Asís* went aground off Cadiz. To escape the same fate, *Rayo* anchored, but lost her masts and had to surrender to the *Donegal*. Her salvation was temporary, being driven ashore on 26 October.

With Cosmao-Kerjulien back in Cadiz and the storm abating, Collingwood could turn his mind to urgent matters within the fleet. A major concern was the numbers

---

Loss of the Redoutable

Extract from Captain Lucas to the Minister of Marine

We spent the whole of that night [21 October] at the two pumps which were all that remained workable, without, however, being able to keep the water under. The few Frenchmen who were able to do duty joined with the English party on board in pumping, stopped several leaks, blocked up the port holes and boarded in the poop of the ship, which was ready to cave in. Indeed, no toil was too hard for them. In the middle of all the turmoil and horrible disorder on board, just keeping the ship above water, with the 'tween-decks and batteries encumbered with dead, I noticed some of my brave fellows, particularly the young midshipmen, of whom several were wounded, picking up arms which they hid on the lower deck, with the intention, as they said, of retaking the ship. Never were so many traits of intrepidity, of valour and daring, displayed on board a single ship; the whole history of our navy can show nothing like them.

Next morning the captain of the Swiftsure *sent a boat to take me on board, together with Lieutenant Dupotet and Midshipman Ducrest, and we were duly conducted there. At noon the* Redoutable *lost her foremast, the only mast she had left. At five in the evening the water continued so to gain on the pumps that the prizemaster made signals of distress, and all the boats of the* Swiftsure *were lowered to rescue the crew. It was blowing very hard at the time, and the sea ran very high, which made the getting out of the wounded very difficult. These poor fellows, on its being seen that the ship was going down, were nearly all brought up and laid on the quarter-deck. They were able to save several of them. At seven in the evening the poop was entirely submerged. The* Redoutable *sank with a large number of the wounded still on board. They met their death with courage worthy of a better fate. A hundred and sixty-nine men, forming the remainder of the brave crew of the* Redoutable, *found themselves together on board the English ship. Seventy of the number were badly wounded and sixty-four of the rest had less serious wounds. All the wounded were sent into Cadiz under a flag of truce, and in the end only thirty-five men from the* Redoutable *were taken to England as prisoners of war.*
Source: Fraser (1906), pp. 170–3.

Collingwood to W Marsden
Euryalus, *off Cadiz,*
24 October, 1805

In my letter of the 22nd I detailed to you, for the information of my Lords Commissioners of the Admiralty, the proceedings of His Majesty's squadron on the day of the action and that preceding it; since which I have had a continued series of misfortunes; but they are of a kind that human prudence could not possible provide against, or my skill prevent.

On the 22nd, in the morning, a strong southerly wind blew, with squally weather, which, however, did not prevent the activity of the officers and seamen of such ships as were manageable from getting hold of many of the prizes (thirteen or fourteen), and towing them off to westward, where I ordered them to rendezvous round the Royal Sovereign, in tow by the Neptune. But on the 23rd the gale increased, and the sea ran so high that many of them broke the tow-rope, and drifted far to leeward before they were got hold of again; and some of them, taking advantage of the dark and boisterous night, got before the wind, and have perhaps drifted upon the shore and sunk. On the afternoon of that day, the remnant of the combined fleet, ten sail of ships, which had not been much engaged, stood up to leeward of my shattered and straggling charge, as if meaning to attack them, which obliged me to collect a force out of the least injured ships, and form to leeward for their defence. All this retarded the progress of the hulks; and the bad weather continuing, determined me to destroy all the leewardmost that could be cleared of the men, considering that keeping possession of the ships was a matter of little consequence, compared with the chance of their falling into the hands of the enemy; but even this was an arduous task in the high sea which was running. I hope, however, it has been accomplished to a considerable extent. I intrusted it to skilful officers, who would spare no pains to execute what was possible. The captains of the Prince and Neptune cleared the Trinidad, and sunk her. Captains Hope, Bayntun, and Malcolm, who joined the fleet this morning, from Gibraltar, had the charge of destroying four others. The

HMS *Victory* jury rigged. (Warwick Leadlay Gallery)

Redoutable sunk astern of the Swiftsure,
while in tow. The Santa Anna *I have no
doubt is sunk, as her side is almost entirely
beat in; and such is the shattered conditions
of the whole of them, that, unless the weather
moderates, I doubt whether I shall be able to
carry a ship of them into port. I hope their
Lordships will approve of what I (having only
in consideration the destruction of the
enemy's fleet) have thought a measure of
absolute necessary.*

*I have taken Admiral Villeneuve into this
ship. Whenever the temper of the weather
will permit, and I can spare a frigate (for
there were only four in the action with the
fleet,* Euryalus, Sirius, Phœbe *and* Naiad;
the Melponeme *joined the 22nd, and the*
Eurydice *and* Scout *the 23rd), I shall collect
the other flag-officers, and send them to
England with their flags (if they do not go to
the bottom) to be laid at His Majesty's feet.*

*There were two thousand troops embarked,
under the command of General Contamin,
who was taken with Admiral Villeneuve in
the* Bucentaure.

Source: Collingwood, pp. 133–5.

of Spanish wounded aboard the British ships. Accordingly he wrote to the Marquis de Solana, Governor of Cadiz on 27 October, requesting that boats be sent out to receive them and transfer them to hospitals ashore. Responding to this compassionate gesture, Solana replied next day, indicating that he would send out the frigates of the Combined Fleet to receive the wounded. He also requested that all the Spanish and French prisoners be sent into Cadiz on parole. In exchange he determined to send out all the fit British officers and seamen who had been in the prizes that had been blown or sailed into Cadiz or had been shipwrecked on the shore during the storm. Any that were ill would be looked after until recovered.[134] Collingwood eventually handed over to the Spanish authorities in Cadiz 1,087 wounded Spaniards, 253 wounded Frenchmen, plus 210 Spanish officers and 4,589 Spanish seamen taken prisoner and now released on parole. Nearly 3,000 French prisoners, including Villeneuve, Magendie, Infernet and Lucas, were conveyed to England.

The heavily damaged ships of the British fleet now began to arrive at Gibraltar. On 28 October *Tonnant, Revenge, Colossus, Thunderer, Bellerophon* and *Victory* arrived, the latter bearing the preserved body of Lord Nelson. *Royal Sovereign, Defiance* towing *Téméraire* and *Orion* arrived on 2 November. That day the first prize arrived, *San Ildefonso* assisted by the *Defence*. The other three remaining prizes arrived shortly, the French *Swiftsure*, and the Spanish *Bahama* and *San Juan Nepomuceno*. After organising temporary repairs to the most damaged ships, those that had led the two lines, Collingwood began to send them home for more extensive work. On 5 November *Belleisle, Victory* and *Bellerophon* began their journey home, escorted by the frigate *Boadicea*. Four days later *Revenge, Mars, Defence* and four other 74s were under way. They were followed on 19 November by *Royal Sovereign, Téméraire, Leviathan, Colossus, Tonnant* and *Spartiate*. Collingwood, now flying his flag in the 98-gun *Queen*, sailed on 22 November with *Prince, Dreadnought, Orion, Swiftsure* and *Thunderer*, to continue the relentless naval war by blockading a Spanish fleet in Cartagena.

SIR RICHARD STRACHAN'S ACTION

On 21 October four French ships from the van of the Combined Fleet, under the command of Rear Admiral Dumanoir de Pelley, had escaped the battle largely intact. His flagship, the 80-gun *Formidable,* was last seen heading south followed by the three 74s *Duguay Trouin, Mont-Blanc* and *Scipion,* towards the Straits of Gibraltar and presumably on to Toulon. In fact Dumanoir had turned north on the 25th to head for Rochefort where a squadron under Zachaire Allemand was stationed. At this moment Allemand was at sea wreaking havoc among British merchantmen and threatening homeward and outward bound convoys. It was essential that these two fleets be prevented from joining together.

There were several detached squadrons searching for these missing ships. With intelligence that Allemand had been seen in the Bay of Biscay heading northwards towards the end of October, Captain Thomas Baker's *Phoenix* came upon several enemy ships off Cape Finisterre on 2 November. Setting a course for Dumanoir's ships, Baker was fired at and chased away by *Duguay Trouin,* but he remained in contact with the enemy squadron until he could find a British fleet. But Baker's was not the only frigate at sea looking for Allemand; *Boadicea* and *Dryad* had also stumbled across the Trafalgar survivors. In attempting to chase the squadron these two frigates were outrun by Dumanoir who made to flee the area for the safety of Ferrol.

In fact, on 2 November Dumanoir, his ships still taking in water despite attempts to stem the leaks, had actually passed inshore of a British squadron under the command of the energetic but headstrong Sir Richard Strachan. Unaware of the battle of Trafalgar and the escape of Dumanoir, Strachan had taken up a position off Cape Finisterre in case Villeneuve tried to bring the Combined Fleet north.

Phoenix now made contact with Strachan's flagship, the 80-gun *Caesar*, passing on the information that he thought he had seen Allemand. Strachan took up the chase and *Phoenix* was tasked with collecting the scattered British squadron. Hoping to prevent the French fleet getting into Ferrol during the night of 2 November, Strachan maintained his pursuit, despite losing Dumanoir in the thick weather on more than one occasion. At dawn on the 3rd the enemy could still be seen fleeing in the distance. Baker had managed to round up several of the British ships, so that Strachan now had four ships-of-the-line: *Caesar, Hero, Courageux* and *Namur*, but the 74-gun *Bellona* lagged behind the faster vessels and took no part in the ensuing action.

Using his four frigates, *Santa Margarita, Æolus, Révolutionnaire* as well as the *Phoenix*, to pursue and slow Dumanoir's flight, by noon on 3 November Strachan had closed the distance to about fourteen miles. Three hours later the fast *Phoenix* and *Santa Margarita* were catching up with Dumanoir's rearmost ship, *Scipion*. With Strachan blocking passage to Ferrol, Dumanoir decided to cross the Bay of Biscay and make for Rochefort.

Daybreak on 4 November found *Phoenix* and *Santa Margarita* within range of *Scipion*, with *Caesar* a little farther astern. Utilising superior mobility, speed and seamanship, the frigates avoided *Scipion*'s heavy broadside guns, hanging off her blind spots on her stern quarters, while sending shot into the rigging and sails of the French ship to slow her down. Strachan's chasing ships-of-the-line were now about six miles astern of Dumanoir and closing fast. Forming into line ahead, by 11.45 a.m. Strachan's *Caesar, Hero* and *Courageux*, with *Namur* trailing fourteen miles behind, were so close that Dumanoir was forced to turn and form a line of battle or risk losing *Scipion*.

Instead of following the orthodox practice of his lead ship engaging the windward enemy ship, the rest of the attack then passing under cover of the first ship and engaging the next ahead in the enemy line, Strachan attacked *à la* Nelson. He aimed to crush the centre and rear of the French line, his heaviest ship *Caesar* leading the attack and aiming for the French flagship *Formidable*. *Hero* and *Courageux* made for the *Mont-Blanc* and the much-beleaguered *Scipion*, respectively. The attack began at about midday. *Caesar* opened fire fifteen minutes later and *Hero* and *Courageux* shortly after that. At 12.50 p.m. Strachan hoisted the signal for close action. Five minutes later Dumanoir signalled the squadron to tack in succession. At the head of the line *Duguay Trouin* tacked to starboard, taking up a raking position across *Caesar*'s bows but was foiled by a swift counter movement. *Caesar* and *Hero* now fired upon *Duguay Trouin* at close range while the rest of the French fleet manoeuvred to provide support. In executing the movement *Formidable* moved from third to second in the line and despite some difficulties Dumanoir's squadron had shifted to the port tack in an attempt to shake of their assailants. Strachan's ships followed suit at 1.20 p.m., but with *Caesar* slowing because of damage aloft, he signalled the fast-arriving *Namur* to head straight for the enemy van while instructing *Hero* to lead the attack of his three other ships.

Just before 2 p.m. the next round began with *Hero* emptying a starboard broadside into *Scipion*, bringing down the main topmast. *Scipion* drifted a little to leeward and was engaged from windward by *Courageux* and from leeward by the frigates *Phoenix* and *Revolutionnaire*, the latter having come up during the course of the first encounter. *Hero* now closed with and fired into *Formidable* until 2.45 p.m. when *Namur* arrived to take her place, *Hero* moving on to tackle *Mont-Blanc*. With *Caesar* coming back into the fight and about to fire into *Formidable*, the French flagship struck, followed shortly by the *Scipion*. *Duguay Trouin* and *Mont-Blanc* had begun to form another line ahead of *Scipion*, but on seeing their comrades surrender the two ships fled. It did not take long for *Hero* and *Caesar* to overhaul them and, after 20 minutes of hard pounding, forced them to surrender at about 4 p.m.

Dumanoir was criticised for attempting to flee rather than turning to fight Strachan before *Namur* arrived on the scene, but perhaps it was too much to expect such aggressive tactics from someone who had recently seen at close hand the superiority of British gunnery and seamanship. Moreover, Dumanoir was outnumbered in frigates, four to nil, of which the British made great use. Finally *Formidable* had been shorn of fifteen of her guns, three of which had been put out of action at Trafalgar, while another twelve had been heaved over the side to lighten the ship during Strachan's pursuit.

The harassment and slowing down of *Scipion* caused by the masterful attacks of *Phoenix* and *Santa Margarita* forced Dumanoir to turn back and attempt to save his rearmost ship. This cost him the squadron and the lives of 750 killed and wounded men, Dumanoir himself being among the latter. Strachan's ships lost a total of 24 killed and 111 wounded, further testimony to the superiority of British close-quarter gunnery. The four captured ships had suffered damage aloft: *Duguay Trouin* and *Scipion* were completely dismasted, *Formidable* and *Mont-Blanc* had only their foremasts standing. They were all taken into the Royal Navy, *Duguay Trouin* being renamed *Implacable*. She was one of the last remaining wooden walls, but was scuttled in post-war cutbacks in 1949, her stern flying the white ensign and tricolour as she slipped beneath the waves.

On 4 November 1805 Sir Richard Strachan fell in with Dumanoir's survivors from Trafalgar. Attacking *à la* Nelson, Strachan seized four French battleships. (From Jenkins' *Naval Achievements* reprinted by Sim Comfort Associates)

For mopping-up one of the loose ends after Trafalgar, Strachan, already a hereditary baronet, was awarded the Order of the Bath and granted £1,000 a year. His promotion after the battle to flag rank, as Rear Admiral, was due entirely to seniority. After his celebrated action Strachan was appointed to command the naval element of a disastrous attack on Walcheren in 1809, which cost thousands of British lives for little material gain. The exploits of Strachan and the Army commander, the Earl of Chatham, with whom Strachan regularly quarrelled, were 'celebrated' by an anonymous wit:

Great Chatham with his sabre drawn
Stood waiting for Sir Richard Strachan
Sir Richard, longing to be at 'em
Stood waiting for the Earl of Chatham.

It is interesting to note that until Dumanoir actually set foot aboard *Caesar*, Strachan thought he was fighting a part of Allemand's squadron. In fact Allemand, evading all the squadrons looking for him, returned to Rochefort on 25 December 1805. Now aboard *Caesar*, Dumanoir could inform Strachan of the general outcome of the battle fought on 21 October. At the same time as Strachan was finding out about the great engagement off Cape Trafalgar, people at home in England were just about to hear the glorious but tragic news.

Key

British

1 Caesar
2 Hero
3 Courageux
4 Namur

French

5 Duguay Trouin
6 Formidable
7 Mont Blanc
8 Scipion

About 11am

About 12 noon

About 1 pm

About 1·30 pm

About 2·45 pm

Strachan's action. (CPL)

The News of Trafalgar Arrives in England

Entering Falmouth harbour on the morning of 4 November 1805 was the schooner *Pickle* under the command of Lieutenant John Lapenotière. Keen observers would have noticed that she was flying the signal 'I have urgent dispatches'. Because of the storms off Trafalgar it was not until 9.00 a.m. on 26 October that Collingwood could order Lapenotière to his flagship to take dispatches to the Admiralty. Blackwood in *Euryalus* had hoped he would be the bearer of the news, but Collingwood needed all the frigates to remain with the fleet. Built in Bermuda and taken into the Royal Navy in 1800, the small 120-ton *Pickle* was a very fast ship. Lapenotière had played no material part in the battle of 21 October, but in the aftermath *Pickle* had dragged more than a hundred men from the water and had saved a French woman named Jeanette. Lapenotière had made Lieutenant in 1794, but without a great deal of patronage had spent most of the next eleven years in cutters and schooners, joining *Pickle* in 1802. Boarding Collingwood's flagship that morning, he knew that it was tradition that the bearer of dispatches from a successful battle would receive promotion and honours.

Captain Sir Richard Strachan to the Honourable William Cornwallis, Admiral of the White, and Commander in Chief

Caesar, *west of Rochefort 264 miles, November 4, 1805, wind S.E.*

Sir, Being off Ferrol, working to westward, with the wind westerly, on the evening of the 2d we observed a frigate in the N.W. making signals; made all sail to join her before night, and followed by the ships named in the margin, [Caesar, Hero, Courageux, *and* Namur. Bellona, Æolus, Santa Margarita, *far to leeward in the south-east.*] *we came up with her at eleven at night; and in the moment she joined us, we saw six large ships near us. Captain Baker informed me he had been chased by the Rochefort squadron, then close to leeward of us. We were delighted. I desired him to tell the captains of the ships of the line astern to follow me, as I meant to engage them directly; and immediately bore away in the* Caesar *for the purpose, making all the signals I could, to indicate our movements to our ships; the moon enabled us to se the enemy bear away in line abreast, closely formed; but we lost sight of them when it set, and I was obliged to reduce our sails, the* Hero, Courageux, *and* Æolus, *being the only ships I could see. We continued steering to the E.N.E. all night, and in the morning observed the* Santa Margarita *near us; at nine we discovered the enemy of four sail of the line in the N.E. under full sail. We had also everything set, and came up with them fast; in the evening we observed three sail*

astern; and the Phoenix *spoke me at night. I found that active officer, Captain Baker, had delivered my orders, and I sent him on to assist the* Santa Margarita *in leading us up to the enemy. At day-light we were near them, and the* Santa Margarita *had begun in a very gallant manner to fire upon their rear, and was soon joined by the* Phoenix.

A little before noon, the French finding an action unavoidable, began to take in their small sails, and form in a line, bearing on the starboard tack; we did the same; and I communicated my intentions, by hailing the captains, "that I should attack the centre and rear," and at noon began the battle: in a short time the van ship of the enemy tacked, which almost directly made the action close and general; the Namur *joined soon after we tacked, which we did as soon as we could get the ships round, and I directed her by signal to engage the van; at half past three the action ceased, the enemy having fought to admiration, and not surrendering till their ships were unmanageable. I have returned thanks to the captains of the ships of the line and the frigates, and they speak in high terms of approbation of their officers and ships' companies. If anything could add to the good opinion I had already formed of the officers and crew of the* Caesar, *it is their gallant conduct in this day's battle. The enemy have suffered much, but our ships not more than is to be expected on these occasions. You may judge of my surprise, Sir, when I found the ships we had taken were not the Rochefort squadron, but from Cadiz. Source: Naval Chronicle, vol. III, p. 241.*

Pickle and Lapenotière lived up to Collingwood's expectations, making the passage to Falmouth of more than 1,000 miles in just eight days. With fast horses to cover the 260 miles to London, he presented himself at the Admiralty at about 1 a.m. on 6 November, greeting the Secretary William Marsden with the words: 'Sir, we have gained a great victory. But we have lost Lord Nelson.' In view of Barham's ire at not being roused four months earlier when *Curieux* had arrived with dispatches, Marsden wasted no time in waking the First Lord and informing him of the news. It must have been with mixed emotions that Barham read the first words of the opening paragraph: 'The ever to be lamented death of Vice Admiral Lord Viscount Nelson, who, in the late conflict with the enemy, fell in the hour of victory.' Reading on, Barham would have immediately realised the magnitude of victory that had been achieved by the late, great Admiral. In a short time copies of Collingwood's dispatch were rushed off to King George III, the Cabinet and the press.

As the news spread the nation reacted with shock. Nelson's loss seemed to overshadow the great victory that had been achieved. In London a *'Gazette Extraordinary'* was published on 6 November printing Collingwood's dispatches, which were also printed in *The Times* of 7 November, which did not know 'whether to mourn or rejoice' at the news. The battle was 'the most splendid and decisive Victory that has ever graced the naval annals of England: but it has been dearly purchased. *The great and gallant Nelson is no more'*.[135] The Covent Garden Theatre provided a 'hasty, but elegant' compliment, consisting of the principal actors, surrounded by medallion of the 'Naval Heroes of Great Britain', casting their eyes to the heavens 'from whence a half-length portrait of Lord Nelson descended'. All across London lights appeared in windows as a signal for mourning. The main thoroughfares organised a 'general blaze of refulgence'. Perhaps fittingly for someone as conscious about his public image as Nelson had been, the theatres took the lead in commemorating the great hero. At Drury Lane transparent lamps spelled out the late Admiral's initials, 'LN' placed over an anchor and all enveloped in a wreath. The Covent Garden Theatre 'presented a brilliant 'N', surmounted by an anchor in gold-coloured lamps'.[136]

It was reported that on hearing the news King George III was stunned to absolute silence for five minutes while other members of the Royal Family wept. On 7 November the King issued a Royal Proclamation giving thanks 'to Almighty God for the recent and signal interposition of His good Providence'. It finished by declaring 'a General Thanksgiving to Almighty God for these His mercies be observed throughout those parts of our United Kingdom called England and Ireland, on Thursday the fifth day of December'.[137]

The diplomat Lord Malmesbury exclaimed 'not one individual who felt joy at this victory, so well-timed and complete, but first had an instinctive feeling of sorrow… I never saw so little public joy.' He had dined with Pitt the night after the news arrived. He recalled that the Prime Minister had confided that he had been called up at various hours in his eventful life by the arrival of news of various hues, but that, whether good or bad, he could always lay his head on his pillow and sleep again. On this occasion, however, the great event announced brought with it so much to weep over, as well as to rejoice at, that he could not calm his thoughts, but at length

'Britons! Your Nelson is dead!' In many of the official publications and private reports the sense of shock at the loss of Nelson is tangible. Even Collingwood's post battle dispatch began by mentioning the death of Nelson before detailing that a great victory had been won at Trafalgar. (Warwick Leadlay Gallery)

got up, though it was three in the morning'.[138] On hearing the news, John Henry Slessor of the 35th Sussex Regiment of Foot confided in his diary: 'Great rejoicings for the Battle of Trafalgar, tho' a victory dearly purchased by the death of the immortal Nelson. His memory must ever be dear to an Englishman.'[139]

As the bearer of successful dispatches Lapenotière was made commander. The Lloyds Patriotic Fund presented him with a sword of honour. He went on to serve at the bombardment of Copenhagen in 1807, and was finally promoted to captain in 1811. He was not the only beneficiary in the aftermath of Trafalgar as rewards and promotions were handed out *en masse*, creating a log-jam of senior officers that would cause problems for years to come. In an extraordinary move the Admiralty created a new flag grade, Rear Admiral of the Red. Collingwood was made a Baron, given £2,000 per annum for life and promoted from Vice Admiral of the Blue to Vice Admiral of the Red, with the Earl of Northesk moving up from Rear Admiral of the White to Rear Admiral of the Red. The two acting commanders, Lieutenants Pilford and Stockham, of *Ajax* and *Thunderer* respectively, were both made Captain on 25 December. Behind them on the list of seniority were two Lieutenants who had taken command of their ships upon the death of their captains: William Hennah of *Mars* and William Cumby of *Bellerophon* were both promoted on 1 January 1806. Promoted to commander, an intermediary before captain, were Lieutenants John Pascoe, Edward Williams and John Yule, all from *Victory*. The flagship's First Lieutenant, John Quillan, was made commander and then captain. All the First Lieutenants present at Trafalgar were promoted to commander.

On 3 December a Special Meeting of the Committee of the Patriotic Fund, held at Lloyds Coffee House, resolved to make a plethora of rewards. Lady Viscountess Nelson, Earl Nelson and Collingwood all were to receive specially commissioned vases worth £500. Northesk and Strachan were to receive vases valued at £300. The surviving ships' captains were each to be presented with a ceremonial sword costing £100. Lieutenants, Captains of Marines and other second class officers were to be awarded £100 if severely wounded and £50 if slightly wounded. Each severely wounded third-class officer was to receive £50 or £30 if slightly wounded. Fourth class officers were to be presented with £40 for a severe wound and £25 for a slight wound. All seamen and marines who had lost a limb or suffered some other form of permanent disability were awarded £40; if only severely wounded £20, or if slightly wounded £10. Moreover, the Committee decided to offer relief to all those widows, parents and orphans of men who had fallen in the action.

Nelson's brother, the Reverend William, was raised to the peerage as Baron Nelson of the Nile and Burnham Thorpe and was also created Viscount Merton and Earl Nelson of Trafalgar and Merton. William was provided with £90,000 to buy a suitable estate to match his titles and a pension of £5,000 per annum. The two women in Nelson's life fared a lot worse. Nelson had cut Josiah Nisbet and Fanny, now the Dowager Viscountess Nelson and Duchess of Bronte, completely out of his will. Nevertheless, Fanny was granted by Parliament £2,000 per annum until her death in 1831. In the codicil to his will, Nelson left Emma and Horatia to the care of the nation. They received nothing. Emma rapidly fell into debt, and despite selling the house at Merton, was incarcerated. Attempting to start a new life in France, and accompanied only by Horatia, she died in poverty at Calais in January 1815. Horatia returned to England and in 1822 married Philip Ward in Burnham. She named her eldest son Horatio Nelson Ward, but denied she was Emma Hamilton's daughter until her death in 1881 at the age of 80.

Lady Bessborough to Granville Leveson Gower,
6 November 1805

Good heavens! What news! How glorious if it was not so cruelly damp'd by Nelson's death! How truly he has accomplished his prediction that when they meet it must be to extermination. To a man like him he could not have pick'd out a finer close to such a life. But what an irreparable loss to England! I wish they would do what the Courier proposes – order a general mourning for him. Courage and perseverance like his cannot be too highly honour'd and it will encourage others to follow his noble career of glory. I can think of nothing else, and hardly imagin'd it possible to feel so much grief for a Man I did not know. Mr. Mander says he liv'd to hear of his Victory, and gave signs of joy tho' he could not speak. Do you know, G., it makes me feel almost as much envy as compassion; I think I should like to die so. Think of being mourn'd by a whole Nation, and having my name carried down with gratitude and praise to the latest generations.

Source: Leveson Gower, II, p.131.

EPILOGUE –
NELSON'S FUNERAL

HMS *Victory*, carrying the body of Lord Nelson, arrived at Spithead on 4 December. All the ships lying in the anchorage and the harbour lowered their flags and pendants to half-mast in respect. The next day the nation observed the General Day of Thanksgiving: 'All the Churches and Chapels were crowded; all distinctions of sects were done away; and Christian, Jew, Catholic and Protestant, all united in the expression of one feeling of piety and gratitude to the Almighty'. Collections were held for the wounded, the widows and orphans of the dead, the total received was in excess of £100,000.[140]

On 10 December, after more running repairs, *Victory* sailed for the Thames. Hit by gales, she anchored off Dover in the evening of 12 December. On the 15th Nelson's body was removed from the cask and laid in a plain elm coffin. Apart from a small amount of discoloration to his left ankle, the brandy had done its job; his body was excellently preserved. Reaching the Downs on the 17th, some visitors were allowed on board to view the body. *Victory* sailed for the Nore on the 19th and after a tortuous passage arrived on the 22nd, but could go no farther because of contrary winds. The body was transferred to the yacht *Chatham* to be taken to Greenwich on the morning of the 23rd. On the way up river all the vessels lowered their colours while Tilbury and Gravesend forts fired minute-guns in respect. Arriving at Greenwich later that night, Nelson's body was received by the aged Lord Hood and taken to a private room until the Painted Hall had been made ready for the lying in state. The plain coffin was now encased in a specially commissioned casket, covered with highly decorative gilt designs. Throughout this time Nelson's corpse was accompanied by Alexander Scott who, wracked with grief, refused to part from his

Lady Bessborough to Granville Leveson Gower,

10 November 1805

… I must still rave to you of Nelson; it has taken possession of every one's Mind. Mr Pitt had been writing a long dispatch to him and was just gone up to bed; about two in the morning he was call'd up again with the news. He was most extremely affected, for in this last time of N's being in England he had seen a great deal of him, and his opinion of his merit and great conception was higher than it had ever been before. Almost every body wears a black crape scarf or cockade with Nelson written on it – this is almost general high and low; indeed enthusiasm is general beyond anything I ever saw.

Source: Leveson Gower, vol. II, pp. 131–3.

beloved friend. The funeral was set for 9 January, and on the 4th the coffin was moved to the Painted Hall. Hundreds of candles had been positioned in sconces and huge black drapes covered the wall-paintings, creating a highly charged emotional atmosphere. The doors were opened to the public on Sunday, 5 December.

From *Victory*'s crew, 300 men had been selected to attend the funeral, each provided with a blue jacket and trousers, a black hat and armband. On 7 January a picked group of 46 seamen and fourteen Marines were collected from Chatham by the brig *Elizabeth and Mary* and taken up river to Greenwich. Met by Lord Hood, who ordered the 'Heroes of Trafalgar' to be brought ashore, the seamen were warmly greeted by a large group of spectators. This small group were allowed to pay their respects to their former commander in a private viewing of the body. Many of the weather-beaten faces left the room with tears streaming down their cheeks.

Wednesday, 8 January saw a large flotilla assembled on the Thames for the transfer of the coffin to the Admiralty. At 12.30 Nelson's coffin was placed on a Royal Barge dating from the reign of Charles II. The cortège moved slowly off, 'the flags half-staff high, and the boats of the River Fencibles firing minute-guns'. Both banks of the Thames were crowded with thousands of spectators standing in eerie silence. At about 2.45 p.m. the procession reached the Tower of London, its passing saluted by the firing of minute-guns from the shore, to which the River Fencibles gunboats responded by firing at intervals. In extremely windy conditions the funeral procession progressed slowly up the river, arriving at Whitehall stairs at precisely 3.30 p.m. The coffin was transferred to the Captain's Room at the Admiralty, placed on a platform and covered with black velvet. An armed guard from the Tower had been stationed to protect the Admiralty from the large numbers of people who gathered outside hoping to catch a glimpse of the coffin. Long into the night preparations were being made for the unprecedented spectacle that would take place on the morrow.

On Thursday, 9 January, Nelson's coffin was placed on a specially designed ornate funeral carriage:

…decorated with a carved imitation of the Head and Stern of His Majesty's Ship the *Victory*, surrounded with escutcheons of the Arms of the Deceased, and adorned with appropriate Mottoes and emblematical Devices; under an elevated Canopy, in the form of an upper part of an ancient Sarcophagus, with six sable Plumes, and the Coronet of a Viscount in the centre, supported by four columns, representing palm trees, with wreaths of natural laurel and cypress entwining the shafts; the whole upon a four wheeled carriage, drawn by six led horses, the caparisons adorned with armorial escutcheons.[141]

Nelson's funeral procession sets off from Greenwich in a raging gale against a heavy swell. Inset: the funeral carriage. (Warwick Leadlay Gallery)

All along the processional route from the Admiralty to St. Paul's Cathedral thousands of people had been gathering since three in the morning to be assured a good view. An hour before daybreak troops were lining the route and carriages were prevented from using the roads to be used by the procession.

The solemn cortège snaking through the crowded streets was so long that the head had reached the Cathedral before the tail had left Whitehall. *The Naval Chronicle* could not help but praise the conduct of all those in the streets: 'During the whole of this solemn ceremony, the greatest order prevailed throughout the metropolis; and as the remains of the much-lamented hero proceeded along, every possible testimony of sorrow and of respect was manifested by an immense concourse of spectators of all ranks.'[142] Upon reaching the Statue of King Charles at Charing Cross, the funeral car paused. 'Every hat was off, every

sound was hushed, and the most awful silence prevailed.' The majority of the procession was actually composed of soldiers, the only naval members being forty-eight Greenwich pensioners and forty-eight seamen and twelve Marines from *Victory*. The seamen carried *Victory's* battle-scarred ensigns, holding them open occasionally to show the holes caused by the enemy shot. When the funeral carriage arrived at St. Paul's Cathedral the coffin was removed by twelve of the *Victory's* seamen before being passed to the pall-bearers.

The doors of St. Paul's had been thrown open at 7 a.m. and the principal ticket holders had occupied their seats very swiftly. They were in for a long wait because the cortege did not arrive until a few minutes after 1 p.m. At 1.30 p.m. General Sir David Dundas marched in at the head of 300 soldiers, who took up positions lining the route to be taken from the Western Gate, along the aisle and circling the catafalque located directly beneath the dome where the sarcophagus would rest before burial. Inside St. Paul's special arrangements had been made: stands had been erected and a large hexagonal lamp suspended from the dome provided a central lighting source in the gathering gloom of the short January afternoon. At 2 p.m. the procession began to enter but it was not until 4 p.m. that the tail had entered the choir, where the coffin was placed during the service. After the service the coffin was moved from the Choir to the catafalque and at precisely 5.33 p.m. was lowered into the crypt as Sir Isaac Heard read out Nelson's titles and decorations. It was here that in the highly charged emotional service the *Victory's* crew deviated from the script. Instead of folding up *Victory's* colours and placing them on top of the disappearing coffin, they ripped off a large section, dividing it up between them as a permanent memento. At the signal of the body being lowered, artillery companies and soldiers outside fired off three volleys in salute. 'Thus terminated', *The Naval Chronicle* stated in its lengthy description, 'one of the most impressive and most splendid solemnities that ever took place in this Country, or perhaps in Europe.' With the ceremony finally ending at 6 p.m., it was not until three hours later that the Cathedral had emptied of mourners.[143]

Sir Isaac Heard, Garter King at Arms

Thus it hath pleased Almighty God to take out of this transitory life, unto His divine mercy, the Most Noble Lord Horatio Nelson, Viscount and Baron Nelson of the Nile, and of Burnham Thorpe, in the County of Norfolk, Baron Nelson of the Nile, and of Hillborough, in the same County; Knight of the Most Honourable order of the Bath; Vice Admiral of the White Squadron of the Fleet, and Commander-in-Chief of His Majesty's Ships and Vessels in the Mediterranean: also Duke of Bronte in Sicily; Knight Grand Cross of the Sicilian Order of St. Ferdinand and of Merit; Member of the Ottoman Order of the Crescent; Knight Grand Commander of the Order of St. Joachim; and the Hero, who in the moment of Victory, fell covered with immortal glory! – Let us humbly trust, that he is now raised to bliss ineffable, and to glorious immortality.
Source: Nicolas, VII, p. 417.

CONCLUSION

Trafalgar was tactically the most decisive battle fought under sail and no other sea battle can come close for drama and heroic tragedy. Nelson's 'pell-mell' battle was designed to take advantage of superior British gunnery, discipline, seamanship, cooperation and morale. In the latter notion he was wrong; Villeneuve did not flee and the French and Spanish officers and men put up a desperate resistance that surprised many British observers. If Nelson was sure that the enemy would stand, he might have taken a little more time to order the attack. As this had to be carried out swiftly, Collingwood's column could not deploy fully which left many ships, including his own *Royal Sovereign*, isolated. The light winds also delayed the advance, leaving some heavy ships, for example *Prince* and *Dreadnought*, towards the rear of the attack. Despite all the difficulties, Nelson gained the victory by making clear to his officers the result he wanted and how it was to be achieved.

Moreover, by accident the Combined Fleet managed to deploy in the one formation, a near double line, that was ideal for receiving Nelson's style of attack. If the Franco-Spanish Fleet had been well handled by its commanders and its seamen, highly experienced and in good morale, Nelson's tactics would have been disastrous. Here the long advance into battle came into play. For several hours the officers and men had time to think about what would happen that afternoon, which would have a great influence on morale. For the British this was largely a good thing, as they were expecting to win. For the French and Spanish, many were looking, including Villeneuve, to simply retrieve some credit after the disastrous events of 22 July. Once the hard fighting began, several ships dropped out of battle and headed for Cadiz, while the van under Dumanoir did not come round quickly enough to provide tangible support. One cannot imagine either of these important events occurring in a British fleet under the command of Nelson.

From a total of thirty-three, eighteen ships-of-the-line of the Combined Fleet were captured, destroyed or wrecked. In addition to the normal ship-building programmes, the capture of enemy ships was a traditional way of strengthening the Royal Navy. French ships in particular were well designed and built, some designs being so successful that they were often copied, providing a blueprint for future British designs. But of the enemy ships taken at Trafalgar only four were taken into the Royal Navy. When added to the four captured by Strachan and the two Spaniards seized by Calder, this gives a total of ten. But during the Trafalgar campaign Nelson's object was not to seize ships but to annihilate the enemy's naval capability to prevent them challenging the Royal Navy's use of the sea. For Nelson understood that battles were only a means to an end. The British way of fighting France was not to deliver a knockout blow in the style of a Napoleonic decisive battle. British strategy was more subtle, relying on maritime strength to wage a long-haul war of economic attrition, and decisive naval actions could influence the grand strategic situation in the context of the wider war with France.

First, the battle of Trafalgar did not put a stop to Napoleon's invasion plans. He heard of the battle on 18 November, but no reference was made to the defeat in any official publication. Any doubts as to his supreme military talents would be shortly dispelled by his brilliant victory of Austerlitz. In the short term it was Calder's action of 22 July that prevented Villeneuve from entering the Channel and covering the invasion flotilla. Napoleon decided to abandon the plan to invade England, at least temporarily, and use his *Grande Armée* to attack Austria instead. Trafalgar did not prevent the war on land going very badly for Britain, as the continental powers were steam-rollered by Napoleon's war machine. It took another ten years of hard fighting by the major European powers and a British Army to be committed to continental Europe to bring the wars to an end.

Another fallacy is that Trafalgar put an end to French naval ambitions. It did not. After 1805 'Napoleon had not given up using his fleet to good effect'.[144] French ships continued to escape from port, wreaking havoc among British merchantmen and causing great consternation at the Admiralty. One was caught and defeated by Sir John Duckworth on 6 February at Santo Domingo in the West Indies.[145] According to Barham that victory 'puts us out of all fear from another predatory war in the West Indies'.[146] At the same time another French squadron was cruising between South America and the coast of Africa intercepting British trade.[147] On 25 September 1806 Commodore Samuel Hood intercepted a French frigate squadron from Rochefort bound for the West Indies, and captured four fine 40-gun frigates which were taken in to the Royal Navy.[148] Again, in 1806 a French squadron had cruised off the African coast and then headed for South America.[149] 'Though largely ineffective and ultimately costly to the French,' one source has noted, here was clear evidence of 'the potential danger to British trade from the West Indies, India and China posed by their presence at large in the Atlantic'.[150] In 1807, while blockading Cadiz, Collingwood was concerned that the French and Spanish would escape, perhaps heading for the Mediterranean, East or West Indies.[151] In February 1808 a fleet of ten battleships, sailed from Toulon, and cruised at will around Corfu, the Ionian Islands, Sicily and Sardinia, before finally anchoring in Toulon on 10 April.[152] Clearly Trafalgar had not brought an end to the war at sea.

If existing enemy squadrons were a short-term threat to Britain, a long-term danger was posed by French naval building plans. Although Napoleon had seemingly abandoned his plans to invade the British Isles in 1805, there was a continuing real threat that France might gain local naval superiority at some point vital to British interests. Napoleon's determination to reconstruct his naval forces would be achieved by an ambitious rebuilding programme and attempts to seize the navies of the European neutral powers. In the years immediately after Trafalgar, on paper at least, Britain had a total of 296 ships (136 ships-of-the-line and 160 frigates) while France and her allies could muster 167 ships (96 ships-of-the-line and 71 frigates).[153] But French rebuilding plan began to bear fruit during from 1806 to 1808 when 24 ships-of-the-line were launched or acquired.[154] France continued to lay down new ships at an alarming rate: in 1806 eight to the five laid down by the Royal Navy; in 1807 the figures were 12 and 11 respectively. It was not until 1808 that French shipbuilding slackened, laying down only three new battleships to the seventeen laid down for the Royal Navy. Overall in the years 1804 to 1808, Britain laid down 50 battleships to the 45 laid down in French and Dutch yards.[155] By 1807 Napoleon could theoretically call on 62 French and allied ships-of-the-line ready for action against British interests. Apart from the escape of squadrons noted above, the French fleet was mainly held in port and gained little sea experience after 1805. But this served to preserve the fleet 'in being' as there were no serious losses compared to those of 1794 to 1805. Moreover, the navies of smaller powers were all vulnerable to French ambitions. William James has argued that Napoleon could have a French, Dutch, Swedish, Danish and Russian fleet of at least 60 sail-of-the-line operating in Northern waters, while only half this number were needed to convoy a possible French invasion of Ireland.[156] The French navy, along with those of her allies, still posed a long-term threat, not just in the war but possibly in a post-war climate. This threat had to be countered by the Royal Navy to preserve and guarantee the future of British maritime supremacy and the commercial life of the nation.[157]

Trafalgar was the last major fleet battle fought by the Royal Navy during the wars (and in fact for more than a century until Jutland in 1916), but the navy did not remain idle after 1805. A prime object was to remove warships from the clutches of Napoleon. In the years 1806 to 1810 Britain added 101 captured warships to the Royal Navy.[158] At Copenhagen and Lisbon in 1807, swift and decisive British action denied Napoleon the use of naval forces. These operations were, with regard to the wider maritime war, more important than Trafalgar. Temperley succinctly noted that 'Nelson destroyed nearly twenty men-of-war at Trafalgar. Canning [now Foreign Secretary] obtained more than thirty from Denmark and Portugal.'[159]

Trafalgar did not directly help Britain achieve key war aims. Britain was not fighting to overthrow Napoleon or even to decisively defeat France. British war aims were to safeguard the Low Countries and to limit French expansion in Western

Europe and overseas. These aims could only be achieved with the help of the Great European powers, but French military success continued to knock Austria, Prussia and Russia out of the wars. With peace unlikely, Britain continued to stand alone facing the combined might of Imperial France aligned alongside virtually the whole of continental Europe until, two and a half years after Trafalgar, the Spanish uprising became the first major check to Napoleon's continental plans.

Maritime power provided Britain with the cash not just for her own ever-increasing expenses, but to provide financial assistance to possible European allies. But Britain could not and would not follow the French model. British economic strength was built on overseas trade and colonies, protected by the might of the Royal Navy. By blockading enemy fleets in ports and aggressively pursuing them if they escaped, and by launching maritime based expeditions in Europe and overseas to preserve maritime supremacy, Britain continued to fight. Unable to strike at Britain directly, Napoleon attempted to dominate the European markets and hit the British economy by excluding British commerce from the continent. But France also needed to fight aggressive wars in order to make war pay, through booty and placing indemnities on defeated powers. Moreover, her massive army could not be sustained on French soil, and had to live off other nations. All this created an expansionist dynamic which would lead to a long, bloody and ultimately unsuccessful commitment to Iberia during 1808–1814 and the disastrous, fatal invasion of Russia in 1812.

So if Trafalgar did not save the British Isles from invasion or put an end to the naval war, what did the battle achieve for Britain? Trafalgar provided the Royal Navy with only the most recent example of the superiority of British gunnery and discipline. It was a crushing psychological blow for the French navy and even more so for the Spaniards, spreading loathing for the French among the Spanish population and government well before the Peninsular War. Trafalgar did go some way to guarantee the security of the British Isles and raise morale at home by reinforcing the belief that Napoleon could not invade. More importantly it allowed the Royal Navy to concentrate on protecting and expanding overseas trade and possessions, without which the country would have been brought to its knees by financial exhaustion, and ensuring that when the war did come to an end she was the premier world power. After 1805 British policy was concerned not necessarily with winning the war, but more with winning the peace that would eventually come.

In the years after Trafalgar the Royal Navy began to change, not only in numbers but also in form. Looking at the figures the most remarkable fact is the increase in cruiser types after 1805; this was the beginning of a trend that would be evident throughout the nineteenth century. The battlefleet served to protect home security, it was the smaller ships that promoted and protected British influence and trade overseas. The key to this was a chain of strategic naval bases, allowing the Royal Navy to project power on a global scale. Some of these bases were in British hands, such as Gibraltar, Malta, Bermuda and English Harbour in Antigua, but others were under the control of other powers, such as Port Mahon, Palermo, Livorno and

Lisbon. The operations of British maritime commerce and the Royal Navy were dependent on such bases.

The European Navies 1805–1810				
	1805		1810	
	Battleships	Cruisers	Battleships	Cruisers
French	41	46	46	38
Spanish	40	50	28	27
Russian	47	16	35	14
Danish	20	16	2	–
Swedish	12	11	13	8
Dutch	15	13	13	9
Portuguese	12	18	11	14
Total	187	170	148	110
The Royal Navy	135	192	152	245
Source: Glete, II, pp. 396–400.				

After Trafalgar Britain would continue to fight to preserve and expand maritime trade, the lifeblood of the nation, to allow her to come out of the war in a favourable position. Not favourable in narrow strategic terms of conquest, but favourable in terms of maritime trade and finance. What in the nineteenth century would be recognised as an informal Empire. British statesmen simply could not allow the economy to be a victim of French continental hegemony. Long-term borrowing and taxation, to pay for increasing British war expenditure and to provide the means to subsidise European allies, was the cornerstone of British fiscal strategy. This could only work if British trade continued to flow and expand to take into account ever-increasing war expenditure. Although Britain was willing to accept some spheres of influence within Europe, France in Western and Central Europe and Russia in the East, any actions that threatened the British Atlantic economy were resisted with vigour. Moreover, Britain could not let her enemies steal a march in these regions, hence Nelson's extreme worry at Villeneuve's expedition to the West Indies. It is only in this wider context, of a long haul maritime war based on trade, colonies and naval power, that the true significance of the battle of Trafalgar and its place in British history can be understood.

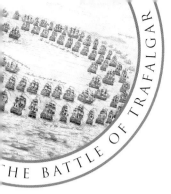

APPENDICES

Nelson Today

Although the battle of Trafalgar was fought nearly 200 years ago, there are numerous relics and interesting sites where one can capture the flavour of the period. These given below are by no means an exhaustive list, but form a useful starting-point in the British Isles. Dates and times are subject to change and readers are strongly advised to check before visiting attractions and events.

Most famously Lord Nelson's flagship HMS *Victory* remains in commission, as the Flagship of the Royal Navy's Second Sea Lord in Portsmouth. The only remaining three-decker in the world, she is restored to her 'fighting' condition of 21 October 1805. Open to the public all the year round, *Victory* provides a tangible link to the 'Wooden Walls' of the past.
www.hms-victory.co.uk

Two frigates of the 'Leda' class, designed in 1812 but representative of those of seven years earlier, remain in existence. HMS *Trincomalee*, now located in Hartlepool, was built in India of teak, oak being in short supply in England. The second frigate is HMS *Unicorn*. Launched in at Chatham in 1824, she now resides in Dundee.
www.hms-trincomalee.co.uk
www.frigateunicorn.org

In London, Trafalgar Square has Nelson's Column with the four gigantic lions at its base.

Nelson's sarcophagus, together with Collingwood's final resting-place, can be seen directly below the middle of the Dome in St. Paul's Cathedral, London (www.stpauls.co.uk).

The Nelson Society examines the life and story of Nelson himself, within the context of the Georgian period. Run by enthusiasts, it provides an excellent resource including a list of answers to frequently asked questions. The 1805 Club exists for the purpose of preserving monuments and memorials relating to Nelson and seafaring people of the period; promoting research into the Royal Navy and Nelson; and organising cultural and historical events.
www.nelson-society.org.uk
www.admiralnelson.org

On-line editions of some of Nelson's dispatches and letters as edited by Nicolas, particularly those relating to October 1805, can be found at the *War Times Journal*. UK and Ireland Genealogy (GENUKI) contains the names of some 1,640 officers and men who served in the various ships of the British Fleet at the Battle of Trafalgar.
www.wtj.com/index_flash.htm
www.genuki.org.uk/big/eng/Trafalgar/

2005 is the year of the sea in Britain, a whole host of nation-wide events are being organised by a number of bodies, of which Trafalgar and Nelson celebrations are just a part.

www.seabritain2005.com
www.trafalgar200.com
At the National Maritime Museum, Greenwich, London, many Trafalgar relics can be viewed. Perhaps most poignant is Nelson's undress coat worn on the day of the battle. The hole caused by the fatal musket ball can still be seen. The Museum is hosting a special exhibition entitled 'Nelson and Napoleon' from 7 July to 13 November 2005. It is the first time the parallel lives of the two great men have been portrayed together in such detail. With the most significant and extensive set of permanent exhibitions devoted to Nelson in the UK, including his Funeral barge, the Sailing Navy and the Battle of Trafalgar, the Royal Naval Museum Portsmouth will be a hub of events, including the Battle of Trafalgar 'Experience'. The Museum's website also acts as a link to many events which will take place in Portsmouth during the year.
www.nmm.ac.uk
www.royalnavalmuseum.org

GLOSSARY

Abeam: the point at right angles with the ship's mainmast.

Aboard: the inside of a ship. To fall aboard is to strike against another ship. To haul aboard the main tack is to bring the clew of the mainsail down to the chess-tree.

About: the situation of a ship immediately after she has tacked, or changed her course, by going about, and standing on the other tack.

Abreast: synonymous with Abeam.

Adrift: the state of a ship or vessel broken loose from her moorings, and driven without control, at the mercy of the wind, sea, or current.

Aft, After: behind, or near the stern of a ship.

Aloft: up in the tops, at the mast-head, or anywhere about the higher yards or rigging.

Alongside: close to the ship.

Amidships: the middle of the ship, either with regard to her length or breadth.

Astern; behind the ship.

Athwart: across the lay of the ship's course or its keel.

Bar: a shoal running across the mouth of a harbour or river.

Bear up, or bear away: to change the course of a ship, in order to make her run before the wind, after she has sailed some time with a side wind, or close-hauled.

Beating: the operation of making progress at sea against the direction of the wind, in a zig-zag line, or traverse; beating, however, is generally understood to be turning to windward in a storm, or fresh wind.

Bow: the rounding part of a ship's side forward, beginning where the planks arch inwards, and terminating where they close at the stem or prow. On the bow, an arc of the horizon, not exceeding 45°, comprehended between some distant object and that point of the compass which is right ahead, or to which the ship's stem is directed.

Braces: ropes fastened to the extremities of the yards to brace them about.

Brails: ropes applied to the after leeches of the driver, and some of the stay-sails, to draw them up.

Bring to: to check the course of a ship by arranging the sails in such a manner that they shall counteract one another, and keep her nearly stationary.

Bulkheads: partitions in the ship.

Cable: a large rope by which the ship is secured to the anchor.

Cable's length: a measure of 120 fathoms, or 240 yards.

Capstan: a machine by which the anchor is weighed.

Cat-head: a strong bracket projecting from the forecastle on each bow, furnished with sheaves or strong pulleys, and to which the anchor is lifted after it has been hove up to the bow by the capstan.

Close-hauled: the arrangement or trim of a ship's sails when she endeavours to make progress in the nearest direction possible towards that point of the compass from which the wind is blowing.

Fill: to fill the sail that has been shivered or hove aback, to bring the ship to.

Gun-shot: implies, says Falconer, 'the distance of the point-blank range of a cannon-shot'. With submission, we take a gun-shot distance to mean long, and not point-blank range: if this be correct, a ship is within gun-shot of another when she is within a mile or a mile and a quarter of her.

Haul the wind: to direct the ship's course as near as possible to that point of the compass from which the wind arises.

Hawse: generally understood to imply the situation of the cables before the ship's stem, when she is moored with two anchors out from the bows; viz., one on the starboard, and the other on the larboard bow. It also denotes any small distance ahead of a ship, or between her head and the anchors by which she rides.

Hawse-hole: hole through which the cables pass.

Hawser: a small cable.

Heave to: synonymous with bring to. Heaving to an anchor, is when all the cable is taken in until the ship is directly over her anchor, preparatory to its being weighed out of the ground.

Knot: synonymous with one nautical mile.

Larboard: a name given by seamen to the left side of the ship, when looking forward from the stern (this term was abolished in 1844).

Lie to: synonymous with Bring to, Heave to.

Luff: the order to the helmsman to put the tiller towards the lee-side of the ship, in order to make the ship sail nearer to the direction of the wind.

Musket-shot: distance, from 300 to 400 yards.

Offing: implies out at sea, or at a good distance from the shore.

Overhaul: to examine; also to overtake a ship in chase.

Pistol-shot distance: about 50 yards.

Plying: turning to windward.

Port: a name given by seamen to the left-hand side of the ship. Used instead of larboard, on account of the affinity of sound between the latter word and starboard.

Quarter: that part of a ship's side which lies towards the stern, or which is comprehended between the aftmost end of the main chains and the side of the stern, where it is terminated by the quarter-pieces.

Rake a ship: is when the broadside sweeps another's decks fore and aft, either by lying athwart her bows or her stern.

Stand on: maintain the same course .

Starboard: the right-hand side of the ship, when looking forward, or towards the head.

Stay: to stay a ship, is to arrange the sails and move the rudder, so as to bring the ship's head to the direction of the wind, in order to get her on the other tack.

Tack: to change the course from one board to another, or to turn the ship about from the starboard to the larboard tack, or vice versa, in a contrary wind.

Wake of a ship: is to be immediately behind or in the track of her. It also means when a ship is hidden from view by another ship.

Weather a ship, headland, &c.: to sail to windward of it. The weathergage implies the situation of one ship to windward of another when in action, etc.

Wear, or veer ship: to change her course from one board to the other by turning her stern to windward.

Weigh: to heave up the anchor of a ship from the ground in order to prepare the ship for sailing.

Work a ship: to direct her movements, by adapting the sails to the force and direction of the wind. To work to windward is a synonym of beat, tack, turn to windward, etc.

GUIDE TO FURTHER READING

This is by no means an exhaustive review of the literature available on Trafalgar. Instead, it is a guide to a few hand-picked published primary and secondary sources, which will be most useful to those intending to undertake further research while building on the ideas expressed in this book. For a more comprehensive list of sources, see the bibliography.

Although biographies of Nelson are legion, several are worthy of particular note. Immediately after Trafalgar the historical literature produced concentrated on the story of Nelson. Surgeon Beatty's *Authentic Narrative of the Death of Lord Nelson* appeared in 1807. James Stanier Clark and John Macarthur, with the support of Earl Nelson and the Prince of Wales, produced the official biography in 1809. Large parts of Nelson's letters were 'tidied up' and the work as a whole is unsatisfactory and of little use to modern scholars. In response to Clark and Macarthur's poor effort, Robert Southey embarked on another biography, which appeared in 1813 and was a massive hit with readers. Setting to rights many of the errors in the earlier works, but providing a balanced account, Southey combined Nelson's own writings with his own formidable literary skill to portray his subject as the flawed hero. Following Southey, the next major work of note was Sir Nicholas Harris Nicolas' *Dispatches and Letters of Lord Nelson*, seven volumes of immense historical importance completed in less than two years and published in 1844–6. Previously only available in specialist libraries, a recent paperback reprint allows scholars easy access to Nelson's own words and thoughts in the run up to Trafalgar. Carola Oman's *Nelson*, despite the passage of half a century, remains one of the most accessible, affordable, entertaining and accurate of biographies. More recently Andrew Lambert's excellent *Nelson: Britannia's God of War* has made it clear that Nelson still has many things to say to the twenty-first century.

The operations of the British Royal Navy and the actions of Nelson have dominated the study of the campaign and battle of Trafalgar. The battle itself, together with the Nile and Copenhagen, has often been portrayed as the ultimate examples of decisive battle in the age of sail. William James, writing shortly after the Napoleonic Wars, produced a remarkable work of scholarship, which remains important. His emphasis is purely naval, and therefore, despite his in-depth examination of Calder's action, Trafalgar and Cape Ortegal, does not cover the wider aspects of the Trafalgar campaign. Despite the pioneering work of James in the 1820s, it was not until nearly a hundred years after Trafalgar that historians began seriously to examine naval warfare from a scientific basis. In *The Influence of Seapower upon the French Revolution and Empire, 1793–1812*, A. T. Mahan's emphasis was on the decisive nature of battle and the importance of blockade. With this agenda, he concluded the majority of his study at the year 1805, regarding Trafalgar as the ultimate naval battle and the natural culmination of naval warfare in the age of sail. Writing in a period of naval aggrandisement and apparent threat from Germany, Julian Corbett's *Campaign of Trafalgar* remains one of the core texts on Trafalgar. Corbett dispelled the myth that Nelson had been lured to the West Indies, when in fact Nelson had processed the information available to him and decided to head to the Caribbean to safeguard British trade and possessions. Nelson's following of Villeneuve did not leave the British Isles open to invasion, a moot point considering the strategic situation contemporary with Corbett where a possible German invasion was an apparent threat.

Vital for examining the trends in fleet development is Jan Glete's statistical analysis *Navies and Nations*. Most importantly, his work enables the reader to analyse the fleets of the other major powers of the period. When consulted with Otto von Pivka's *Navies of the Napoleonic Wars*, a more balanced view of naval warfare in the period can be obtained. From the French and Spanish perspectives much work remains to be undertaken. Readers will find immense benefit from Desbrière's *The Trafalgar Campaign* and Fraser's *The Enemy at Trafalgar*. For the Spanish navy in particular, John Harbron's *Trafalgar and the Spanish Navy* is more than just a

study of the battle. Using Spanish archival material, he provides a full history of the Spanish navy before Trafalgar, examining ship design and building, infrastructure as well as personnel.

With regard to the course of the battle, Jackson's *Logs of the Great Sea Fights* provides detailed transcripts of the actual ship's logs during the course of the day. Corbett's *Fighting Instructions* examines fleet battle tactics by analysing documentary evidence of fighting instructions, placing them into context with regard to their genesis, intention, and significance to present a picture of how naval warfare was actually conducted. One important point raised by Corbett is his assertion that the concept of breaking the line of enemy ships in order to defeat parts of that fleet in detail was already in practice before Nelson's victory at Trafalgar. Admiral Rodney in 1782 at the battle of the Saintes, Admiral Lord Howe at the Glorious First of June in 1794, and Admiral Duncan at Camperdown in 1797 had all successfully used this tactic. The important difference in Nelson's concept was in overtly implementing the tactic as a means to force a battle where the superior British discipline, gunnery, and ship handling, as opposed to superior numbers, would guarantee victory. When used in conjunction with Tunstall and Tracy's *Naval Warfare in the Age of Sail: The Evolution of Fighting Tactics*, and Tracy's *Nelson's Battles*, the reader will be fully apprised of developments in naval tactics before Trafalgar.

Of the recent studies of Trafalgar, Alan Schom's *Trafalgar Countdown to Battle* relies heavily on Corbett's work and is an immensely readable and readily available study. Robert Gardiner (ed.) *The Campaign of Trafalgar*, as well as providing an excellent account of the battle and the wider naval situation in 1803–5, contains many excellent illustrations providing a valuable visual history. Clayton and Craig's *Trafalgar, The Men, The Battle, The Storm* is an enjoyable work, but gives little space to the overall campaign, a failure also evident in Roy Adkins' *Trafalgar: Biography of a Battle*. Nevertheless, the easy style and the gripping narratives of these studies will appeal to many modern readers.

Tom Pocock's *The Terror Before Trafalgar* provides an excellent account of the threat of French invasion during the years 1801–5. For the years following Trafalgar, Corbett's 'Napoleon and the British Navy after Trafalgar' is a short but masterful account of how the Royal Navy was employed after the battle. After this heavy defeat, Napoleon re-instituted a ship-building programme and attempted to add to his fleets by seizing the neutral navies of Denmark, Sweden, and Portugal.

Faced with this threat, the Royal Navy was used to prevent France from gaining additional naval power. This was achieved by securing the neutral navies of Denmark and Portugal, blockading French fleets, and undertaking opportunistic strikes on French naval facilities. As one would expect, Corbett stressed the important relationship between naval and commercial history, a subject that forms the basis of a number of important works by Michael Duffy (1987, 2001).

Finally, mention should be made of a work of naval fiction. Bernard Cornwell's *Sharpe's Trafalgar*, despite containing fictitious characters and ships, nevertheless culminates with a breathtakingly atmospheric account of the battle of Trafalgar, placing the reader firmly on deck surrounded by whizzing musket balls, screaming roundshot, deadly splinters and smashed human bodies.

Manuscript Sources

The National Archives, Kew (formerly PRO)
Admiralty Papers (ADM)
National Maritime Museum, Greenwich
   Nelson Papers
British Library
   Nelson Papers
   Additional Manuscripts (Add. Mss.)
Moniteur
The Times
Cobbett's Parliamentary Debates (London: T. C. Hansard, 1808)

Published Documents

Bourchier, J. *Memoir of The Life of Admiral Sir Edward Codrington*, 2 vols. London, 1873

Collingwood, G. L. Newham (ed.). *Correspondence and Memoirs of Vice-Admiral Lord Collingwood*. London, 1829

Corbett, J. S. (ed.). *Fighting Instructions, 1530–1816*. London, 1905

Granville, Countess (ed.). *Lord Granville Leveson Gower Private Correspondence, 1781–1821*, 2 vols. London, 1916

Historical Manuscripts Commission. *Reports on the Manuscripts of J. B. Fortescue Preserved at Dropmore, 1892–1927*. London, 1912

Hodges, H. W., and Hughes, E. A. *Select Naval Documents*. Cambridge, 1936

Hughes, E. (ed.). *The Private Correspondence of Admiral Lord Collingwood*. London, 1852

Jackson, T. S. (ed.). *Logs of the Great Sea Fights*, 2 vols. London, 1899–1900

Lambert, A. (ed.). *Letters and Papers of Sir John Knox Laughton*. Aldershot, 2002

Laughton, J. K. (ed.). *Letters of Lord Barham*, 3 vols. London, 1909–1910

Longford, E. *Wellington: The Years of the Sword*. London, 1969

Mackenzie, R. H. *The Trafalgar roll*. London, 1913

Minto, Countess. *Life and Letters of Sir Gilbert Elliot, First Earl of Minto, from 1751–1806*, 3 vols. 1874

Morris, R. (ed.). *The Channel Fleet and the Blockade of Brest, 1793–1801*. Aldershot, 2001

Nicolas, Sir Nicholas Harris (ed.). *The dispatches and letters of Vice Admiral Lord Viscount Nelson*, 7 vols. London, pbk edn., 1997

Tracy, N. (ed.). *The Naval Chronicle: The Contemporary Record of the Royal Navy at War*, 5 vols. London, 1999

Warner, O. *The life and letters of Vice-Admiral Lord Collingwood*. OUP, 1968

Books

Addis, C. P. *The men who fought with Nelson in HMS Victory at Trafalgar*. London, 1988

Adkins, R. *Trafalgar: Biography of a Battle*. London, 2004

Allen, J. *The Life and Services of Sir William Hargood*. Greenwich, 1861

Beatty, W. *The Authentic Narrative of the Death of Lord Nelson*. 1807

Broadley, A. M. and Bartelot, R. G. *Nelson's Hardy: his life, letters and friends*. London, 1909

Clark, J. S. and McArthur, J. *The Life of Admiral Lord Nelson K.B. from his Lordship's Manuscripts*. 2 vols., London, 1813

Clarke, J. D. *The men of HMS Victory at Trafalgar including the muster roll of HMS Victory, casualties, parliamentary grant, prize money, Lloyd's Patriotic Fund rewards, medals, pay rates*. Dallington, 1999

Clayton, T. and Craig, P. *Trafalgar: The Men, The Battle, The Storm*. London, 2004

Corbett, J. S. *The Campaign of Trafalgar*. London, 1910

— *Some Principles of Maritime Strategy*. London, 1911

Cornwell, B. *Sharpe's Trafalgar*. London, 2000

Deane, P. and Cole, W. A. *British Economic Growth, 1688–1959: Trends and Structure*. Cambridge, 1962

Desbrière, E. *The Campaign of Trafalgar*, 2 vols. (trans. C. Eastwick). Oxford, 1933

Duffy, M. *Soldiers, Sugar and Seapower*. Oxford, 1987

Ehrman, J. *The Younger Pitt, Volume One: The Years of Acclaim*. London, 1969

Emsley, C. *The Longman Companion to Napoleonic Europe*. London, 1993

Fenwick, K. *HMS Victory*. London, 1959

Fortescue, J. W. *A History of The British Army*, 13

vols. London, 1899–1930

Fraser, E. *The Enemy at Trafalgar*. London, 1906, rp, 2004

— *The Sailors Whom Nelson Led*. London, 1913

Gardiner, R. (ed.). *The Campaign of Trafalgar, 1803–1805*. London, 1996

Glete, J. *Navies and Nations: Warships, Navies, and State Building in Europe and America, 1500–1860*. 2 vols., Stockholm, 1993

Goodwin, P. *Nelson's Ships: A History of the Vessels in Which He Served*. London, 2002

Harbron, J. D. *Trafalgar and The Spanish Navy: The Spanish Experience of Sea Power*. London, 1988

Harding, R. *Seapower and Naval Warfare, 1650–1830*. London, 1999

Hayther, A. (ed.) *The Backbone: Diaries of a Military Family in the Napoleonic Wars*. Bishop Auckland, 1993

Hibbert, C. *Nelson: a personal history*. London, 1995

Howarth, D. *Trafalgar: the Nelson touch*, London, 1969

James, W. *The Naval History of Great Britain During the French Revolutionary and Napoleonic Wars*, 6 vols. London, rp, 2002

Keate, E. M. *Nelson's Wife*. London, 1939

Kennedy, L. *Nelson and his Captains*, London, 1975

Kennedy, P. *The Rise and Fall of British Naval Mastery*. London, 3rd edn, 1991

King, D. *Every Man Will Do His Duty*. London, 1997

Lambert, A. *Nelson: Britannia's God of War*. London, 2004

Lavery, B. *Nelson's navy: the ships, men and organisation 1793–1805*. London, 1989

— *Nelson's Fleet at Trafalgar*. London, 2004

LeFevre, P. and Harding, R. *Precursors of Nelson: British Admirals in the Eighteenth Century*. London, 2000

Mahan, A. T. *The Influence of Seapower upon History*. Cambridge, 1892

— *The Influence of Seapower upon the French Revolution and Empire, 1793–1812*, 2 vols. London, 1893

— *The Life of Nelson: The Embodiment of the Sea Power of Great Britain*. London, 1899

Oman, C. *Nelson*. London, pbk edn, 1968

Pivka, Otto von. *Navies of the Napoleonic Era*. Devon, 1980

Pocock, T. *Nelson's Women*. London, 1999

— *Horatio Nelson*. London, 1987

Popham, H. *A Damned Cunning Fellow, The eventful life of Rear-Admiral Sir Home Popham 1762–1820*. Tywardreath, 1991

Richmond, H. W. *Statesmen and Sea Power*. Oxford, 1946

Robinson, H. *Sea Drift*. Portsea, 1858

Russell, J. *Nelson and the Hamiltons*. London, 1969

Russell Lord. *Knight of the Sword: The Life and Letters of Admiral Sir William Sidney Smith*. London, 1964

Schom, A. *Trafalgar: Countdown to Battle, 1803–1805*, London, 1990, pbk edn, 1992

Talbot, J. E. *Pen and Ink Sailor: Charles Middleton and the King's Navy*. London, 1998

Temperley, H. W. V. *Life of Canning*. London, 1905

Tracy, N. *Nelson's battles: the art of victory in the age of sail*. London, 1996

Tunstall, B. and Tracy, N. (eds). *Naval Warfare in the Age of Sail: The Evolution of Fighting Tactics, 1650–1815*. London, 1990

Vincent, E. *Nelson: Love and Fame*. London, 2002

Walker, R. *The Nelson Portraits*. Portsmouth, 1998

Warner O. *Trafalgar*. London, 1959

White, C. (ed.). *The Nelson Companion*. Stroud, 1995

— *The Nelson Encyclopædia*. London, 2002

Woodman, R. *The Victory of Seapower, Winning the Napoleonic War, 1806–1814*. London, 1998

HMSO. *Report of a Committee appointed by the Admiralty to consider the tactics employed at Trafalgar*. HMSO, 1913

Articles

Corbett, J. S. 'Napoleon and the British Navy after Trafalgar', in *Quarterly Review*, 1922

Duffy, M. 'The establishment of the Western Squadron as the linchpin of British naval Strategy', in M. Duffy (ed.). *Parameters of British Naval Power, 1650–1850*. Exeter, 1992

— 'World-Wide War and British Expansion, 1793–1815', in P. J. Marshall (ed.). *The Oxford History of the British Empire: Volume Two, The Eighteenth Century*. Oxford, pbk edn, 2001

Goodwin, P. 'Where Nelson Died: an Historical Riddle Resolved by Archeology', in *Mariner's Mirror*, vol. 85, 1999

Horsfall, L. F. 'The West Indian Trade', in C. Northcote Parkinson (ed.). *The Trade Winds: A Study of British Overseas Trade during the French Wars, 1793–1815*. London, 1948

Marthinsen, S. 'French Sail-of-the-Line in the Napoleonic Wars (1792–1815)', in *Warship*, 1994

Tracy, N. 'Sir Robert Calder's Action', in *Mariner's Mirror*, vol. 77, 1991

White, C. 'Nelson's 1805 Battle Plan', in *Journal of Maritime Research*, 2002

NOTES

1 See Mahan (1793), vol. II, pp. 116–17.
2 Gardiner, p. 64.
3 Schom, p.77.
4 Gardiner, pp. 57, 64; Lavery (2004), pp. 26–7.
5 Schom, p. 72.
6 Mahan (1893), II pp. 112–14; Lavery (2004), pp. 28–9.
7 Gardiner, pp. 64–5.
8 Robinson, p. 208.
9 Collingwood to Lord Radstock, 12 Dec 1805, *Collingwood*, p. 165.
10 Mahan (1893), II, pp. 131–3.
11 Mahan (1893), II, pp. 124–5.
12 Mahan (1893), II, p. 118.
13 Goodwin (2002), p. 188.
14 James, IV, p. 283.
15 Mahan (1893), II, p. 119.
16 See Morris, pp. 1–6, quotation from p. 6; Duffy (1992), pp. 60–81.
17 Cited in Gardiner, pp. 69–70.
18 Mahan (1893), II, p. 119.
19 Hayther, p. 75.
20 Schom, p. 58.
21 Cited in Lavery (2004), p. 39.
22 Nelson to Stewart, 8 Oct 1805, Nicolas, VII, p. 87.
23 *Naval Chronicle*, III, pp. 59–61. See also Popham, p. 117.
24 Popham, p. 119.
25 Smith to Keith, 29 Sept 1805, Keith's reply, 3 Oct 1805, Lord Russell, pp. 104–6.
26 Lord Russell, pp. 110–11.
27 Mahan (1893), II, p. 129.
28 Telegraph Ganteaume to Napoleon, 24 Mar 1805; Telegraph Napoleon to Ganteaume, Hodges and Hughes, p. 208.
29 Nelson to Lord Mayor, 1 Aug 1804, Nicolas, VI, pp. 124–5.
30 Nelson to Elliot, and to Acton, 30 Jan 1804, Nicolas, V, pp. 395–6.

31 See Nicolas, III, pp. 231–4, especially Nelson to Campbell, 14 Jan 1799, pp. 232–3, and Nelson to Acton, 15 Jan 1799, p. 233.
32 Nelson to Niza, 27 Feb 1799, Nicolas, III, pp. 271–2.
33 Nelson to Sidmouth, 11 May 1805, Nicolas, VI, p. 436.
34 Recent research has shown that by 1815 the emphasis of the Empire had shifted from the Atlantic to a very different; kind of empire centered in the East Indies and India in particular, see Duffy (2001), pp. 184–207.
35 Deane and Cole, p. 34.
36 Ehrman (1969), p. 332.
37 Duffy (1987), quotation from p. 5, see also p. 10.
38 Kennedy (1991), p. 152.
39 Emsley, pp. 132–3.
40 Horsfall, p. 163.
41 Fortescue, IV, pt. 1, p. 79.
42 Auckland to Grenville, 6 June 1806, Fortescue, VIII, p. 181; Horsfall, pp. 158–161.
43 Collingwood to Carlyle, 2 July 1805, Hughes, p. 159.
44 Nelson to Simon Taylor, 10 June 1805, Nicolas, VI, pp. 450–1. See also Nelson to Davison, 7 May 1805, Nicolas, VI, p. 427.
45 Duffy (1987), p. 19.
46 Cited, L. Kennedy, p. 309.
47 Bourchier, pp. 47, 70.
48 Collingwood to J. E. Blackett, 4 Feb 1805, Collingwood, p. 100.
49 Nelson to Marsden, 12 June 1805, Nicolas, VI, pp. 452–3.
50 Nelson to Fitzgerald, 15 June 1805, Nicolas, VI, pp. 455–6.
51 Nelson to Marsden, 20 July 1805, Nicolas, VI, p. 473.
52 James, IV, p. 360 states captains of *Atlas* and *Formidable*, whereas Villeneuve states Deperrone killed and Rolland wounded, Tracy, Naval

Chron, vol. 3, p. 162.
53 James, IV, pp. 6, 359.
54 *Naval Chronicle*, III, p.166. James, IV, p. 359 details the damage sustained by Calder's fleet.
55 Lady Bessborough to Granville Leveson Gower, 20 Aug 1805, Granville, II, p. 106.
56 Nelson to Barham, 30 Sept 1805, Nicolas, VII, p. 56.
57 Nelson to Fremantle, 16 Aug1805, Nicolas, VII, p. 5.
58 Lady Bessborough to Granville Leveson Gower, Sept 1805, Granville, II, p. 111.
59 For Calder's letters to Nelson see Nicolas, VII, p. 119–20, n. 8.
60 Nelson to Emma, 11 Oct 1805, Nicolas, VII, p. 385; Nelson to Collingwood, 14 Oct 1805, Nicolas, VII, p. 121.
61 Naval Chronicle, III, p. 164.
62 Naval Chronicle, III, p. 166.
63 Naval Chronicle, III, pp. 169–70.
64 Warner (1959), p. 41.
65 Naval Chronicle, III, p. 153.
66 Lyon, 'Calder's Action', in Gardiner, (1997), p. 129.
67 Tracy (1996), p. 163.
68 Desbriere, II, pp. 90–4 for the state of Villeneuve's fleet in Sept 1805.
69 In fact on 14 Oct 1805 Nelson informed Blackwood that if the Combined Fleet did not come out he was expecting 'three stout Fire-Ships from England'. 'I should not be surprised if Mr. Francis and his catamarans were sent, and Colonel Congreve and his rockets.' Nicolas, VII, pp. 121–2.
70 Desbriere, II, p. 102.
71 Fraser (2004), pp. 49–52.
72 Gardiner, p. 131.
73 Fraser (2004), pp. 54–5.

74 Nelson to Davison, 24 July 1805, Nicolas, VI, p. 494.
75 Nelson to Cornwallis, 25 July 1805, Nicolas, VI, p. 500.
76 Minto, II, p. 368.
77 Nicolas, VI, p. 26.
78 See Longford, pp. 110–11.
79 Nicolas, VII, p. 35.
80 Nicolas, VII, p. 117, n.7.
81 Collingwood to Nelson, 6 Oct 1805, Collingwood, p. 114.
82 Nelson to Castlereagh, 5 Oct 1805, Nicolas, VII, p. 76.
83 For a discussion of the effects of Trafalgar upon 19th- and early 20th-century naval history see Lambert (2004), chpt XVIII.
84 Nelson to Rose, 6 Oct 1805, Nicolas, VII, p. 80.
85 Tracy (1996), p. 175
86 Augustus Phillimore to Laughton, 28 Oct 1891, Lambert (ed) (2002), p. 76. See also Lavery (2004), pp. 81–2.
87 Nicolas, VII, p. 67, n. 3.
88 Tracy (1996), p. 178.
89 Nicolas, VI, pp. 467–8.
90 Nelson to Collingwood, 30 Sept 1805, Nicolas, VII, p. 57; Duff to his wife, 1 Oct 1805, *Naval Chronicle*, III, pp. 191–2.
91 Duff to his wife, 10 Oct 1805, *Naval Chronicle*, III, pp.191–2.
92 Note in margin of original, 'The Enemy's Fleet is supposed to consist of 46 Sail of the Line – British fleet of 40 – if either is less only a proportionate number of Enemy's ships are to be cut off; B to be ¼ superior to the E cut off.
93 White (2002), pp. 236–7; see also White, 'Nelson's 1805 Battle Plan'.
94 Nicolas, VII, p. 134.
95 Fraser (2004), p. 101–96 Nicolas, VII, p. 139
97 Goodwin (2002), p. 145; White (2002), p. 147 has recently argued that just

backing the mizzen topsail would not have slowed the ship sufficiently; therefore more sails must have been backed.
98 Collingwood, p. 124.
99 Goodwin (2002), p. 257.
100 White (2002), pp. 118–19.
101 Nicolas, VII, p. 150.
102 Nicolas, VII, p. 35.
103 Nelson to Rose, 6 Oct 1805, Nicolas, VII, p. 80.
104 Nelson to Stewart, 8 Oct 1805, Nicolas, vol. VII, p. 87.
105 'The Dreadnought certainly sails very ill', Collingwood to Nelson, 12 Oct 1805, Nicolas, VII, p. 115, n.4.
106 See Memorandum 10 Oct 1805, Nicolas, VII, p. 104. Collingwood's ships, as he was Vice Admiral of the Blue, should have flown Blue Ensigns but following Nelson's memo his division flew White Ensigns.
107 Collingwood to Marsden, 22 Oct 1805, Collingwood, p. 120.
108 Collingwood, p. 127.
109 Collingwood to Lord Radstock, 12 Dec 1805, Collingwood, p.165.
110 Fraser (1913), p. 256; Lavery (2004), p. 179.
111 Collingwood to Duke of Clarence, 12 Dec 1805, Collingwood, pp. 163–4.
112 Allen, pp. 279–81.
113 Jackson, II, p. 245.
114 King, p. 162.
115 Jackson, vol. 2, p. 244.
116 Cited in Gardiner, p. 159.
117 See Clayton and Craig, p. 172; Schom, p. 321.
118 Jackson, II, pp. 183, 219.
119 See Goodwin (2002), p. 259 for the suggestion of the speaking-tubes.
120 Beatty, pp. 28–9.
121 Fraser (1913), pp. 301–2; Gardiner, p. 153.
122 Lavery (2004), p. 168.
123 Codrington to his wife, 31 Oct 1805, Bourchier, vol. I, pp. 64–6; Lavery

(2004), p. 174.
124 Nicolas, VII, pp. 168–9.
125 Lambert, 2004, p. 311.
126 See Beatty's narrative reproduced in Nicolas, VII, pp. 244–62.
127 Figures from Lavery (1989), p. 187.
128 See Bourchier, I, p. 71; Schom, p. 355.
129 Lavery (2004), p. 185.
130 Collingwood to Marsden, 22 Oct 1805, Collingwood, p. 123.
131 Lambert (2004), p. 307.
132 Tracy, *Naval Chronicle*, vol. III, p. 231.
133 Goodwin (2002), p. 261.
134 Collingwood to Solana, 27 Oct 1805; Solana's reply 28 Oct 1805, Nicolas, VII, pp. 22–8.
135 Cited in Gardiner, p. 179.
136 *The Times*, 7, 8, Nov 1805.
137 Nicolas, VII, p. 303.
138 Nicolas, VII, pp. 302–3.
139 Hayther, p. 78.
140 Nicolas, vol. VII, p. 308.
141 Nicolas, vol. VII, p. 409.
142 *Naval Chronicle*, III, p. 255.
143 Nicolas, VII, pp. 416–17.
144 Harding (1999), p. 270.
145 See James, IV, pp. 184–91.
146 Citation from Woodman, p. 24.
147 James, IV, p. 203.
148 James, IV, p. 264.
149 James, IV, p. 265.
150 Woodman, p. 18.
151 Collingwood to Purvis, 17 Feb 1807, Hughes, pp. 201–2.
152 James, V, pp. 3–9; Collingwood to Lady Collingwood, 15 May 1808, Collingwood, pp. 355–7.
153 Harding, p. 270, table 10.1.
154 Marthinsen, pp. 15–21; James, IV, p. 283.
155 Glete, II, pp. 386–7.
156 James, IV, pp. 283–4.
157 James, IV, p. 283; Glete, II, p. 389.
158 Glete, II, pp. 384–5.
159 Temperley, p. 81.

INDEX